JOSSEY-BASS TEACHER

Jossey-Bass Teacher provides educators with practical knowledge and tools to create a positive and lifelong impact on student learning. We offer classroom-tested and research-based teaching resources for a variety of grade levels and subject areas. Whether you are an aspiring, new, or veteran teacher, we want to help you make every teaching day your best.

From ready-to-use classroom activities to the latest teaching framework, our value-packed books provide insightful, practical, and comprehensive materials on the topics that matter most to K–12 teachers. We hope to become your trusted source for the best ideas from the most experienced and respected experts in the field.

D0556252

SUPPORTED LITERACY FOR ADOLESCENTS

Transforming Teaching and Content Learning for the Twenty-First Century

CATHERINE COBB MOROCCO
CYNTHIA MATA AGUILAR
CAROL BERSHAD
ANDREA WINOKUR KOTULA
ALISA HINDIN

CO-PUBLISHED WITH THE
EDUCATION DEVELOPMENT
CENTER, INC.

JOSSEY-BASS
A Wiley Imprint
www.josseybass.com

Published by Jossey-Bass
A Wiley Imprint
989 Market Street, San Francisco, CA 94103-1741—www.josseybass.com

Readers should be aware that Internet Web sites offered as citations and/or sources for further information may have changed or disappeared between the time this was written and when it is read.

Limit of Liability/Disclaimer of Warranty: While the publisher and author have used their best efforts in preparing this book, they make no representations or warranties with respect to the accuracy or completeness of the contents of this book and specifically disclaim any implied warranties of merchantability or fitness for a particular purpose. No warranty may be created or extended by sales representatives or written sales materials. The advice and strategies contained herein may not be suitable for your situation. You should consult with a professional where appropriate. Neither the publisher nor author shall be liable for any loss of profit or any other commercial damages, including but not limited to special, incidental, consequential, or other damages.

Jossey-Bass books and products are available through most bookstores. To contact Jossey-Bass directly call our Customer Care Department within the U.S. at 800-956-7739, outside the U.S. at 317-572-3986, or fax 317-572-4002.

Jossey-Bass also publishes its books in a variety of electronic formats. Some content that appears in print may not be available in electronic books.

Library of Congress Cataloging-in-Publication Data.

Supported literacy for adolescents : transforming teaching and content learning for the twenty-first century / Catherine Cobb Morocco . . . [et al.].
p.   cm. — (Jossey-Bass teacher)
Includes bibliographical references and index.
ISBN 978-0-470-22269-0 (pbk.)
1. Literacy—United States.   2. Teenagers—Education—United States.   3. Curriculum planning—United States. I. Morocco, Catherine Cobb.
LC151.S86 2008
302.2'244—dc22

2008018497

Printed in the United States of America
FIRST EDITION

PB Printing   10 9 8 7 6 5 4 3 2 1

CONTENTS

PREFACE

In writing this book, our author group held many conversations about what the future holds for the adolescents of today and how we can best prepare them to live and work in a global society. Our young people are using 'phones, computers, and iPods to network across the country with each other; they link to sports, music, and information in ways that we could not have imagined for ourselves as adolescents. They understand that a tsunami thousands of miles away may show up as waves lapping our own shores.

We asked ourselves, "What does a fifteen- or eighteen-year-old need to know and be able to do in a volatile and changing world? What does it mean to be a 'literate' young person? What ways of using literacy are important for these times?"

This book is our attempt to answer these questions. The first two chapters present a teaching framework that identifies the competencies that all adolescents need in a global world and the specific literacy tools that adolescents can use to develop those competencies. Many twenty-first-century learning reports have outlined the competencies that a global society requires of students. These reports emphasize that the ability to manage information and understand complex issues will be prized in the workplace. They argue that inquiry is rigorous when students are engaging in competencies that include conceptual understanding, critical thinking, creative thinking, and collaboration and communication with culturally diverse peers. In most of the rest of the chapters, the book brings these competencies into the classroom and links them with a set of "multiliteracy tools" that students need to develop and engage in these competencies. Reading to understand, writing to think, accountable talk, and digital and media fluency provide the students the means by which to hone their twenty-first-century competencies in all the content areas they encounter.

The book brings together the content area competencies and literacy tools in lessons and curriculum units organized around some of the most compelling questions of our times. In the science classroom, students use digital and multimedia images to ask "What is the evidence of climate change in our country and across the world?" They use writing, drawing, and peer discussion to investigate what our human role is in global warming. In history and literature class, they engage in peer discussion of historical texts and a memoir of a Japanese family after World War II, asking what impact war has on families and what countries and families themselves do to survive war. In their English class, they follow the development of a character who is struggling to fit into her peer group and also hold on to her self-respect. They write and support their interpretations about the characters in persuasive essays. And in the social studies class, they read articles, pose questions, and create podcasts about immigration to explore the questions of why people leave one country for another and how immigration affects communities.

The book shows teachers engaging their students in these big twenty-first-century questions as critical inquiries that involve thinking about the causes of conflict for individuals and families. Within the Supported Literacy framework, critical inquiries involve all students, including those with disabilities, struggling readers, and English language learners, in using their minds actively. Students find personal connections to the questions. (For example, What is *my* family's own immigration history? What is the carbon footprint of *my* school?) Critical inquiry is active and goes beyond simply gathering inert information. It links personal development with social critique and action.

But what about the sixth- or ninth-grade reader who still struggles to make sense of the written word? In addition to addressing the needs of typically developing learners, the Supported Literacy Intensive component addresses the needs of these struggling readers. And the book shows how a special education teacher, whose students have moderate cognitive difficulties, teaches her students the reading and peer collaboration skills they need to compare and contrast characters in a novel. This book takes the stand that all teachers in a school need to be connected and to work toward supporting all their students.

At a time when teachers are pulled in many directions and schools are seeking to provide professional development, Supported Literacy provides an accessible resource. This book includes classroom snapshots that capture the creative decision-making processes teachers use in developing their lessons. You can hear the voices of many teachers and students across different content domains and grade levels as they engage in a series of lessons from an extended curriculum unit. The book provides examples of curriculum units that can structure learning in a whole content area, building twenty-first-century competencies through a coherent and connected set of lessons.

Over the past decade, we authors developed the Supported Literacy framework through a series of collaborations between our organization, Education Development Center, Inc., in Newton, Massachusetts, and teams of teachers and administrators in Massachusetts and New York State and in the Southern states of Arkansas, Mississippi, and Louisiana. We supported these teams in working as learning communities to refine ideas, to use the framework to design sample curriculum units, and to develop new ways of integrating twenty-first-century competencies and literacy tools into content teaching. These teachers are the heart of the story; we hope they inspire you as they use the Supported Literacy framework to take their students into the twenty-first century.

Catherine Cobb Morocco and Cynthia Mata Aguilar
Newton, Massachusetts
March 2008

THE AUTHORS

Catherine Cobb Morocco is senior scientist and associate director at Education Development Center, Inc. (EDC) in Newton, Massachusetts. Her work focuses on improving students' writing, comprehension, and discourse skills and teachers' instructional expertise in literacy. As principal investigator of the REACH Institute (a five-year program funded by the U.S. Department of Education, Office of Special Education Programs, she coordinated the work of three university partners to design instructional materials for content area classrooms, and oversaw the development of a schoolwide literacy approach—Supported Literacy™—for the language arts classroom. Through additional grants, she and her colleagues expanded the classroom component of Supported Literacy to a tutorial model to provide additional tutoring for adolescents lacking foundation reading skills of phonemic awareness, decoding, word identification, and comprehension skills. She has also directed or served as principal investigator for a series of studies of middle schools and high schools that have strong participation and positive results for their students with disabilities. She was first author of a recent a book, *Visionary Middle Schools: Signature Practices and the Power of Local Innovation Disabilities,* with colleagues Cynthia Aguilar and Nancy Brigham, and also produced a special journal issue, "Good High Schools for Students with Disabilities." She has published in numerous scholarly journals and regularly presents at national conferences. She received her doctorate in language and literature from Harvard University.

Cynthia Mata Aguilar is a senior project director and adolescent literacy specialist at EDC. Her expertise includes adolescent literacy, special education and inclusive practices, school reform in the middle and high school, and diversity, multicultural, and anti-racism training. She is the author of several research articles and publications, including *Visionary Middle Schools: Signature Practices and the Power of Local Invention.* The August 2006 issue of *Learning Disabilities: Research & Practice* features "Good High Schools for Students with Disabilities," another of Aguilar's projects. Currently, she is adolescent literacy team leader for the New York and New England Comprehensive Centers, federally funded technical assistance centers that support states' efforts to raise the academic achievement of secondary school students and meet the goals of No Child Left Behind. Her experience as a teacher, union president, researcher, and professional development specialist informs her work. She is the co-writer for several Supported Literacy curriculum units including "How Far Would You Go to Fit In?"

Carol Bershad brings more than twenty-five years of experience in developing curricula, books, simulations, and online courses in science, literacy, health, leadership, and school change, as well as designing and conducting professional development for educators. Carol was a co-writer for the Supported Literacy curriculum unit titled "How Far Would You Go to Fit In?" and designed and conducted Supported Literacy professional development for teachers and coaches. Carol has also written other middle school curricula integrating literacy and life skills, including a literacy-based module titled "Taking Action to Stop Bullying." Bershad has co-written books on nutrition and fitness for children, including *Bodyworks* (Random House). She also wrote an online teacher course for the WGBH public broadcasting station's series titled *Evolution* (www.pbs.org/evolution). In addition, Carol has been a consultant for systemic school change, conducting national workshops and presentations for educators using the simulation she co-developed, Systems Thinking/Systems Changing™. She is currently completing two other simulations, one on leadership and academic achievement and the other on professional development design for science, "Building Systems for Quality Teaching and Learning in Science," funded by the National Science Foundation. Bershad earned her M.S. in biology from the University of Michigan and has eight years of classroom experience teaching biology in the Newton Public Schools, Newton, Massachusetts.

THE CONTRIBUTORS

Andrea Winokur Kotula is a project director and literacy specialist at EDC. She is completing a study, funded by the U.S. Department of Education, Office of Special Education Programs, to develop a model of intensive differentiated reading instruction for the lowest quarter of readers at an urban middle school. This model has become a part of the Supported Literacy framework. She works with EDC's technical assistance team in the New York Comprehensive Center to provide assistance to New York City and New York State literacy leaders and professional development to literacy coaches and leadership teams on implementing scientifically based reading research. Kotula's special expertise is the diagnosis and correction of reading difficulties. Prior to coming to EDC, she was the director of reading and educational resources at the Franciscan Hospital for Children, where she trained and supervised staff who conducted educational evaluations as part of multidisciplinary teams. She has teaching experience at the elementary level, as a reading specialist, and at the undergraduate and graduate levels. She earned a doctorate in reading, language, and learning disabilities at Harvard Graduate School of Education, where she was a research assistant to Jeanne S. Chall, a world-renowned expert on reading instruction, reading disability, and readability. She has been the president of the International Reading Association's Special Interest Group on Readability since 1997 and frequently presents at national conferences.

Alisa Hindin is an assistant professor of educational studies at Seton Hall University (New Jersey), where she teaches courses in literacy and teacher education. Her research interests include literacy instruction, teacher preparation in literacy, and family literacy. She was a research associate for the REACH Institute at Education Development Center, Inc. (EDC), where she played a major role in the development and field testing of Supported Literacy, providing professional development support to teachers in the project, and writing and publishing journal articles related to the work. Her most recent journal publications are forthcoming in the *Journal of Literacy Research* and *Teachers and Teaching: Theory and Practice*. Her doctorate is from Boston University.

ACKNOWLEDGMENTS

The authors wish to thank the many people, particularly teachers, principals, and coaches, who contributed to this book. *Supported Literacy for Adolescents* was created with and for classroom practitioners working with EDC staff, and reflects the realities of what teachers cope with and accomplish daily in their work with young people. Each chapter includes the voices of teachers and other professionals who were part of developing and applying the Supported Literacy framework.

Teachers from Worcester East Middle School and Sullivan Middle School in Worcester, MA opened their classrooms to the EDC team and worked many hours after school to design initial curriculum units. Three Sullivan Middle School teachers, Terry Palumbo, Claire Scanlon, and Lilla Robinson, made additional contributions by allowing us to videotape their students in Supported Literacy lessons. These teachers and their students are the focus of the detailed stories in several chapters. Caprice Kopka from Worcester East Middle School stepped in at the end of the process to give us feedback on several chapter drafts. Principals John Bierfeldt and Kevin Keany encouraged all of these teacher contributions and made Supported Literacy an integral part of their schools.

In Mississippi, Arkansas, and Louisiana, teachers in every content area, including mathematics and foreign language, used Supported Literacy to develop their school-wide literacy coaching skills. We thank those teachers and their principals and the staff of Atlas in the Middle (AIM), who organized and supported that year-long training process. The AIM director, Glenda Copeland, and coordinators Ruby Midkiff and Barbara Hunter-Cox connected us with schools through these southern states, including Lincoln Middle School and Lake View Middle in Forrest City, AR; Henderson Intermediate School and Armstrong Middle School in Starkville, MS; Magnolia Middle School in Meridian, MS; and Martin Luther King, Jr. Middle School in Monroe, LA.

Teachers and administrators from Collins Middle School in Salem, MA and Morton Middle School in Fall River, MA collaborated with doctors Kotula and Morocco in designing and piloting the Supported Literacy Intensive program described in Chapter Six. Principal Mary Manning and Assistant Principal Nancy Pelletier from Collins Middle School took on scheduling and staff development challenges in order to develop an intensive tutorial program for low reading students in grades 6 through 8.

Many people, in addition to our Worcester teachers, contributed to the content area curriculum adaptations we describe. For the social studies examples (*Immigration* in Chapter One and *War and People* in Chapter Two) we would like to thank Greg Hurray, K-8 English language arts coordinator for the Newton Massachusetts Public Schools, for sharing information about the integration of literacy into content areas in middle school classrooms. We thank Robert Parlin, Newton South High School history teacher, for sharing his immigration unit and teaching experiences, and Janet Buerklin,

K-8 social studies coordinator, for talking with us about teaching about immigration and integrating literacy skills into history teaching. We treasure the contribution of Yoko Kawashima Watkins, author of *My Brother, My Sister, & I*, to our work with that text; she shared her life and her heart in a unit that became *War and Families*.

Many people contributed to Chapter Three, on applying Supported Literacy to teaching climate change. Two 17-year-old students, Floryn Honnett and Teddy Rosenthal, helped us understand how adolescents think about global warming. Michael Ernst, director of information systems at the Woods Hole Research Center, generously provided up-to-date graphs on climate change. Susan Mundry, associate director of mathematics, science, and technology programs at WestEd, and Deborah Haber, a former science teacher and now director of the Center for School and Community Health Programs at EDC, both provided helpful feedback on the climate chapter and science inquiry learning. Ruth Krumasi, an earth sciences teacher and member of EDC's curriculum development staff, shared her curriculum and experiences teaching climate change. Jackie Miller and Marion Pasquale, also of EDC's Science Center, allowed us to consult their Earth Science Curriculum Project and provided thoughtful feedback on Chapter Three. Karen Worth shared her science literacy curriculum for younger students and has been a partner in discussing science and literacy for many years.

Many other staff in our EDC brain trust have helped us over the years. Thank you to David O'Neil, director of publishing, for fostering our relationship with Jossey-Bass; to Nancy Ames for her great vision, insightful feedback, and draft of the final chapter; and Judy Zorfass and her Literacy Matters staff, for their help in bringing Supported Literacy to the country. Sherry Anderson coordinated book production, Andrea Goguen creating the early graphics, and Laurie Rosenblum edited the references. Cerelle Morrow reviewed several chapters. Emily Arwen Mott was an invaluable EDC research assistant during our early years of piloting the program in Worcester. We appreciate David Riley's help in seeing the implication of the work for students with disabilities and providing us many opportunities to share the Supported Literacy work with teachers across the country in conferences of the Urban Special Education Collaborative.

Kim Elliott is the most extraordinary editor, whose developmental editing and deep copy editing immensely strengthened our manuscript.

Our work would not be possible without the contributions of our funders, both federal and foundation. The Office of Special Education Programs (OSEP) of the U. S. Department of Education provided the original grant for a five-year institute to look at curriculum for diverse students as well as a second grant to that focused on struggling readers. The first two authors directed the institute and developed Supported Literacy in that context. The Office of Elementary and Secondary Education (OESE) supported the comprehensive school reform work with AIM literacy coaches in the South. The MetLife Foundation funded the development of a unit that applied Supported Literacy to a curriculum unit on health and social studies.

Finally, we dedicate the book to all middle and high school teachers as they work together to prepare their students for a world with formidable problems and infinite opportunities. We hope that you will find some powerful ideas and tools in this book to help you engage all of your students in critical inquiry and in advocating for their ideas.

EDUCATION DEVELOPMENT CENTER

Education Development Center, Inc. (EDC) is an international, nonprofit organization that conducts and applies research to advance learning and promote health. EDC currently manages 325 projects in thirty-five countries. Our award-winning programs and products, developed in collaboration with partners around the globe, address nearly every critical need in society, including early child development, K–12 education, health promotion, workforce preparation, community development, learning technologies, basic and adult education, institutional reform, medical ethics, and social justice.

CHAPTER

1

A NEW VISION OF ADOLESCENT LITERACY

CLASSROOM CLOSE-UP

A Twenty-First-Century Classroom

Tom Howard's eleventh graders are using a fishbowl format to discuss an immigration crisis in their community. The students vary in their reading and writing skills as well as in their cultural backgrounds, but most of them love this talking format. All are aware that U.S. immigration policies are a big subject of debate in the country—they know, because many students in the school have recently immigrated from Central and Latin America or Asia. Also, their town is grappling with an immigration crisis. Federal immigration officers raided a factory in their community that employs several hundred Mexican women, most working in the United States illegally, and quickly deported many of them to an immigration detention center in Texas. The eight students in the inner circle are talking about what happened and how this current immigration conflict relates to earlier waves of immigration to the United States. Fifteen other students are sitting in a larger circle around the speakers, listening and taking notes.

Mr. Howard: Okay, you in the fishbowl, from your reading and Internet search of press releases and reports, what happened at the New Rialto leather factory?

John: Immigration authorities burst into the plant and hauled away workers.

(Continued)

1

Tomas: Just ones who couldn't show papers, but it was over three hundred people. And the factory was paying practically nothing and had terrible work conditions. And the factory is still open!

Teresa: They put hundreds on planes to Texas to detention camps. Some of the women have little children.

Oscar: Detention centers aren't prisons, though they can have bad conditions. Social service people flew to Texas to see who has kids and needs to be home.

Ruben: Some parents have kids in our school. I've been to meetings with them.

Emma: We feel badly for these workers, but you know, *they're illegal* [speaker's emphasis]. My uncle is here *legally,* and he should have one of those jobs!

This discussion comes at the end of an eight-week unit on the causes and impact of immigration to the United States since the end of the nineteenth century. The unit is organized around questions of current interest: Why do people emigrate to another country? What different waves of immigrants have come to the United States, and why have they come? What issues and conflicts are arising around current immigration to the United States? The students have constructed family trees at home to learn about their family histories and to be able to bring their family and cultural identities into their understanding of present-day immigration issues.

They are using a multiplicity of literacy tools. They are reading textbooks and reading and listening to primary sources focused on more than a hundred years of immigration to the United States from Southern and Eastern Europe, Asia, Mexico, Central and South America, and Africa. The readings included narratives of earlier immigrants published in print books and on the Internet, online newspaper accounts of earlier immigration issues, and court briefs. They are writing summaries and analyses of their readings, and they bring that writing to peer discussions. Groups of four or five students have studied different immigrant waves and posted write-ups on the class *blog* (a Web site designed for students to post observations and comments) after presenting their findings to the class. Each group investigated why people came, how they were treated when they arrived, their economic situations, and how they fit into the economy at that time. For example, they contrasted the reasons why poor Mexicans are coming into the country now with the reasons why poor Irish settled here in the 1800s.

Mr. Howard encourages his students to connect what they've read about earlier immigrations with what is happening in their own community:

Ruben: It's *nativism* [local people's fears that immigrants will disrupt their jobs and way of life]. Like we discussed from studying the Irish immigrations. People are afraid they'll lose their jobs to new people.

Teresa: And it's economic. Earlier groups also came for work. I'm from California and illegal immigrants pick our grapes and oranges.

Tomas: My group read the Homeland Security Documents on how to treat immigrant detainees. Fine, the rules aren't so bad, but we can't just hold people. My grandparents came here from Russia and they're citizens. How should people get to be Americans?

Mr. Howard: When you write up your group investigations next week, find as many connections as you can to this crisis in our own community. We'll record your presentations and post them as a *podcast* [a digital sound file] on our class blog.

The students continue the discussion on the class blog. Emma offers to start the discussion of whether or not illegal immigrants should be allowed some route to legal citizenship. Over the next few weeks, students from two California-Mexico border towns who are also studying immigration issues—as well as living on the front lines of the debate—join the online discussion.

Mr. Howard's students are grappling with a complex topic that affects their community and is part of many of their own family histories. Looking at their family trees fueled their curiosity and influenced their reading, writing, and talking about U.S. immigration history. These students are using the traditional literacies of reading, writing, listening, and discussing in new ways and using new technologies to gather information and communicate with each other and with audiences beyond their classroom.

Their readings come not just from libraries and textbooks but from digitized materials on the Internet that include print, oral histories, podcasts from other classrooms, photographs, video, and film. They are writing in ways their parents never experienced in school—on computers as well as on paper, and to each other and to adolescents anywhere in the world who read their blog, not just to their teacher. Some of the texts they compose integrate oral and visual materials and links to Web sites. But they are not just communicating in cyberspace. Their classroom discussions and interactions are honest and respectful of all students' ideas.

WHAT IS A PREPARED ADOLESCENT?

The content of Mr. Howard's teaching—immigration history and policies—reflects state and national social studies standards and twenty-first-century issues. His students use a wide variety of literacy practices and tools to investigate the complex question of why people move from one part of the globe to another. Mr. Howard believes that all of his students need to wrestle with historical questions and connect those questions with the present. Like you, and like many teachers across all of the content areas, Mr. Howard wants his teaching to be relevant for a different kind of world than the one in which he grew up.

Mr. Howard's teaching responds to a call for change from education and economic groups in this country and abroad. In *America's Perfect Storm: Three Forces*

Changing Our Nation's Future (2007), Educational Testing Service (ETS) calls this a pivotal time in history, in which we depend on education as never before to prepare students to live and work in a global, international society. Reports such as *Tough Choices, Tough Times: The Report of the New Commission on the Skills of the American Workforce* from the National Center on Education and the Economy (NCEE, 2007) and *Results That Matter: 21st Century Skills and High School Reform* from the Partnership for 21st Century Skills (2006) make a strong case to reform education to better serve students. In *A Global Imperative: The Report of the 21st Century Literacy Summit,* the New Media Consortium (NMC) argues that the use of digital and media forms are enhancing learning and that "as young people create casual multimedia, they are also creating the opportunity to experiment, learn, take risks, and become fluent" (2005, p. 3).

These reports urge us to rethink what and how adolescents are learning and what kind of literacy skills they need. The reports converge around the ideas that schools need to reflect the globalized world in which adolescents will work and live as citizens (Gardner, 2006; Suarez-Orozco & Qin-Hilliard, 2004). We use *globalization* here to refer to the process by which countries become more integrated with one another as a result of movements of goods, capital, labor, and ideas (Bloom, 2004). All these global movements pose challenges and present vibrant opportunities:

- *Movements of people.* Recent waves of immigration to the United States from Asia, Central and South America, the Caribbean, and the Middle East are generating diverse U.S. communities and classrooms that reflect the larger world. As we write this, young people from 190 countries or more are getting up to go to school in New York City today (Linares, 2006). Many small town classrooms now have that same diversity. Does yours?

- *Movements of capital.* Since 1990, three billion people in China, India, and the former Soviet Union have moved from closed economies to participating in a global economy (Wilson, 2005). Already, one in five jobs in our country is tied to international trade (U.S. Census Bureau, 2004). Your students' future employers will prize employees who understand economics and can collaborate with colleagues of varied cultural backgrounds and status.

- *Movements in science and technology.* Scientists work in international teams, sharing databases to understand complex scientific questions and create innovative solutions in medicine (Friedman, 2005). They research issues—the spread and responses to infectious disease, the causes and impact of climate change—that have global implications. Your students need a rigorous science and technology education to enter these fields.

- *Movements in popular culture.* Young people around the world wear similar clothes and follow global sports heroes like David Beckham, an English soccer player who lives in Los Angeles (Suarez-Orozco & Sattin, 2007) and Daisuke

Matsuzak ("Dice-K"), a Japanese pitcher for the Boston Red Sox. Because of Internet radio stations, music sites, and iTunes, your students live in a rich world of talk, music, and online discussions. In using social networking sites like MySpace, Friendster, and Facebook, adolescents are part of a larger global community where they discuss a plethora of topics including common interests, international events, and politics.

Your students are part of a generation of Millennials—youth born between 1982 and 1998—that has almost unlimited access to information and to different perspectives to spark their imaginations. According to the National Center for Education Statistics (NCES, 2005a), almost every K–12 U.S. classroom has been connected to the Internet since 2000. Many teens have access at home, libraries, and in community centers (Bruce, 2005). At the same time, many teens lack the skills, aptitudes, and competencies they need to benefit from these opportunities for global learning. Their teachers need to help them think critically about the abundance of information available to them. They need teachers who cultivate their curiosity and knowledge about other cultures.

Mr. Howard engages his students in investigating questions about U.S. history that expand their views of themselves as individuals. While other teachers and schools are also working to educate students to be engaged citizens and ethical human beings, too many schools remain "out of sync with the realities of a global world" (Suarez-Orozco & Sattin, 2007, p. 58).

More than ever before, your students need help to master important information, not as an end in itself but as a foundation for inquiry into questions that are important in your content area and in a global society. But inquiry is not only a process by which individuals develop and learn, it is the way a democratic society examines and renews itself. When Mr. Howard's students connect their investigation of immigration history to themselves, their community, and their country's federal policies, they are engaging in a process called *critical inquiry,* linking history with personal identity and social critique. The process deserves that name because it is active and goes beyond simply gathering inert knowledge (Beach & Bruce, 2005).

In arguing for a more relevant way of teaching for a challenging new time, the twenty-first-century learning reports noted earlier emphasize that rigorous inquiry encompasses four kinds of competencies:

- Conceptual understanding

- Critical thinking

- Creative thinking

- Collaboration and communication

The following paragraphs present a brief description of each of these competencies. Because each requires literacy skills—the ability to use reading, writing, discussion, and digital and media skills for inquiry—we use the bulk of this chapter to define a set of *multiliteracy* tools that students need to build and engage in the four competencies of critical inquiry.

Conceptual Understanding

Mr. Howard's students' critical inquiry into U.S. immigration leads them to historical information and concepts such as nativism, immigration policy, and the causes and consequences of immigration. Prepared adolescents are able to build a deep understanding of that information and connect those concepts. To be prepared to work and live in the twenty-first century, your students must have a conceptual understanding that encompasses concepts in the traditional subject areas of history, science, literature, and mathematics, as well as new content in areas such as finance, world economics and business, and international humanitarian law.

Your students will develop deep conceptual understanding from asking questions and investigating them in ways that are distinctive in each content area. Scientists pose questions about the world, come up with tentative classifications and theories, design experiments to produce data that test those theories, and revise current theories in light of new findings. Historians investigate the past from existing data—albeit frequently scattered and contradictory fragments of information (Gardner, 2006, p. 28). Regardless of the field, to understand is to be able to apply an idea or concept in a new context (Blythe, 1998). In Mr. Howard's classroom, students apply the concept of nativism first to a historical study of immigration, and then to a current immigration crisis in their own city.

Critical Thinking

Prepared adolescents have skills in analyzing the source and accuracy of print and digitized information. Your students need to be able to question data, evaluate the quality of the evidence provided for a finding, and determine why the author is providing that particular piece of evidence. They need to consider multiple perspectives on an issue or problem and test alternative views or hypotheses. These are all skills of critical thinking.

Your students also need to be able to detect patterns in information and synthesize information from many different sources. Mr. Howard encourages students to do this as they compare the participants in, and causes and impacts of, different waves of immigration. Howard Gardner argues that "the ability to knit together information from disparate sources into a coherent whole is vital" in a world where accumulated knowledge might double every few years (2006, p. 46). Daniel Pink (2006) argues that the workplace of the future will prize *symphony,* a term he uses for ability to see relationships between seemingly unrelated events or ideas.

As members of the twenty-first-century workforce, your students will need to go beyond gathering and synthesizing information related to a question to taking a stance and arguing their point of view with evidence and logical reasoning. Supporting an argument brings the individual beyond analysis to problem solving and lays the groundwork for social or political action.

Creative Thinking

Creativity encompasses innovation to sustain economic competitiveness, ingenuity in scientific research, resourcefulness in building human relationships, and imaginative expression in the arts. While the synthesizer puts together what is known into a useful form, the creator extends what we know and "ruffles the contours of a genre" (Gardner, 2006, p. 98). Creativity is the spirit of risk taking, which sends us in new directions and brings us "out of our minds" (Robinson, 2001). Mr. Howard's students open themselves to new ways of understanding immigration by posing their discussions on a blog and getting responses from students in California.

An international leader in the development of creativity, Robinson (2001) argues that schools are a crucible for helping individuals find their creative abilities and that these abilities take varied forms and show up in different learning styles. He describes Gillian Lynne, the choreographer for the Broadway shows *Cats* and *The Phantom of the Opera,* whose parents took her to a psychiatrist as a child because she would not sit still in school. Fortunately, Robinson jokes, the doctor told the parents that Gillian was a dancer and should go to dance school rather than take medication (Robinson, 2006). Creativity is also highly interactive; original ideas that are important (Robinson's definition of creativity) emerge in multidisciplinary settings, where people examine issues or dilemmas from very different perspectives.

Effective Collaboration and Communication

Many twenty-first-century issues extend across national boundaries and disciplines and require people with different knowledge bases, perspectives, and cultures to work together to investigate problems. Prepared adolescents are accustomed to and adept at working with others on a complex question to bring all elements of a problem into its solution.

Teachers like Mr. Howard help build students' capacity to collaborate by modeling the role of facilitator as students work with each other on inquiry projects. His teaching practices give students responsibility for their learning and promote attitudes of respect for others' cultural histories and ideas. His use of a class blog extends their inquiry into immigration issues beyond the classroom.

To participate in collaborative problem solving, your students must, like Mr. Howard's, learn and adhere to standards of ethics and moral behavior (Stewart, 2007). Howard Gardner defines the *ethical mind* for the workplace and for citizenship as "a conviction that one's community should possess certain characteristics of which one is proud and a commitment personally to work toward the realization of the virtuous community" (2006, p. 129). Ethical collaboration is important in both distant and face-to-face work. Digital and media tools give students unprecedented access to other thinkers and also require that they use and share information with an ethical stance.

■ ■ ■

When you support students in developing these four areas of competence, you prepare them for rigorous and imaginative inquiry in their work and lives beyond school. They acquire the abstract reasoning and problem-solving skills to evaluate what they hear and read. They build their capacity to communicate well and to work with others of different cultural backgrounds. From their experience of collaborating with peers, they cultivate the habit of being open to and curious about new ways of thinking. They carry the moral and ethical stances they develop while they investigate issues in your classroom beyond the school walls, helping preserve the democratic values that define the U.S. national culture.

But what literacy skills can you teach to support their critical inquiry into important content areas and global issues and problems? While it is probably true that, as the National Adolescent Literacy Coalition (NALC, 2007) observes, "literacy will divide winners and losers" in efforts to prepare adolescents for the economies and problem solving ahead, what should those literacies be? Is reading still important to your students' future? How should we define a text, and what reading skills do your students need for critical inquiry, given the many kinds of print and digital texts they access? Can your students learn to "read" visual texts—those that integrate print, video, photographs, and sound? Given the new tools for communicating information and expressing ideas, what classroom writing and discussion practices can you engage your students in to prepare them to work, participate, and reflect in a connected society? If digital and media literacies have value and energy far beyond casual communication and entertainment, what is their role in critical inquiry?

Figure 1.1 portrays literacy (or, as we name it, *multiliteracy*) as the core area of competence that supports students in developing and using the other four competencies. The section that follows defines the particular kinds of multiliteracy skills that students need to engage in critical inquiry and build the other four twenty-first-century competencies.

SUPPORTED LITERACY FOR NEW TIMES

Supported Literacy is an instructional framework to guide your students' classroom learning. It is also a curriculum framework that you can use to create rigorous and relevant new units in any subject or to modify and enrich existing units to better address the four key twenty-first-century competencies. The framework provides you with teaching strategies that help academically diverse groups of students gain a deep understanding of important ideas and concepts in traditional content areas and emerging fields. The strategies focus on fostering students' use of *multiliteracies*—intellectual tools and techniques that enable learners to access, process, and communicate information and ideas—that extend and enrich their critical inquiry. Using the Supported Literacy Meaning-Making Cycle, you and your students can investigate essential questions that create the conditions that promote critical inquiry and develop the use of multiliteracies.

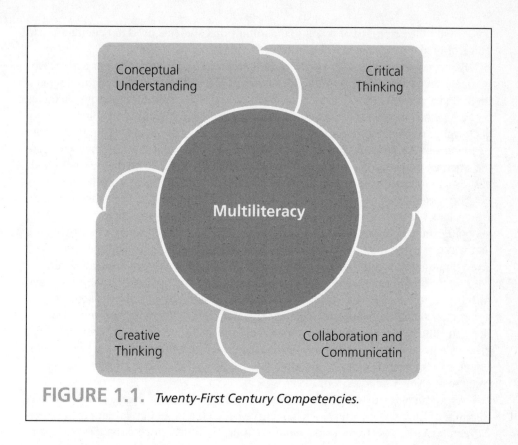

FIGURE 1.1. *Twenty-First Century Competencies.*

Over the past decade, we developed the Supported Literacy framework through a series of collaborations between our organization, Education Development Center, Inc., in Newton, Massachusetts, and teams of teachers and administrators in Massachusetts, New York State, and the Southern states of Arkansas, Mississippi, and Louisiana. We supported these teams in working as learning communities to refine ideas, to use the framework to design sample curriculum units, and to develop new ways of integrating twenty-first-century competencies into content teaching (Hindin, Morocco, Mott, & Aguilar, 2007; Kotula & Morocco, 2006; Morocco, Hindin, Mata-Aguilar, & Clark-Chiarelli, 2001). Today, we continue to provide training and technical assistance to enable schools nationwide to use the Supported Literacy framework.

The framework's concept of multiliteracies draws from three areas of literacy research and practice. One area is National Institute of Child Health and Human Development research on reading comprehension that focuses on how students acquire the cognitive processes—such as phonemic awareness, decoding, word attack, and comprehension strategies—they need to understand print texts (NICHD, 2000). The No Child Left Behind legislation emphasizes reading as literacy and has pushed for basic reading skills in all groups of students. While Supported Literacy agrees with the centrality of reading, it assumes that students need to acquire a broad range of literacies for twenty-first-century learning.

A second area is research on *multiple literacies*—competence in using new technologies such as digital texts, Internet search engines, film and video, and integrated multimedia presentations. These researchers assert that print and nonprint literacies occur together in students' lives outside school and that students build their reading and writing skills, as well as their sense of personal identity, as they use a wide range of literacies (Alvermann, 2007). Many teachers espouse this view as they integrate the Internet, blogging, *Web quests* (guided information searches on the Internet), podcasts, and multimedia tools into their teaching.

Supported Literacy multiliteracies also reflect a third area, new literacy research, which looks at the social contexts in which literacy occurs—in school, on the Web, shopping, and applying for a job. These contexts call for varied forms of participation and ways of using reading, writing, talking, listening, and digital and media activity (New London Group, 1996; Pahl & Rowsell, 2005). New literacy uses the term *discourses* to refer to the norms for how members participate, interact, and use language in these different contexts (Gee, 1999a, 1999b, 2003). Researchers in new literacy assert that students' literacy reflects the skills and discourses they learn in their families and cultural groups, at school, on the Internet, and in peer groups. They posit that schools will be more equitable, motivating, and successful if teachers encourage adolescents to bring their diverse literacy-related skills and discourses through the classroom door (New London Group, 1996).

As a strategic fusion of these three strands of literacy research and practice, Supported Literacy encompasses cognitive, social and cultural, and technological components. The framework identifies four multiliteracies that students need to master:

- Reading for deep understanding

- Writing to build and express meaning

- Accountable talk

- Digital and media fluency

Teachers will not always be engaging students in critical inquiry and in the kind of extended investigations that we present in this book. When they do, these four multiliteracies have a core role to play and a wide application across the different content areas. They support students' inquiry by helping them "extract meaning from experience as they engage in efforts to address questions meaningful to them" (Beach & Bruce, 2005, p. 153). As you engage your students in content inquiry, these tools support the kinds of questioning, drive to understand, critical and creative thinking, and communication and collaboration that are the hallmarks of twenty-first-century learning.

Reading for Deep Understanding

As historical texts become rich and conceptually dense, readers may slow down—not because they fail to comprehend but because the very act of comprehension demands that they stop to *talk* with their texts (Wineberg, 2001, p. 69).

Almost every existing text is becoming available through scientific and historical Web sites, Web archives, school and online libraries, publishing companies, family archives, and blogs. Those texts bring a variety of data sources and different perspectives that can shape an inquiry. While acquiring basic decoding skills and fluency will continue to be important for some adolescents (see Chapter Six), reading instruction needs to focus on higher-order reading skills and on questioning the meaning of the text. It is especially important for students with reading difficulties to grasp the ideas in the texts and to connect those ideas to scientific, historical, and literary questions. To gain a deep understanding of a text, *all* students must develop the skills to read strategically, notice how texts are organized, think critically about the text, and build word meaning.

Read Strategically. To read hard-copy or online texts of all genres, your students need to acquire the habit of strategic reading. A number of comprehension strategies have a strong research base, including asking questions to help make sense of what students read and to connect the text to their big questions, as Mr. Howard's class does in asking, "Why do people want to come to the United States?" (See this chapter's Classroom Close-Up, p. 1.) Strategic readers connect their reading with what they already know about a topic. They predict what might happen next in a reading, identify the most important ideas, summarize what they understand, and organize information visually with graphs and charts (NICHD, 2000). They notice their thinking as they read and they use that *metacognitive awareness*—or "ability to monitor one's current level of skill or understanding and decide when it is not adequate" (Bransford, Brown, & Cocking, 2000, p. 47)—to choose a better strategy when they bog down.

Notice How Texts Are Organized. To read for deep understanding, your students must recognize how different kinds of writing are structured. They should be aware that a history textbook often organizes the material chronologically and uses a time line as shorthand for that chronology. They should know that many science texts use a research report structure that begins with a purpose or question, provides background research, and presents a hypothesis, data-gathering procedure, data from empirical studies, and analysis and discussion. Good readers look for other kinds of patterns, such as the argument form, in which an author presents a position and then supports the position with evidence and reasoning. Comparison and contrast is a text pattern that occurs in almost every content area: comparing waves of immigration (history), results of experiments (science), or characters in a novel (literature). Attending to these patterns can be a good strategy (Langer, 1986).

Think Critically About the Text. Your students need to be able to evaluate the source, accuracy, and completeness of what they read in a print or nonprint text. Students tend to think that texts are the truth, that they have the *right answers* to their questions, rather than seeing texts as "live artifacts with a story and system behind them" (Pahl & Rowsell, 2005). In the history classroom, students need to go beyond finding the main idea of a document to noticing the language the writer uses to convey a point of view. Sam Wineberg (2001) has his students notice that their textbook writer uses the word *atrocity* to label an early skirmish in the Revolutionary War and the word *patriot* to describe the farmers involved. Without noting who fired the first shot, the writer is constructing the event as a massacre by the English. Wineberg wants his students to read texts as authors' voices to decode and "keys to unlocking the character of human beings, people with likes and dislikes, biases and foibles, airs and convictions" (p. 74).

Build Word Meaning. As you guide your students in considering twenty-first-century questions, they will encounter new technical vocabulary. Knowing the term *nativism* helps Mr. Howard's students read and understand local reactions to the factory raid in their community. Science texts include technical language having to do with scientific inquiry such as *data, evidence, hypothesis,* and *claim* and with particular fields—astronomy, earth science, or biology. A host of texts and teacher guides offer strategies for vocabulary development, such as using unfamiliar words as springboards for increasing content knowledge. For example, Allen (2007) observed a teacher pre-select challenging new words before starting a science unit on digestion and engage students in building background knowledge through interesting short readings and writing activities.

Writing to Build and Express Meaning

"Meaning is remarkably elusive. . . . Putting an idea into written words is like defrosting the windshield: The idea, so vague out there in the murk, slowly begins to gather itself into a sensible shape" (Zinsser, 1988, pp. 14–16).

Writing is the companion of deep reading and the workshop of thought during critical inquiry; it causes students to make connections and see patterns. With reading, observation, and scientific experimentation as raw materials, "writing exercises the intellect as it moves from amorphous understanding toward precision and practical application. In the end, committing thinking to paper pushes us to discover and produce thought in its clearest and most potent form" (Schmoker, 2006, p. 64). It stimulates deeper thinking than conversation or inner reflection.

In a twenty-first-century inquiry, students' writing practices go beyond writing final lab reports, essays, and tests (presentational writing) to writing throughout an investigation. They write to summarize several articles and documents, to prepare for a small group discussion, to express their ideas informally to others and get feedback, to give others access to their ideas, and to change or deepen their own understanding (exploratory writing). They also post their writing on a class blog to continue

SNAPSHOT

Reading for Deep Understanding in Your Classroom

To emphasize deep reading for inquiry learning, you need to teach and talk about specific comprehension strategies with your students because most students do not learn them otherwise (RAND Reading Study Group, 2002). You cue your students to the important features of the text that help them build meaning, for example, the structure of a lab report, the chronology embedded in a history article, or the story elements—setting, plot, climax, resolution—that underlie a work of fiction. When a reading includes technical terms and new concepts, you introduce them before students read, and you ask them to talk about the new concepts in their discussion. To build students' critical inquiry skills, you usually refrain from telling them what a text means. Instead, you encourage them to struggle for meaning through reading, writing, and discussion. You demonstrate critical thinking about texts by thinking aloud your agreements and disagreements with the text and how it advances the class inquiry.

Just as Mr. Howard's questions stimulate his students ("What does this writer say—or mean—about why natives may dislike new immigrants in their community?"), your comments push your students to connect what they read to their key questions. And you are explicit about the kind of talk—discourse—you expect around a text. For example, you support students in talking about where writers agree or disagree on a point. Visitors to your classroom see students sharing divergent points of view, contesting interpretations, and negotiating the interpretation of texts (King & O'Brien, 2005).

conversations after class, as do Mr. Howard's students. In *Education Leadership,* a teacher wrote, "What I didn't realize was how powerfully revising scripts for broadcasting would improve students' writing" (Dlott, 2007). The increasing use of writing for blogs and podcasts in middle school classrooms is motivating students to write comments, broadcasts, and arguments with distant audiences in mind. To successfully build and express the meaning of ideas, students need to master several writing skills. They must be able to use writing and drawing to comprehend texts, use writing to think critically about content, and write clearly for many purposes.

Use Writing and Drawing to Comprehend Texts. Writing and drawing aid students' comprehension (Applebee, 2000; National Writing Project & Nagin, 2006). Written comprehension strategies include students' writing summaries of what they read, posing and answering questions to activate their critical thinking, and connecting new content with what they know. Organizing information in a chart helps students remember it. Using these writing strategies makes students grapple with the meaning of a print text.

Students can also use writing strategies to make sense of visual texts such as graphs, data tables, still media images and photographs, and moving images. They can write their interpretations of information in a numerical graph or data table. They can write about their emotional responses to a film and also describe the strategies they used in making meaning from it. These strategies might include the prior knowledge they brought to the film, their predictions about what would happen, and the inferences they made about a character's thoughts and emotions from dialogue, facial expressions, and actions.

Use Writing to Think Critically About Content. Writing is a natural medium for synthesis and analysis; we associate one event with another as we write and see connections that we did not consider previously. In charting the different sources, points of view, and data sources of three Civil War documents, students prepare to articulate the explicit and implicit messages these documents contain. In using writing to engage in critical thinking, students learn the academic language of a content area. In science, students use writing to represent data visually in charts or graphs, articulate hypotheses, summarize data, and discuss conclusions. In writing about the themes of a novel, students use the academic language of literature study, including terms such as *character development, point of view, scene, plot, image, theme,* and *metaphor.*

Write Clearly for Many Purposes. In twenty-first-century classrooms, students understand the different features of an effective story, technical manual, Web page, book review, editorial, memoir, biography, oral history, podcast, multimedia presentation, or persuasive essay. They consider what form will be the most effective way to communicate their messages to a particular audience; they can give form to feeling and thought with poetry, drama, memoir, and fiction.

Comparison and contrast, a kind of thinking that can be used as a critical reading strategy, is also an important way to organize a piece of writing. In Chapter Five, a special education teacher teaches that structure for students to use in reading and writing about a novel. Another genre that is important in critical inquiry is argument—taking a position or claim and supporting it with evidence and logical reasoning. Lisa Delpit (2006) writes that argumentative literacy defines intellectual maturity and prepares us for an adult life. A supported argument draws on many twenty-first-century competencies, particularly conceptual understanding, considering multiple perspectives, and synthesizing information to take a stance. Each content area has a version of this important genre, which requires learners to take a stance on what they have read and explain it to others. In a democracy, this form of writing is a basis for policy, legislation, and community action.

SNAPSHOT

Writing to Build and Express Meaning in Your Classroom

To help students vary their writing appropriately, you provide them with models of good writing. You respond with specific feedback to their writing, so that their writing moves forward and uses evaluation criteria that fit the purpose of the writing. You integrate group writing—texts on the board or on chart paper that connect and synthesize many students' ideas—into discussions that you facilitate with all your students. You teach your students to use technology tools and multimedia environments as well as paper and pencil to express what they learn and to move their audiences to action. You help students master the tools of grammar and punctuation to strengthen their public writing. Including all your students, you build a writing community whose boundaries extend beyond students' local—classroom, school, community—world to embrace a global community of authors and readers.

Accountable Talk

Accountability to rigorous thinking involves both the teacher's efforts to promote students' reasoning to support their ideas and the students' own elaboration of their logic (Wolf, Crossen, & Resnick, 2006).

Expressing ideas and building on others' ideas is a foundation of critical inquiry into twenty-first-century issues. Discussion is *accountable* when students not only express their ideas out loud but do so in a way that builds on others' comments and ideas (Wolf et al., 2006). Discussions that stimulate thinking and build understanding are also authentic, in that they are exchanges of ideas without a predicted outcome. They extend over time and push participants' thinking as they "make predictions, summarize, link texts with one another, and with background knowledge, generate and answer text-related questions, clarify understanding, muster relevant evidence to support an interpretation, and interrelate reading, writing, and discussion" (Applebee, Langer, Nystrand, & Gamoran, 2003, p. 693).

Accountable conversations have results. Students who talk about their positions and arguments with each other before they write about them produce better essays than students who write without discussion (Reznitskaya et al., 2001). In an urban seventh-grade classroom, we observed a group of students from low-income families, many of whom were members of underrepresented groups and two of whom had learning disabilities, argue about whether a character in a novel had any choice in how her peers treated her. In the novel, students harass the character for her dark color and her independent ways of dressing. From a close analysis of the seventh graders' discourse, we found that they were asserting interpretive claims, elaborating interpretations, questioning each other's statements, and revising their interpretations—high-level argument skills that are critical to intellectual growth (Morocco & Hindin, 2002). Typical students, students with disabilities, and English language learners all learn more content when they engage in classroom discussion (Nystrand & Gamoran, 1991).

Technology-based tools such as e-mail, blogs, and online discussion environments open unlimited opportunities for conversations that extend beyond the classroom. They enable students to express their own perspectives and seek perspectives from other communities. Other oral language practices besides peer- and teacher-facilitated discussions can also help build students' understanding and engage them in critical and creative thinking. For example, students can dramatize a scene from a play to represent an interpretation of the meaning of a scene. They can present an oral monologue to express a point of view of a historical figure or a literary character. Or they can collect oral histories that provide resources for understanding a historical issue.

It is possible for every school to realize a vision of twenty-first-century classrooms in which students direct their own conversations about the issues they are investigating. To reach that goal, however, students must master several discussion skills. They need to know how to use conversations to make sense of a text, to manage responsible roles in peer discussion, and to engage in critical or creative thinking through discussion.

Use Conversations to Make Sense of a Text. Authentic, accountable talk helps students think about what they read, understand it better, and comprehend better on their own (Beck & McKeown, 2006). Discussion engages adolescents intellectually and emotionally in their reading and in assignments (Guthrie & Humenick, 2004). Regardless of the content area or global learning topic, asking questions that call for students to make inferences and comparisons invites them to judge and evaluate the content of the text, makes the text relevant to their lives, and helps them comprehend more deeply (Probst, 2007, pp. 52–53).

Manage Responsible Roles in Peer Discussion. Peer discussion formats can include literacy circles, critical friends groups, group projects, or group exhibitions. Skills in setting ground rules, facilitating a peer conversation, documenting ideas contributed, presenting results to the class as a whole, and evaluating the group's productivity help the group collaborate to investigate a complex topic. Skills in getting the floor and recognizing others' contributions make the conversation more accessible. If small working groups in science classrooms are not taking up worthwhile ideas of students with identified disabilities, for example, "the guided inquiry process has been turned into a form of popularity contest" (Cutter, Palincsar, & Magnusson, 2002, p. 192).

Engage in Critical or Creative Thinking Through Discussion. Conversation is a visceral and social form of thinking. When adolescents participate in thinking creatively

SNAPSHOT

Accountable Talk in Your Classroom

Your students build deep understandings of what they read and investigate as you create opportunities for them to build on one another's ideas ("Do you want to add . . . ?") and reformulate students' comments ("So what I hear you saying is . . . "). In your coaching, you help students follow each other's ideas (Wolf et al., 2006, p. 12). You teach students the various roles they can play in peer discussions, give them challenging discussion tasks, and monitor the quality of student participation. You support students in using online discussion environments to extend their talk beyond the classroom and to listen to podcasts from other students. You also encourage students to use creative oral language forms to express their ideas, such as dramatizing a scene from a novel or play. Students are comfortable bringing their voices to your classroom.

and critically about concepts and issues aloud with their peers frequently over time, they begin to integrate those processes into their own thinking.

Content areas require somewhat different ways of thinking. As a result, critical thinking conversations will sound different from classroom to classroom. For example, in a science conversation about sinking and floating, students talk about what they observed, and they examine different claims about what makes things sink. In a literature circle, they take on a challenging question about a character, state their interpretations of the text, listen to different interpretations, and reword their own interpretations. Discussion is a tool and medium for engaging in the synthesis and perspective taking that characterize a prepared adolescent. In thinking aloud with others, in a common physical or virtual space, around a common topic, students practice the critical thinking skills that will serve them well in future learning communities.

Digital and Media Fluency

"Using the Wikibooks.org Web site, we [eleventh-grade English class] . . . set up an annotated text to work alongside our study of the novel. . . . By the end of our study of the novel, we'd created a readers' guide to *The Stranger* that was multi-modal, completely owned by each of the students in the class, and receiving a large, and validating number of hits each day. . . . Sam explained, 'I think that makes this the first book I've really *read*'" (Kadjer, 2007, p. 223).

New technology tools have several benefits for critical inquiry. They are practical, designed by the very people who need and use them, including teachers and students (and even dropouts, jokes Bill Gates, who dropped out of Harvard to invent Microsoft). They are integrated, in that many tools converge in a learning environment that includes ways of gathering, organizing, and analyzing and representing information related to an issue. They are also democratic, in that they give individuals control over how they interpret information, in contrast with the control exercised by, as one teacher put it, "media empires and moguls . . . who have the power to both entertain, inform, and manipulate" (Mustacchi, 2007).

These environments and tools bring an almost unlimited array of continually changing literacy practices inside and outside the classroom and take advantage of the collective intelligence of a group of students. For example, Wikis, Wikipedia, wikiquote, and wikibooks—which Kadjer (2007) describes in the quote just presented—are Web sites that are entirely created, edited, and monitored for inaccurate information by users. Students can also use online environments to retrieve and organize information, including conducting Internet searches and using graphics to display information. They can share ideas with others in remote communities by designing blogs, e-mailing peers worldwide, and developing multimedia projects. They can use software such as PowerPoint and Photoshop to create print and multimedia documents. And they can learn concepts through simulations and model building and distributing documents and events such as blogs and podcasts.

Online learning environments can bring new forms of collaborative investigation, by linking students' individual thinking with ideas from their classmates and from communities beyond the classroom. Jim Burke's (2007) high school students use corporate style discussion facilitation tools like Open Space (www.openspaceworld.org) and Save the Last Word for Me (www.nsrfharmony.org/protocol/doc/save_last_word .pdf) to guide them in substantively reading, writing, and talking about their chosen topics. His students carried on a threaded discussion of summer reading about strong women characters and feminist issues on School Loop (www.schoolloop.com), an integrated communication service for students and teachers. Other new practices support students' efforts to organize and connect ideas. Computer-supported collaborative learning (CSCL) tools help students organize their ideas around the key questions of their inquiry. Sentence starters such as "I hypothesize that . . . " and "I observe that . . . " prompt students to communicate like scientists. In a Midwestern middle school organized around science inquiry, all sixth- through eighth-grade students use a CSCL tool called Knowledge Forum to post their questions for a unit on pollution (for example, "What is pollution?" "What is humanity's role in causing it?" "What can we do?"). They link the information they gather to those questions in a Web format (Morocco, Brigham, & Aguilar, 2006).

These technology practices help students build their conceptual understanding and collaboration and communication competencies. At the same time, these practices require students to develop new skills. Students must learn how to use technology tools to represent complex concepts in multiple ways (Roschelle, Pea, Hoadley, Gordin, & Means, 2000) to sort, categorize, and attribute information, and to compose with digital and media tools.

Represent Complex Concepts in Multiple Ways. As they jointly conduct lab experiments, students need to learn the various ways that technology tools can organize, manipulate, and display their data. They can learn to rotate the planets and observe them from different positions in space, examine and rotate a DNA molecule, and view a virtual night sky from any point on earth. With Protein Explorer, a program for Grade 9 through college, students can visualize the three-dimensional structure of protein, DNA, and RNA macromolecules and their interactions.

Students can use digital technology to represent geography concepts visually. Google Earth enables students to explore absolute and relative location, and the British Broadcasting Center's Landscapes enables students to build maps. The *National Geographic*'s World Music Web site allows students to learn about a country through its art by searching music by country, region, and category. The River City Project is a virtual world where students can collect data and use the scientific method to explore the causes of a town's health problems.

Sort, Categorize, and Attribute Information. Students can choose from a rich array of sources that provide them with varied perspectives, and digital and media skills are an invaluable aid in this process. Yet they must be able to deftly sift through this data and identify and discard inaccurate or incomplete information. They must also be able to categorize the importance of information—what is more essential and what is less essential. And they must understand how to properly attribute sources—what they can include from the Internet in their own work and how to fairly credit Internet sources.

Compose with Digital and Media Tools. Students need to be able to use multiple forms of representation to make their results and ideas accessible, understandable, and relevant for others. By understanding the visceral and emotional immediacy of a presentation such as Al Gore's movie, *An Inconvenient Truth,* students can reflect on the personal impact and the messages that they communicate using multimedia tools. These skills transform students from consumers to authors who can themselves use new forms of communication to reach audiences beyond their own classrooms. The New Media Consortium, author of *A Global Imperative,* argues that twenty-first-century literacy includes creative fluency as well as interpretive facility: "21st century literacy implies the ability to articulate and create ideas in these new forms, as well as to understand the layers of meanings they may convey" (2005, p. 2). Thinking about who will hear their podcasts keeps students focused on how to make their messages clear and, where appropriate, emotionally powerful. They "learn first hand how writing is a communicative act; they learn to take responsibility for their words, to defend and modify them based on reaction from the real people sitting around them" (Kutz & Roskelly, 1991, p. 263, quoted in Kadjer, 2007).

Integrating the Multiliteracies

As Figure 1.1 indicates, the multiliteracies described in this chapter are the core competency that links all twenty-first-century competencies for critical inquiry. Reading

SNAPSHOT

Digital and Media Fluency in Your Classroom

In your classroom, the Internet is one source of information, along with libraries, museums, professional experts in the community, hands-on experimentation, and students' own experiences. Your students move seamlessly from print to nonprint forms, from communicating with their classmates face-to-face to communicating with others through e-mail, podcasting, and video broadcasting. You teach students to use a wide variety of tools to express themselves, and you help them learn how to select the best medium for their messages. You work with other teachers, the school, and your community to make all these tools for gathering information and expressing ideas available to all of your students.

for deep understanding, writing to build and express meaning, accountable talk, and digital and media fluency will help your students grapple with complex issues and learn and think together about their world. These are the intellectual tools and techniques for building conceptual understanding, for critical and creative thinking, and for collaborating and communicating in inquiry. Students draw on all these multiliteracies in understanding issues well enough to take a position and argue it with reasoning and evidence. For critical inquiry, they need to move nimbly from one multiliteracy skill to another—to shift from deciphering graphs on climate change to writing a summary of the trends shown in those graphs to explaining that data to another person. Like Mr. Howard's students, they also need to be able to use their multiliteracy skills to make connections between their personal identities and global issues. This ability not only to master skills but to create and transpose knowledge from one mode to another and from one context to another is the essence of twenty-first-century multiliteracies for learning.

PUTTING IT ALL TOGETHER

Twenty-first-century competencies and multiliteracies are alive in Mr. Howard's U.S. history classroom (in the opening Classroom Close-Up), and we have provided glimpses of what twenty-first-century learning might look like in your classroom. But what does critical inquiry look like in other classrooms and other content areas? How can you build twenty-first-century competencies and multiliteracies into teaching world history, or science, or literature? What does a curriculum unit look like that is organized toward outcomes of conceptual understanding, critical thinking, creative thinking, collaboration, and communication? How can you *teach* the multiliteracies?

Putting this vision of prepared adolescents into practice can seem daunting because of the complexity of the content your students need to learn and the diversity of your students' academic and cultural backgrounds. Across Grades 4–12, eight million students perform below the proficient level on national assessments, and more than 7,000 students drop out of high school every school day, in part because they lack the literacy skills to keep up with an increasingly challenging curriculum (Biancarosa & Snow, 2006; Kamil, 2003; Snow & Biancarosa, 2003). Students with disabilities and students who are learning English as a second language have significantly lower reading and achievement scores than those of their agemates who are keeping up. The achievement gap among various racial, ethnic, and socioeconomic groups continues to be troubling, with 39 percent of white eighth graders proficient in reading compared with 12 percent of black students and 5 percent of Hispanic students (NCES, 2005b).

The old model for building literacy skills, where English teachers took responsibility for students' reading, writing, and speaking skills, allocating a portion of each day or week to separate instruction, is not the answer, because these multiliteracies need to be embedded and developed within every content area. Separating literacy instruction from content learning leaves students unprepared to use multiliteracy skills appropriately in the very contexts where they are needed. Students learn the skills of writing a science report best in the context of *doing* science. They learn to ask questions about the source and credibility of historical documents in the context of grappling with important questions about an important historical event such as World War II. Regardless of the subject that you teach, you can support students' mastery of these multiliteracies by modeling the skills, by having students practice the skills, and by creating learning environments that call upon them to use the skills every day.

In Chapter Two, we describe the Supported Literacy approach to teaching these multiliteracy skills to adolescents so that students can use the skills for critical inquiry. History and literature examples illustrate how you can explicitly teach the multiliteracies by demonstrating them and by integrating them into inquiry. By learning them in the context of a content area investigation, students understand how and when to use the skills as tools for building meaning. Chapter Two describes the instructional core of the Supported Literacy framework—the Meaning-Making Cycle, which structures students' inquiry, and the key framework components that support this kind of learning. The framework includes six components that work together in a twenty-first-century unit: a vision, essential questions, Meaning-Making Cycles, resources for teaching and learning, outcomes, and assessment.

Classroom Close-Ups in Chapter Two show you glimpses of the Meaning-Making Cycle in action, as a teacher uses the Supported Literacy framework to develop and teach a world history and literature unit. The unit moves students through a process of building understanding, using the multiliteracies as their tools. From this Classroom Close-Up, as well as subsequent chapters' Close-Ups that focus on applying the Supported Literacy framework to teaching other content—particularly in science and language arts—and to teaching students with cognitive disabilities, we hope that you will see how you might apply the framework in your own teaching. While it is beyond the scope of this book to provide detailed guidelines for constructing units, we hope that the examples provided will inspire you to further explore the Supported Literacy framework. We encourage you to seek our assistance in implementing the approach in your teaching and in your school.

CHAPTER

2

INSIDE THE SUPPORTED LITERACY FRAMEWORK

CLASSROOM CLOSE-UP

War and Families

Carol: The students in her school call her Rag Doll or Trash Picker because she doesn't have a notebook and uses crumpled up paper from the wastebasket for writing. A girl made a drawing of her picking up trash and wrote on it "Prestigious Sagano School accepts Trash Picker as Student."

Mateo: But why are they mean to her? They're all Japanese. They all survived the war. She's like a refugee in her own country, without a home, like families in Iraq. Why did the war do this to them?

Christine Harris's tenth graders are three weeks into a world literature and history course titled "War and Families." Ms. Harris, together with other history and language arts faculty and EDC staff, used the six components of the Supported Literacy framework (introduced in Chapter One) to design this unit. They aligned their vision of adolescent literacy around that of Supported Literacy. They have organized the unit around two essential questions about the impact of the war, "How did World War II affect the economies and the people of the participating countries?" and "How do families survive war?" To study these questions, Ms. Harris engages her students in

Meaning-Making Cycles that are guiding them in a critical inquiry into an important time in world history—World War II and its aftermath.

So far, her class has used a wide variety of resources—including texts, articles, maps, Web sites, and oral histories—to learn about and discuss the major causes and events of the war. Now they are focusing on postwar Japan as an example. Groups of three to five students have chosen different aspects of postwar Japan to study, such as the economy, government, conflicts with Korea, and culture and people, and each group has shared its findings with the whole class. To give them some insight into how families experienced the war, Ms. Harris has introduced, as a primary source and world literature selection, the memoir of a Japanese girl who survived as a homeless teenager in Kyoto after the war, with her brother, Hideyo, and her sister, Ko.

My Brother, My Sister, and I was written by a Japanese-American writer, Yoko Kawashima Watkins (1994). Yoko was seven years old when Japan entered World War II in 1941. Four years later, in the chaos of Japan's defeat and the rising terror of anti-Japanese hostility, Yoko and her mother, brother, and older sister fled from their home in Name, Korea, and began a life-or-death trek to Seoul and then to Tokyo.

The "War and Families" unit provides compelling topics for this class to discuss because the school is near an air force base, and several students have family members in Iraq or Afghanistan. Yet Ms. Harris finds this topic difficult to teach—not only because it hits so close to her students' lives but also because her students' literacy skills vary greatly. "I have to deal with the gap between our ideal of a global learner who understands and cares about these topics," she says, "and the reality of these students' poor literacy skills and limited knowledge." Her students' reading comprehension skills range from low to high on standard measures. But to meet the outcomes and assessment goals for the unit, they all need to go beyond basic comprehension of their reading to thinking about who wrote the source and why. They need to be able to pull together information from many sources with different perspectives on the war.

Few of the students know much world geography, and most have only a vague knowledge of World War II. Several students immigrated to the United States from Central America, Latin America, and Asia within the past three years. None of these students has brought personal knowledge of Japan or Japanese culture to this tenth-grade unit. Many are familiar with anime and with manga and Internet sites with Japanese-style cartoons, and some are aware of the competition between Japanese and U.S. cars on the market. "Toyota!" two students wrote in listing things they know about Japan before they began the unit.

By engaging her students in this critical inquiry, Ms. Harris is helping them develop the twenty-first-century competencies they will need for their schooling and future careers. Throughout the unit, as they read historical and literary documents, her students are using and working to gain proficiency in the multiliteracies described in Chapter One—reading for deep understanding, writing to build and express meaning, accountable talk, and digital and media fluency.

In the following section, we describe in more detail the six components of the Supported Literacy framework—vision, essential questions, Meaning-Making Cycles, resources, outcomes, and assessment—and we reveal how the components work together to create a unit that builds deep understanding.

COMPONENTS OF THE SUPPORTED LITERACY FRAMEWORK

Figure 2.1 displays the six components you will include when you use the Supported Literacy framework to design or adapt a curriculum unit. Most likely, you already use some or most of these components in your teaching. What might be new to you is the way Supported Literacy draws these components together in one coherent framework, and the way you can apply the framework across many content areas. Also, you will see some examples in this chapter of where and how you might step back during the unit to teach explicitly one or more of the multiliteracy tools for meaning making. In the pages that follow, we describe each of these components and provide an overview of the unit that Ms. Harris has designed. Then, in two Close-Ups of Ms. Harris's classroom, you see the framework in action.

Component One: A Vision of Adolescent Learning

As noted in Chapter One, the Supported Literacy vision of learning hinges on students' mastery of twenty-first-century competencies. In this vision, students are capable of engaging in critical inquiry into important questions in both the traditional content areas and newer global content. They gather, analyze, and synthesize

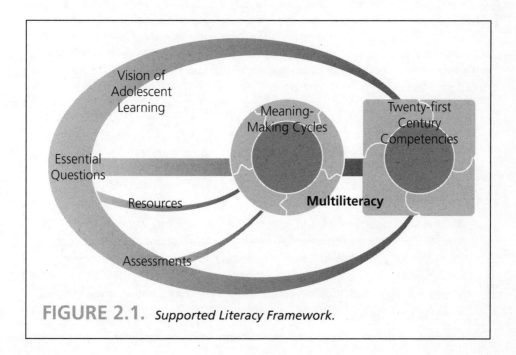

FIGURE 2.1. *Supported Literacy Framework.*

information in science, history, or literature. They build conceptual understanding by thinking critically about what they read and using creative thinking to connect concepts. They work collaboratively with each other and learn to listen and communicate with others in many different ways. This vision is an economic one, in that prepared adolescents are poised to take on the jobs of the twenty-first century. Yet it is also an intellectual and ethical vision of students who are curious about their world and respect other cultures and points of view. When you use the Supported Literacy framework to design curriculum, you identify essential questions, resources for teaching and learning, outcomes, and assessment modes that work in concert to realize this vision of adolescent learning.

Component Two: Essential Questions

To create or modify curriculum units using the Supported Literacy framework, you must develop *essential questions* (Cushman, 1989)—broad questions that are important in a discipline and that propel students into a broad landscape of information and issues—for students to investigate. Essential questions differ from questions that request a factual answer ("Do sharks eat trash?"), a description ("Where is ice melting at the poles?"), or a comparison ("How is melting similar and different at the two poles?") (Guthrie, Wigfield, & Perencevich, 2004). Instead, the essential questions you develop or select, like the ones that organize the content area examples in this book, are the questions that content area experts continue to grapple with, without finding final answers. These include "Why do people emigrate to another country?" "How does war affect economies and people?" "How do humans contribute to climate change?" "How do people learn to stand up for themselves?" They are also the naive questions that children ask. One teacher helped her students see that questions like "Will I live to be a hundred years old?" connect with scientists' investigations into genetics and family history (Bransford et al., 2000, pp. 156–157).

LITERACY NOTE

Essential Questions

What role do questions play in your teaching and in your students' learning? Focusing learning around essential questions gives students a sense of control over what they are learning and a framework for connecting and remembering information. One of the reasons students get dismal results on tests of history details is that they haven't learned the information in a meaningful context (Ravich & Finn, 1987; Van Sledright, 2002).

Component Three: Meaning-Making Cycles

In classrooms that use the Supported Literacy framework, teaching and learning are organized in Meaning-Making Cycles. As shown in Figure 2.2, Meaning-Making Cycles are ongoing cycles of investigation that are driven and energized by the essential questions you develop. A Meaning-Making Cycle includes several phases of building understanding:

- You *engage* students in a content area topic and question.

- Students *respond* individually to texts and other resources related to that question.

- Students *elaborate* and deepen their responses by building ideas with other students.

- Students *revisit* understanding through reflecting on and critically evaluating findings.

- Students *represent* well-formed understandings in ways that communicate to others.

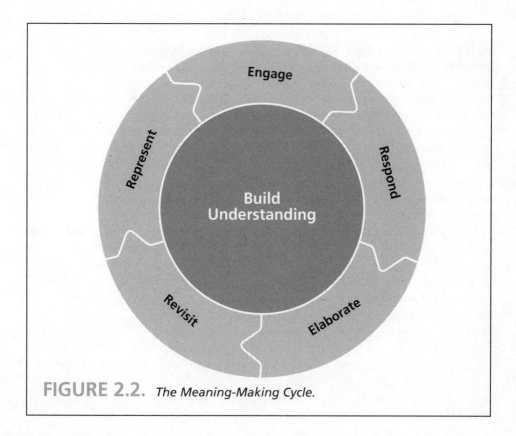

FIGURE 2.2. *The Meaning-Making Cycle.*

The Meaning-Making Cycle reflects an extensive body of research on literacy and human learning that is summarized in reports such as *Making America Smarter* (Resnick, 1999), *How People Learn: Brain, Mind, Experience, and School* (Bransford et al., 2000), *Academic Literacy Instruction for Adolescents: A Guidance Document from the Center on Instruction* (Torgesen et al., 2007), and *Developing Literacy in Second-Language Learners: Report of the National Literacy Panel on Language-Minority Children and Youth* (August & Shanahan, 2006). Those reports and related research converge in the following ideas:

- *Learning is an active and generative process.* People who engage in learning spend time in thought-provoking tasks that lead them to observe, explain, make generalizations, and ultimately take what they have learned and apply it.

- *Authentic tasks and questions motivate learning.* Questions and dilemmas spark interest and arouse students' curiosity so that they care about knowing more.

- *Learners build meaning in a social and collaborative context.* Students want to learn when they have questions that matter and intellectual partners for exploring the questions.

These principles come together in the Meaning-Making Cycle, in which you scaffold active learning by providing your students with the support they need to stretch beyond what they could do on their own and investigate thought-provoking questions. The Meaning-Making Cycle reflects the idea that learning complex content is a generative process that does not happen just through memorizing information. Instead, to understand content, your students must wrestle with a topic by reading and talking about it, puzzling over what is confusing about it, gathering additional background information, discussing issues with others, and forming opinions about the topic. In studying many "beat the odds" schools, whose students face risks associated with poverty, minority status, learning disabilities, and limited English language proficiency, Langer (2001) found that the most successful teachers push students to go beyond the information they have acquired to reflect on what they are learning.

As students cycle through challenging tasks, elaborate their thinking, and revisit important concepts, the Meaning-Making Cycle epitomizes building deep understanding. The cycles encourage students to work on their own as well as with others. Students make sense of what they read, look at their own thinking, and decide how to improve their understanding—practices that increase the degree to which they transfer their learning to new settings and events (Palincsar & Brown, 1984). When you use Meaning-Making Cycles in your classroom, your students will alternate between working under your guidance, working on their own, and working with peers as they build a learning community around the essential questions. In the following sections, we provide an overview of how you use the multiliteracies to support students' learning during Meaning-Making Cycles, and we describe how the cycles support students' mastery of multiliteracy tools.

Multiliteracies Support Meaning Making. When you use the Supported Literacy framework in your classroom, your students use multiliteracy tools throughout the Meaning-Making Cycle to help them investigate an essential question. Reading for deep understanding, writing to build and express meaning, accountable talk, and digital and media fluency provide your students with flexible investigative tools. You facilitate and guide your students' investigations by creating the conditions for them to use particular multiliteracies when they need those tools most.

At the beginning of the unit, you engage your students in the content they will explore. Your goal is to captivate students' interest in the essential driving question. You might choose to begin a unit with an anchoring experience (one that builds students' interest in the topic through images and examples) such as a film, a photographic exhibit, a speaker, an article or short reading, or a dramatization. Or you might read a provocative piece aloud, report on a classroom or school survey, or involve students in a multimedia presentation. You probably use more than one strategy to give your students varied entries into the unit. You want to surface students' knowledge—even fragments of knowledge—about the topic, because conceptual understanding often begins with "fragile and fragmented knowledge" (Alexander, 2003, p. 11). Engagement—being captivated by the subject—builds from those existing fragments. Each class session presents you with the challenge of engaging and reengaging students in working with key concepts and thinking critically about the resources they are using to learn.

After you engage students, you encourage them to respond individually to what they are observing and reading in ways that activate their thinking. If you are a science teacher, you ask students to respond by observing a natural or physical process or writing or drawing a diagram about an observation or experiment in a science notebook. If you are a history or literature teacher, you ask students to write an entry about their reading in their journals, one of the most valuable ways for students to actively process the material you are teaching (see Literacy Note—Journaling). You organize follow-up discussion circles in which students elaborate their individual thinking through accountable talk and build on each other's thinking. In this phase of the cycles, other multiliteracies besides accountable talk might also assist students in elaborating their ideas. For example, they might write a group summary of their various contributions, or they might reread an article together to try to negotiate an agreement about what it says.

Because the purpose of the Meaning-Making Cycle's revisit phase is for students to think critically about their interpretations or findings, you facilitate a discussion in which students report out the results of their peer discussions. Your goal is to have students look at the full range of claims (science) or interpretations (history, literature), and critically examine the reasoning and evidence they are using to support their findings. The point is to balance peer discussions and project work with these evaluative discussions of their results. You might focus on one or two disagreements to deepen students' understanding of the issue. In the revisit phase, you want to support students in linking their findings back to the essential question, so that they can begin the hard work of synthesizing complex information and concepts. "What do we understand now?" is your guiding question during this phase.

As students engage in many inquiry cycles over the course of units that use the Supported Literacy framework, their understanding changes, as do their representations or expressions of their understanding. Your students might express their understanding of topics with a list of questions the first day of class. After six weeks, they might express their expanded understanding with models, formal essays, or refined poster presentations, as the students do at the end of a unit on global warming in Chapter Three. The purpose of the represent phase is for students to communicate their interim answers to the essential questions of the unit, so that they make their thinking visible and others can learn from them. Sometimes students create a group representation—a composite of questions, a model, a summary of findings, a group exhibition—and sometimes individual students represent their particular understanding separately in an appropriate format.

Throughout the Meaning-Making Cycle, you integrate and explicitly teach the multiliteracies that help your students learn content. The art of critical inquiry lies not in the teacher telling and transmitting key concepts to a group of passive learners but in flexible shifting of roles that provides students with the level of support they need to think for themselves and with each other. Nevertheless, *directly teaching* students how to use important multiliteracy tools for inquiry is one of your primary roles in the inquiry cycle. You can also teach these tools within the structure of the Meaning-Making Cycle, as the Close-Up later in this chapter illustrates.

LITERACY NOTE

Journaling

Writing in a journal or notebook builds students' understanding and writing fluency. It reduces nervousness about writing, since entries are not graded for form or published for anyone else to read, and it helps students connect a text with their own experience. Regular writing about their thinking and learning builds *metacognition*—students' awareness of their own thought processes—a characteristic of independent, mature readers and writers. In the context of building conceptual understanding, students collect ideas and examples that they can integrate into a fuller essay. Journals, including science notebooks and history notebooks, also document students' thinking over time and provide an excellent source of informal assessment information (Mayher, Lester, & Pradl, 1983; Raphael, Kehus, & Damphousse, 2001).

Teaching Multiliteracies Within the Meaning-Making Cycle. When you use the Supported Literacy framework, you integrate multiliteracies for learning into Meaning-Making Cycles. These cycles also provide a context for teaching multiliteracy skills. To create an equitable learning community, it is important for you to devote some time to directly teaching multiliteracy tools; few students come into middle or even high school fully proficient in them.

Some students lack the skills they need to write about their ideas in varied forms and for different purposes such as essays, editorials, technical directions, multimedia presentations, persuasive essays, memoirs, stories, or summaries. Other students need to learn strategies to help them comprehend history or science texts, and many flounder during an Internet search when they need to select the most promising addresses from the initial list the search engine provides. As the International Reading Association (IRA, 2006) and the RAND Reading Study Group (2002) have noted, students whose native language is not English—many of them recent immigrants— also need to be explicitly taught these skills.

The traditional view is that language arts teachers are responsible for teaching these kinds of skills, based on the assumption that many of the skills are generic, and that students who acquire the skills in one context can easily transfer them to new contexts. As noted in Chapter One, however, in the Supported Literacy approach multiliteracies take on a specific form and purpose in each subject area. While students might benefit from learning comprehension skills or discussion roles in the English classroom, if you teach another subject, you must also assume responsibility for explicating the relevance and specific uses for multiliteracies within your discipline (NALC, 2007). The goals and ways of learning are particular to each discipline, and so is the discourse of that context (Gee, 1999b). The Meaning-Making Cycle process presents many opportunities to teach the multiliteracies in every topic and in every classroom.

Component Four: Resources for Teaching and Learning

Students use a wide variety of resources for inquiry in units that use the Supported Literacy framework. In our Classroom Close-Ups, resources include textbooks, books and articles, literature, case studies, online summaries and articles, student writings, and primary sources such as speeches, newspapers, diaries, family documents, public documents, and practitioner notebooks. These can include the notebooks of scientists, explorers, fiction writers, pilots, mathematicians, and mountain climbers. For example, in Chapter Three, the Classroom Close-Up focuses on science and features resources such as data from international studies, laboratory materials and equipment for hands-on investigations, and multimedia materials. In your science classroom, you might also use graphs, maps, drawings, film, photographs, videos, and audio interviews and technology tools for building models of scientific processes. Your resources for students with special learning needs might include books on tape to assist blind students or students who struggle with decoding, and text-to-speech technologies to assist students with reading and writing difficulties.

Component Five: Twenty-First-Century Outcomes

Well-defined learning outcomes that reflect the state and national content standards for your school district are a key element of the Supported Literacy framework. The outcomes that you identify as you use the framework to design and modify curricula will also address new global and international fields of knowledge—economics, international relationships, world literature, and research courses in high schools (Morocco & Zigmond, 2006)—recognized by governors' associations and state standards.

The desired result of Meaning-Making Cycles' critical inquiry learning is that your students meet and exceed prevailing standards while developing the twenty-first-century competencies that we described in Chapter One. When you use the Supported Literacy framework, your students learn how to use multiliteracy tools to build an understanding of particular content area concepts, to engage in critical and creative thinking about those concepts, and to collaborate and communicate with each other and with you. The particular multiliteracy tools, concepts, thinking skills, and collaborative process that students need to develop depend on the subject area, unit topic, and the focus of the inquiry. In the example at the beginning of Chapter One, the outcomes had to do with U.S. immigration history. In the examples in this and upcoming chapters, the outcomes are formulated to reflect current standards and issues in world history, science, and language arts.

Component Six: Assessments of Student Understanding

When you use the Supported Literacy framework, you and your students can use several kinds of assessments to gauge their progress in achieving desired learning outcomes. First, you can use standardized test data about students' reading, writing, and content area knowledge as you assemble resources for a curriculum unit. Writing assessment data can, for example, guide your teaching of the writing formats students need for science reports, poster sessions, or analytic history essays. Second, you can use student work to monitor their progress in understanding important concepts. The extensive amount of student writing and discussion in classrooms that use the Supported Literacy framework makes students' thinking visible. By reading students' science or history notebooks and observing discussion groups, you can see how much science or history students understand and readily identify their misconceptions. Finally, culminating assessments, such as an essay, small learning exhibition, dramatization, science report, or other appropriate performance, help you determine how deeply students have investigated an essential question, what they understand, and how clearly they can express their understanding.

In the next section, we return to Ms. Harris's history class to show you an overview of the "War and Families" unit, as well as two Close-Ups of classroom sessions that illustrate how her students use and become proficient in multiliteracies as they learn about post–World War II Japan.

CLASSROOM CONNECTIONS

Supported Literacy Framework

What connections does this framework have to your own content area? Do you use some of these components, but perhaps refer to them with different terms? What aspects of the framework are parts of your current teaching? What concerns do you have about this approach? What questions does it raise for you?

The six components of the Supported Literacy framework interact with each other. The essential questions drive the Meaning-Making Cycles and create a need for particular resources for learning. The desired unit outcomes influence your design of specific activities within Meaning-Making Cycles. Test data on students' reading, writing, and English language proficiency determine the particular reading, writing, and discussion tools you integrate and teach, and the results of your progress monitoring guides your subsequent instruction.

SUPPORTED LITERACY IN WORLD HISTORY AND LITERATURE: UNDERSTANDING THE IMPACT OF WAR

During their development of the "War and Families" unit, and with guidance from EDC staff, Ms. Harris and her team discussed and addressed all six of the framework's components. Identifying their vision, essential questions, resources, desired outcomes, and assessment approaches for the course helped the team develop lessons that make excellent use of the Meaning-Making Cycle to foster students' learning. An overview of the unit the team designed follows.

A vision of adolescent learning: Ms. Harris and her team designed the "War and Families" unit based on their belief that adolescents are capable of investigating challenging questions about world history and linking that study to literature by authors from different areas of the world. The unit provides structured learning experiences and extensive teacher support, yet it assumes that students will take responsibility for learning the multiliteracy skills they need for deep content learning.

Essential questions: The team used the two essential questions described earlier, "How did World War II affect the economies and the people of the participating countries?" and "How do families survive war?" to organize the unit and to focus students' inquiry into post–World War II Japan.

Meaning-Making Cycles: The team organized the lessons in "War and Families," including those portrayed in the Classroom Close-Ups later in this section, around Meaning-Making Cycles that might extend into more than one class period. Ms. Harris and her colleagues have students return to a phase within a cycle when it supports them in building understanding.

Resources for teaching and learning: The team selected a wide range of resources for the unit. These include readings from three history textbooks, illustrated books and articles about Japanese culture, maps of Japan, U.S. and Japanese newspaper articles, and oral histories of Japanese survivors of World War II from the Internet. They also collected historical documents—such as Harry S Truman's Statement on the Atomic Bomb—from a history Web site. Students in Ms. Harris's classroom also look at videos on traditional and contemporary Japanese culture loaned to the school by the Japanese Consulate General. A software program, Skype, enables her students to conduct a video interview with the author of a memoir they read related to postwar Japan.

Twenty-first-century outcomes: For Ms. Harris and her team, important conceptual understandings include knowing the major political and economic events in postwar recovery and the impact of war on countries and on people. The box lists some specific unit outcomes for the "War and Families" unit in terms of each of the major twenty-first-century competencies emphasized in the Supported Literacy framework.

These outcomes articulate with history standards that have been adopted in several states, as well as themes that Ms. Harris's own district adopted from a history commission report (Bradley Commission on History in Schools, 1988) that include personal freedom, individual responsibility, and respect for human dignity. The unit also reflects several standards for English language arts jointly established by the International Reading Association (IRA) and the National Council of Teachers of English (NCTE) (1996). These include, for example, applying a wide range of strategies to comprehend, interpret, evaluate, and appreciate texts (Standard 3), conducting research by generating ideas and questions (Standard 6), and employing a wide range of writing strategies (Standard 5).

Assessment: The team decided that it was important for teachers to know students' standard reading scores in advance, so they could anticipate whether students would have difficulty reading the unit's historical and literary texts. They also decided that, because writing multiliteracies are important to learning in this unit, teachers needed to review state assessments of students' writing scores on persuasive writing to prepare to teach the unit. Then, throughout the unit, journal writing and small group discussions in almost every lesson make students' thinking visible and accessible for progress monitoring. The culminating performance of understanding, a supported argument essay, requires students to synthesize many sources of information and draw on a variety of sources of evidence to support a historical interpretation.

In the pages that follow, we return to Ms. Harris's classroom. In our next Close-Up (p. 36), Ms. Harris's students continue the discussion of the memoir with which we began this chapter. As Ms. Harris uses the Meaning-Making Cycle to support their learning, they try to synthesize—an important twenty-first-century competence—information they have read about the war with this personal family history and with what they know of the current war in Iraq. You will note that Ms. Harris and her team have organized the lesson so that students use a number of multiliteracy tools to help them with this synthesis.

In the second Close-Up (p. 43), Ms. Harris directly teaches a multiliteracy tool—knowing the special features of a genre of writing called a "supported argument essay." Ms. Harris and her team decided to make an essay the culminating

OUTCOMES FOR "WAR AND FAMILIES"

Multiliteracies:
- Understand how to use Internet search engines, such as Google and AltaVista, to find appropriate Web sites for a historical search, and Skype or other comparable tools for videoconferencing.
- Use reading comprehension strategies to understand varied historical texts.
- Develop and argue a position on a historical question in discussion and in writing.

Conceptual Understanding:
- Understand the political and economic changes that accompanied post-war recovery.
- Understand the impact of World War II on economies, cultures, and families.

Critical Thinking:
- Understand processes of historical analysis and consider multiple perspectives.
- Synthesize information about World War II from primary and secondary sources.

Creative Thinking:
- Understand the ingenuity with which families survived the war.
- Connect the memoir to broader historical readings and to current world conflicts.

Collaboration and Communication:
- Cooperate in investigating a specific aspect of World War II in depth.
- Broaden the class discussion to include experts with personal knowledge.

assessment of "War and Families," and she wants to make certain all her students understand what that kind of writing requires. As you read both Close-Ups, consider the teaching choices Ms. Harris is making and her alternatives. Also notice how the various multiliteracies—reading the memoir for deep understanding, writing to build interpretations, discussing their interpretations, and using technology to interview the author of the memoir—work together to assist students in synthesizing historical information and literature about post–World War II Japan. We conclude this chapter with a summary of the benefits of the Supported Literacy framework for teaching and student learning.

CLASSROOM CLOSE-UP

Using Multiliteracies to Synthesize Readings

Ms. Harris's students have been reading background materials on World War II and its aftermath, and they have been reflecting on the unit's first essential question, "How did World War II affect the economies and the people of the participating countries?" In groups of three to five, students have studied different aspects of postwar Japan—the economy, government, conflicts with Korea, its culture and people—and then shared their findings with the whole class. Now, as shown in the beginning of this chapter, students are reading and beginning to discuss a memoir on one Japanese family's struggle following the war, both as a primary history source and as a relevant piece of world literature.

This Close-Up's lesson takes place over two class periods. To push her students to read for deeper understanding and to connect this memoir with their new background knowledge of the war, Ms. Harris asks them to read several chapters while considering the question, "Is this family demonstrating strength or weakness as they struggle to survive?" Students use a number of multiliteracy tools as they take part in the five phases of critical inquiry that make up the Meaning-Making Cycle.

Engage

"Why *is* Yoko being treated badly? What have you learned about the war that could explain this?" Ms. Harris picks up on the earlier discussion between Carol and Mateo (see opening of this chapter) about why Yoko's high school classmates call her "Trash Picker" if she is Japanese, just like them. The students are trying to connect Yoko's personal story with what they have learned about the aftermath of World War II, particularly in the Pacific.

Mateo: Her brother and sister and she lived in a railroad station and a refugee camp. Why don't they have a home?

Carol: They just came from Korea. Their father had a job there. Their grandparents are in the North. Maybe they're dead.

Ivan: Why are they living in an empty warehouse? Washing in a stream! They are Japanese!

Ms. Harris: Think about what we read about Japan and Korea before and during the war. The Kawashima children were caught in the middle of the long conflict between Korea and Japan. How did the war affect Japanese people with jobs in Korea?

Sophie: The Japanese dominated Korea, and so . . . I forget . . .

Michael: The Japanese were dominating Korea, and the Korean people wanted to be free. When the Japanese were losing and were weak, Koreans pushed them out, and Japanese had to escape all down this peninsula [points to a map of Korea].

Ms. Harris draws on her students' emergent knowledge of post–World War II Japan and their even more fragmentary knowledge of homeless adolescents. She has them reread the early chapters as they reflect on a question ("Is this family getting weaker or stronger?") that relates to the essential question about how families survive war. She sets up students' individual and small group work by asking them to reread and skim the first three chapters by themselves or with a partner, take notes, and discuss their findings in their peer discussion circles.

Ms. Harris engages her students, and provides the context for their inquiry, by posing the question about family strengths. They use a multiliteracy tool, accountable talk, to express and build on each other's ideas about why this family struggled to survive in their own country. Their discussion indicates that they own the question and are motivated to read and think further.

Respond

Ms. Harris's students respond to her question about family strength as they reread the memoir and make notes in their history journals. Some students reread silently, and others quietly read aloud with a peer, about how Yoko escaped from Korea to Japan and survived crises along the way:

> Once, at a train station in Korea, a man ordered us to make room for him to sleep. He was about to attack Mother. Then Ko pulled out her peeling knife and almost plunged it into his throat. He left us alone [Watkins, 1994, p. 5].

One chapter describes how Yoko scrounges for food and is able to invent a birthday soup for her brother by boiling discarded daikon greens. Another chapter describes how Ko falls and is injured in a warehouse fire when she runs back to save their few family possessions:

> Ko had gone up for the ashes [their mother's], the sword, and the wrapping-cloth bundle containing mother's and our summer clothes. In the bundle's secret pocket were Father's name seal, Nanam [Korea] school documents, our family's important papers, and some cash Mother had saved. Ko had carried it on her back in the Korean war zone. . . . In the flames I saw Ko at the top of the stairs, holding something to her chest, wanting to come down but trying to avoid the fire [p. 21].

Ms. Harris's question pushes her students to use several multiliteracies to build a deeper understanding of the Kawashima family's dilemma. They use a powerful

(Continued)

comprehension strategy—posing questions about a text—to help them read for deep understanding. They analyze the literature by looking across many scenes to find a pattern in the siblings' behavior. As they take notes on what they read, they use another multiliteracy tool, writing to comprehend a written text and think critically about content area concepts.

Elaborate

Students move into peer groups to elaborate their understanding of this refugee family by talking about the evidence they've found. Ms. Harris hands out one copy of the following chart form to each group and asks them to compile their findings.

Family is getting stronger (Note evidence and page number)	Family is getting weaker (Note evidence and page number)

Ms. Harris reminds her students, "Note your evidence from the text, and think about what you mean by *strong* or *weak*. What is a strong family, anyway?" These peer discussions—a kind of "accountable talk"—engage students in using and building several multiliteracy skills described in Chapter One: using conversations to make sense of a text, managing responsible roles in peer discussions, and engaging in critical thinking through discussion. These skills help students look at each other and explain their ideas in ways that seldom happen when the teacher directs the conversation (Cazden, 2001).

The combination of rereading and journaling, followed by small group discussion, has special benefits for students with learning disabilities, who might not write as fluently or read as strategically as many other students in the class (Graham, Harris, MacArthur, & Schwartz, 1991). The journaling gives students "intellectual capital," valuable ideas they can bring to the peer discussions, where they need to compare and synthesize their findings. Weaker readers can expand on what they've written in their notebooks by hearing the interpretations of stronger readers. English language learners benefit by hearing people who speak English express their ideas (Morocco et al., 2006).

Peer conversations have another benefit in classrooms that use the Supported Literacy framework. You can use these conversations as a source of assessment data because they make students' ideas audible. Ms. Harris hears students interpret the same passage in very different ways, disagreeing on whether an event shows strength or weakness.

Michael: In my notebook, I wrote that Ko shouldn't have run back into the burning building to get things. That's evidence of weakness. She's not taking care of herself. She had to go to the hospital, when they didn't have any money to pay.

Sophie: Gee, I saw that as positive evidence. Their family sword is precious, a symbol of survival. Ko was willing to risk herself to get the sword and her mother's ashes and money. These are their symbols. Even if she got hurt.

Michael: Yes, but living, staying alive, is more important than symbols!

Ms. Harris hears Michael and Sophie using different criteria to evaluate whether the Kawashimas are expressing strength or weakness. Michael is focusing on physical safety, while Sophie is focusing on family and cultural values as a source of strength—an important distinction that Ms. Harris can bring up when they synthesize all of the group findings next.

Revisit

"I heard you defining what *strong* means in your groups," Ms. Harris starts off the review and analysis of her students' small group findings, "now talk about that in your reports."

(Continued)

She facilitates a follow-up conversation about their group charts—not to reveal the correct interpretation but to help her students think critically about their various interpretations and pieces of evidence. She records students' arguments and evidence in a big version of the chart form, so that it becomes a composite of findings.

When Michael and Sophie mention that they disagreed on whether or not the Kawashimas show strength or weakness, Ms. Harris points out that they are using different criteria to define strength. "Michael is using physical endurance and physical protection as his criteria, while Sophie is using cultural beliefs," Ms. Harris observes, as she writes on the board:

STRENGTHS: STAYING SAFE, HOLDING ONTO CULTURAL BELIEFS

"Those are both valid criteria. What other criteria did people use?" Carol and Mateo share a different view.

Carol: In our chart, we said they think up solutions. That's a strength. Like using an apple crate as *both* an altar and an eating table.

Mateo: Yoko finds food for them from garbage cans and gets free radish tops by helping a blind old man who cuts them.

Carol: Yoko sews papers together from the school trash to make a writing notebook.

Mateo: Yoko . . . is *muy ingenioso*. . . [intentionally drawing on his other language, Spanish].

Carol: Really ingenious. They invent new ways.

Ms. Harris slows down students' revisit reports to comment on the word *ingenuity.* "Excellent use of a word we've been studying across the tenth grade. It really describes Yoko's response to poverty. Notice that your group is associating ingenuity and inventiveness with survival, and you are interpreting instances of ingenuity as family strength." She points to the common cognates in the Spanish *ingenioso* and English *ingenious:* "Both of these words contain the Latin stem *gen,* from *gignere,* which means 'to beget' or to 'come into being.'"

Returning to the main discussion thread, Ms. Harris writes on the board:

STRENGTH = INGENUITY IN SOLVING PROBLEMS

She comments that the groups' various criteria and evidence are helping the students answer their bigger question about how families survive war.

This artfully facilitated discussion prompts students to use several multiliteracy tools to help them synthesize their knowledge about family survival. The facilitated discussion, another form of accountable talk, helps them engage in critical thinking about the memoir, and they begin to organize and synthesize their various answers to the question, "Is this family getting weaker or stronger?" While peer discussion pushes students to express and elaborate their thinking, students might surface pieces of the puzzle without a connected understanding. Teacher-facilitated follow-up discussions can improve the depth and quality of students' understanding by getting students to examine their evidence and consider alternative interpretations.

Ms. Harris fits in a very short lesson on English/Spanish cognates when Mateo notices the connection between the Spanish and English versions of *ingenuity*. While this kind of on-the-spot vocabulary building can be helpful to English language learners, it is only one of many strategies you can use to support students in building word meaning (Brisk & Harrington, 2007; Garcia, 2003).

Represent

The class chart and notes Ms. Harris creates during the revisit discussion is a tangible record of what her students understand about family survival at that point. She keeps the charts posted as her students continue cycles of questions, reading, individual reflection, and group analysis. After completing the memoir and further readings about postwar Japan, her students represent a deeper level of understanding in an individual, formal essay on the big question, "What problems did Japanese families face after World War II? How did their governments and the families themselves respond?" (The next Classroom Close-Up, "Teaching a Multiliteracy Skill," addresses that exercise.)

CLASSROOM CONNECTIONS

The Challenges of Using Multiliteracies

In the preceding Close-Up, students use many of the Supported Literacy multiliteracies to build their understanding of how families survive war. The tools work together, sometimes seamlessly and sometimes not so smoothly. As you read this account, which of these multiliteracies are likely to be most difficult for students to learn? Which do you think are the most challenging for teachers to facilitate? In your own classroom, when is peer accountable talk more useful? When is it more useful for you to facilitate whole-class discussions to build your students' understanding?

LITERACY NOTE

Explicit Instruction in Multiliteracy Skills

The general approach to teaching literacy skills is *gradual release,* which involves three steps:

1. Talk with students about how the skill will help them with reading or writing.
2. Teach the skill by "thinking aloud" as you use it with your own writing or reading.
3. Provide practice opportunities in meaningful activities (Torgesen et al., 2007, pp. 27–28).

Small group activities encourage students to discuss what the skill means and how they can use it as a tool for understanding challenging content. Follow small group work with whole-class discussions. Continue to review the skills when they become relevant during a unit, and cue students when it's appropriate to use them.

Group writing offers many useful strategies—charts, lists, board summaries, webs, and diagrams—for synthesizing students' work and also representing their understanding. Deciding on how to represent understanding depends on the stage of inquiry and the purpose of the representation. Early on in a unit, a Meaning-Making Cycle might result in a preliminary concept map or individual student summaries in a journal or science notebook. At the end of a unit, a "performance of understanding" (Blythe, 1998) can take the form of an essay, a podcast or multimedia presentation in social studies, a short story or poem in language arts, or a report, poster presentation, or physical model in science.

This kind of embedded direct instruction introduces students to a valuable multiliteracy—writing to build and express meaning—they can use to synthesize their knowledge and information about the impact of war on families. They are becoming proficient in planning and writing a supported argument essay. By scaffolding the instruction with the Meaning-Making Cycle, Ms. Harris gives her students the chance to observe the skill, try it on a simpler topic, discuss their understanding of the skill with other students, evaluate and correct their understanding, and then use this new genre format for representing their understanding of "War and Families."

When you embed direct instruction in a curriculum, you enable your students to learn a new tool when they most need it. Your students are motivated to master the tool because they need to use it to express what they know. They are more likely to remember and apply it in a new writing situation. Ms. Harris comments that this kind of direct instruction feels "truly like changing the tire as the bus is moving. But students use and remember it because they need it, *now*." Being able to write clearly in many genres and for many purposes is an important twenty-first-century writing skill, and the genre of argument is one that they will continue to use in history and to translate to other content areas and to their lives outside school.

CLASSROOM CLOSE-UP

Teaching a Multiliteracy Tool

For their final "performance of understanding" (Blythe, 1998), Ms. Harris asks her students to write an essay that responds to the questions, "What problems did Japanese families face after World War II? How did their governments and the families themselves respond?" The essay brings them back to the driving, essential questions of the unit and requires that they synthesize their readings and discussions. They must identify one or more problems and support their responses with arguments and evidence from at least four different readings on postwar Japan, including Yoko's memoir. They have been building up to writing this essay by reading articles, books, textbook excerpts, and Internet sources in their discussion groups. They have also completed their reading of *My Brother, My Sister, and I*. Now, to prepare them for their final assignment, Ms. Harris devotes a class period to teaching them the features of a supported argument essay. She uses the Meaning-Making Cycle to provide direct instruction in this skill.

Engage

Ms. Harris reengages her students by asking them to reflect on the work they have done throughout the unit: "Okay, you all said you've never worked on this kind of writing, but actually you have. Look at our big chart of arguments and evidence of family strengths, and look at the notes you made in your notebooks." She points to their responses to the question, "Is this family getting weaker or stronger?" and she asks, "What did your answers to the question include?"

The class is quiet as students review the chart and their journal notes.

Several students: Rereading chapters. Looking for examples. Evidence. We disagreed?

Ms. Harris: And when we disagreed, how did we work that through?

Mateo: Telling our arguments and what in the reading is evidence.

(Continued)

Sophie: We said why they were strong or weak.

Ms. Harris: Explaining your position and arguing for it with reasons and evidence. Listen to me as I think aloud on a real problem I'm facing this week.

She thinks out loud about a forthcoming history faculty meeting where she wants to persuade her colleagues to invest in a certain history book. She thinks aloud about the arguments and evidence she plans to use. "So my *position* is that we need to invest in a new textbook. They'll ask me why they should spend the money. Well, one argument is that students don't have the resources they need for studying the full twentieth century. My evidence is that, look at this table of contents! The two textbooks cover only through World War II. And they don't connect us with the digital and media resources that publishers are now making available. It occurs to me that. . . . " She continues to think aloud her evidence and reasoning, then puts up a poster that lists the features of a supported argument essay.

FEATURES OF A SUPPORTED ARGUMENT ESSAY

A Supported Argument Includes:

1. A statement of your position on a question.
2. Several pieces of evidence that are detailed, specific, interrelated, accurate, and related to your position.
3. Clear explanations of how your evidence supports your position.

Note: You can explain your reasoning and conclusions by using personal experience, examples, point of view, cause and effect, and comparison and contrast.

(Adapted from Morocco et al., 2001)

Respond

Ms. Harris's students practice using this rubric on a real problem of their own choice related to school or their family. They work individually or in pairs, outlining their topic, position, evidence, and explanations and arguments. One pair of girls works on arguments to their families about why they should go on an optional class field trip, and several students work on family homework policies or dilemmas they are encountering in after-school jobs.

Elaborate

Students share their examples in peer discussion circles, using the poster to help them identify each part of their argument: a position, evidence, and reasoning about how the evidence supports the position. They find that the hardest aspect of this kind of writing is the third part—clearly showing how the evidence supports their position. "You need to make the connection," Ms. Harris urges them, "between your evidence and your points."

Revisit and Represent

"How did you do? What did you learn?" The students report out the results of their practice, and Ms. Harris pushes them to translate their work into a historical context, asking "How will your essays on World War II history be like this practice work? How will they be different?" With her prompting, students realize that they need to include evidence from their various readings in their essays, and they need to take into account how the memoir differs from a textbook or a historical research article in providing evidence. As his classmates nod in agreement, Mateo observes, "The textbook is more general and talks about Japan. Yoko is writing just about her family." Ms. Harris's students also notice that they have not all been reading the same materials and might have different positions and arguments.

In a subsequent class, the students work in peer groups to begin to formulate their answers to the essay question. Alex's group mainly talks about economic problems:

Alex: Families have to get jobs. And if they were in the bombing, they have no houses.

Gretchen: If they can't make a living, they are going hungry. The U.S. helped though. The U.S. occupied Japan and gave money.

Ivan: This report says U.S. assistance was $15.2 billion in 2005 dollars. You know, Japan paid some of it back, it says.

Gretchen: "Economic recovery," it says . . . machinery, vehicles, and food supplies, too.

Another group focuses on the psychological impact of war, talking further about Yoko's memoir and reading a book on the impact of other wars on children, *No Place to Be a Child: Growing Up in a War Zone* (Garbarino, Kostelny, & Dubrow, 1991). Some students work on how to integrate the current plight of Iraqi refugee families in the Middle East into their historical study. Keeping the criteria in mind, the students develop responses to the essay question, talk through the evidence, and write their individual essays.

CLASSROOM CONNECTIONS

Teaching with Meaning-Making Cycles

What multiliteracies are your students using? Do they know why they are using them? In the early years of developing Supported Literacy, we did not always explain to students why we were having them use particular tools like writing in journals, participating in discussion circles, or consulting Web sites. When your students are aware of their skills, they can work on them and use them intentionally and creatively. Making multiliteracies explicit, which includes teaching them directly when needed, is one of your most important contributions to your students' learning.

BENEFITS OF USING MULTILITERACIES TO LEARN HISTORY OR LITERATURE

These two Classroom Close-Ups point up several advantages of organizing learning within the Supported Literacy framework. One is that students use multiliteracy tools not simply as ends in themselves but as tools to assist them in learning history and interpreting nonfiction literature as one source for understanding world history. Another benefit is that the different multiliteracies work together and reinforce one another. As one student put it, "This journal writing greases our discussions." Journaling assists reading and discussion, peer discussions assist comprehension, and teacher-led discussions deepen students' understanding of the texts and of family survival. Further, students are building metacognitive awareness—the ability to pay attention to their thinking and to change direction when needed—through these cycles of critical inquiry.

Ms. Harris asks her students to notice their thinking when she says, "Think about what you mean by *strong* or *weak*. What is a strong family?" She wants students to adopt this habit of awareness as a form of internal discourse in which they ask themselves questions and then answer them internally (Bransford et al., 2000). Students notice their thinking when they write about a text and when they listen to other students making different interpretations of the same text. Part of Ms. Harris's role, and your role, is to be explicit continually about the tools students are using, to offer alternatives, and increasingly, over their years in high school, to give them responsibility for deciding how they will use multiliteracies to make sense of new and confusing areas of learning.

The following chapters illustrate what the Supported Literacy framework looks like in other content areas. In the high school Earth Sciences class we depict in Chapter Three, students use a wide range of multiliteracy tools to help them investigate the dynamics of the greenhouse effect and understand our human contribution to global warming. Then, in Chapter Four, seventh-grade students develop skills in understanding the theme of character change in a contemporary novel about adolescent identity development.

CHAPTER

3

USING THE FRAMEWORK TO TEACH CONTENT

A Science Unit

CLASSROOM CLOSE-UP

Understanding Climate Change

Some things that wouldn't normally happen are happening. Like last week, there was a hail storm in Jasper where I go to camp. And it was 70 degrees before that. It was just sort of a very bizarre coincidence. But I've never gotten sunburned in my life before this summer. If you've ever seen *An Inconvenient Truth,* the pictures of polar bears swimming around the water and just dying. And animal life and the change in temperature of water and everything just drastically affects ecosystems. The problem is things like emissions, fossil fuels, like waste, general waste that humans produce, aerosol cans, general chemicals that are harmful to the earth, and UV rays are coming in and it's heating up. The less the ozone there is the more sunlight gets in and the more harmful rays.

—Eva Hernandez's Science Notebook

Everybody's saying that the world is going to end. I was just wondering when? Some people are saying 50 years or something like that. Because all the gases of the world and pollution are creating a hole in the ozone layer. It's because the ozone layer's getting thin, so the sun is coming through with a stronger force. But my dad doesn't believe in it. He says that the trees take up all the extra gases and stuff. The carbon they're producing. He thinks Al Gore just makes things up to try to get attention and stuff. Me, I'm not really interested in it. Some people are crazy, crazy about it. And they do everything they can, and recycle, and everything. I'm not like that at all.

—Ted Violi's Science Notebook

Eva and Ted are responding in their science notebooks to three questions their science teacher, Meg Robbins, has asked them about one of the most important issues of the twenty-first century, climate change (EDC, 2006):

- What evidence do you know of that supports the idea that global warming is happening?

- What have you heard about the potential impacts of climate change?

- Do you think climate change could affect you? If so, how?

While Eva reads more about the problem of climate change than Ted does, and she has some fairly well-developed opinions, Ted worries about the issue. Yet neither of these seventeen-year-olds has a clear idea of the science of climate change or global warming. In fact, both students have two misconceptions that are typical of adolescents' thinking (Driver, Squires, Rushworth, & Wood-Robinson, 2001; Union of Concerned Scientists, 2002)—misconceptions that your students probably share.

First, many adolescents incorrectly believe that global warming is caused by a hole in the ozone layer that allows more heat to come through the atmosphere and warm the earth. Eva implies this when she writes, "the less the ozone there is the more sunlight gets in and the more harmful rays." And Ted has the same idea: "it's because the ozone layer's getting thin, so the sun is coming through with a stronger force." While the ozone layer has thinned as a result of certain human-made chemicals such as chlorofluorocarbons, this thinning does not cause global warming.

Second, adolescents tend to think that all sorts of toxic chemicals are major contributors to climate change. Ted says that "all the gases of the world" and "pollution" cause global warming. Eva says the culprits are "emissions, fossil fuels, like waste, general waste that humans produce, aerosol cans, . . . general chemicals that are harmful to the earth." In fact, while most pollutants from industrial processes—such as carbon monoxide, organic carbons, sulfate, soot, and some oxides of nitrogen—are harmful to the environment, they are not greenhouse gases. Only certain gases, such as carbon dioxide, water vapor, and methane, are greenhouse gases that contribute to warming.

SCIENCE LITERACY AND CLIMATE CHANGE

Scientists are in strong agreement that we are in a period of significant climate change, and we are contributing to it. On TV and the Internet, and in conversations in school and at home, your students hear warnings that our consumption of fossil fuels has triggered long-term climate change and immediate effects such as melting glaciers, droughts, and hurricanes. At the same time, climate science is one of the most complex areas of Earth science for high school students. A fairly young science, climate study is just beginning to have a place in high school curricula. Learning about climate change requires demanding inquiry. Your students need to ask questions, read and analyze data on climate change, consider alternative explanations, and learn how a number of factors can interact to change our climate. If the world is to address this complex challenge effectively, your Millennial students and the generations that follow them must be scientifically literate and must understand the underlying science of climate change.

In this chapter, we focus on climate change because it represents the essence of twenty-first-century learning, and most adolescents understand little about its scientific underpinnings. We provide a unit overview and Classroom Close-Ups of "Understanding Climate Change," a high school Earth science curriculum unit that uses the Supported Literacy framework to help your students develop twenty-first-century competencies, as well as the science literacy capabilities of the National Research Council (NRC). The NRC defines *scientific literacy* in its National Science Education Standards as "the knowledge and understanding of scientific concepts and processes required for personal decision-making, participation in civic and cultural affairs, and economic productivity" (1996, p. 22). As shown in Table 3.1, the specific science literacy capabilities the NRC outlines are consistent with Supported Literacy's twenty-first-century competencies.

Scientific and academic literacy go hand in hand. The Supported Literacy multiliteracies can help your students become scientifically literate, and they are integral to teaching and learning science. By mastering the use of multiliteracies in science contexts, your students can become adults who can "apply a range of scientific skills and knowledge to understand their world and communicate about it. That demands a set of skills that marries knowledge of science facts, concepts, and processes with the ability to use language clearly and precisely to comprehend, articulate, and communicate about scientific issues and ideas" (Thier, 2002).

As students progress through each phase of the Meaning-Making Cycle in the "Understanding Climate Change" unit, they use multiliteracy tools critical to scientific thinking and learning to investigate important questions and to understand concepts related to the greenhouse effect. For example, students write in their science notebooks and think in a variety of nonfiction formats about the climate data they are analyzing. They view powerful images, many in multimedia modes—film, video, photographs, charts—of some of the physical changes taking place on Earth that are related to climate change. They read print articles, reports, and digital texts and

TABLE 3.1. Science Literacy, Multiliteracies, and Twenty-First-Century Competencies.

A scientifically literate person can:	Multiliteracies	Conceptual Understanding	Critical Thinking	Creative Thinking	Collaboration and Communication
Ask for, find, or determine answers to questions derived from curiosity about everyday experiences.	X	X	X	X	X
Describe, explain, and predict natural phenomena.	X	X	X	X	X
Read with understanding articles about science in the popular press.	X	X	X		X
Identify scientific issues underlying national and local decisions and express positions that are scientifically and technologically informed.	X	X	X	X	X
Evaluate the quality of scientific information on the basis of its source and methods used to generate it.	X	X	X		X
Pose and evaluate arguments based on evidence and apply conclusions from such arguments appropriately.	X	X	X	X	X
Engage in social conversation about the validity of the conclusions.	X	X	X		X

Source: Competencies in column 1 are from NRC Guidelines (1996, p. 22).

SCIENCE NOTE

Inquiry Cycles

Science teachers often use inquiry cycles that are similar to Meaning-Making Cycles. The 5 E's Model (Engage, Explore, Explain, Elaborate, Evaluate) developed by Rodger Bybee and the Biological Science Curriculum Study is one such inquiry cycle (Bybee, 1997). Yet the Meaning-Making Cycle process is unique because it highlights the multiliteracies that students use—such as accountable talk and writing in science notebooks to build and express meaning—as well as the class configurations—such as individual, small group, or whole class—that are used to guide inquiry.

datasets from the Internet, using skills of reading critically to assess the credibility of what they are reading. They engage in structured peer group and teacher-facilitated discussions—accountable talk—of difficult concepts, and they develop charts and written summaries of their group work to share with their classmates and to stimulate further analysis and discussion.

The Meaning-Making Cycle integrates appropriate multiliteracy tools at each phase of inquiry. Those tools motivate students and give them multiple ways to represent and interact with science concepts. Students use the tools to process difficult concepts for meaning as they work individually, in pairs, and in small discussion circles where they are given responsibility for their own learning. Through collaborative inquiry as a class, students build a shared foundation of background knowledge, pose questions, and clarify their thinking to collaboratively construct deeper meaning about concepts. The Meaning-Making Cycle facilitates formative assessment since frequent writing and discussion opportunities give the teacher a window into students' understanding and help students clarify what they think and know.

In the sections that follow, we show you how these multiliteracy tools can help your students learn challenging science. You will learn about the following instructional strategies and framework features:

- How you can organize a high school unit on climate change around twenty-first-century competencies and science standards.

- How Supported Literacy, particularly the Meaning-Making Cycle, integrates multiliteracy tools for science inquiry.

- How you can explicitly teach science multiliteracy skills that many adolescents do not possess.

Explicitly teaching science multiliteracy skills is not always easy because science students have varying needs and backgrounds. For example, Ted, who notes in his science notebook that he is "not really interested in" climate change in the opening of this chapter, gets some C's in school because he reads slowly and has difficulty elaborating his ideas in writing (see Chapter Six for further discussion of reading difficulties). Ted writes as little as possible because he makes frequent spelling errors, and he has difficulty organizing his writing. Ted's classmate Eva is verbal and articulates her ideas clearly and forcefully in speaking, but she seems not to use comprehension strategies when she reads. As a result, her understanding of what she reads is sometimes superficial. These two students' limited literacy skills prevent their developing a deep understanding of science concepts. Very likely, many of your students share similar obstacles—such as an inability to read science articles strategically for deep meaning, lack of scientific vocabulary, or an inability to articulate observations and thinking in writing or in discussions—that interfere with their efforts to engage in science inquiry.

If you decide to use the Supported Literacy framework and you already use an inquiry-based science approach, you need not make a large shift in your instructional strategies. However, you must develop a level of awareness of students' literacy practices. You must also provide explicit instruction of the multiliteracies to help your students acquire a tool kit of multiliteracies and to support them in developing the metacognitive awareness to know when to apply these tools and which tool to use.

CLASSROOM CONNECTIONS

Multiliteracies and Content

Whether or not you are a science teacher, what multiliteracies do you think might be particularly valuable for learning science? Which multiliteracy skills described in the first two chapters do you currently use with your students? Which of these multiliteracy tools do you explicitly teach your students? How do you integrate journals and science notebooks into a larger inquiry process, in which students talk about their reading and writing with other students and with you?

SUPPORTED LITERACY IN SCIENCE: UNDERSTANDING CLIMATE CHANGE

The "Understanding Climate Change" unit provides a strong example of how you can use the Supported Literacy framework to further enrich your curricula. We designed this sample Supported Literacy unit drawing on a variety of resources including activities from *Foundation Science: Earth Science Curriculum Project,* funded by the National Science Foundation (NSF) and developed by EDC in 2006, as well as recent scientific reports and online resources including Woods Hole Research Center (2007), the Union of Concerned Scientists (UCS, 2002, 2006a, 2006b), and the Intergovernmental Panel on Climate Change (IPCC, 2007a, 2007b, 2007c). An overview of the unit's six components—vision, essential questions, Meaning-Making Cycles, resources, outcomes, and assessment approaches—follows. At the end of our discussion of the components, we provide an outline of the unit's lessons organized by the essential questions.

A vision of adolescent learning: Designed around the Supported Literacy framework and national science standards, "Understanding Climate Change" envisions adolescents as capable, global learners who can take responsibility for investigating complex concepts. The activities assume that students can learn to use well-informed arguments and reasoning to advocate for research-based action to manage the effects of climate change.

Essential questions: Four essential questions organize the unit and focus students' inquiry into climate change:

- What climate changes are taking place? What is the evidence?

- What causes climate change? How do humans contribute?

- What are the impacts of climate change?

- What can be done about climate change?

Meaning-Making Cycles: The unit's four essential questions drive the Meaning-Making Cycle critical inquiry process. This process integrates multiliteracies and builds students' conceptual understanding of climate change. While the Meaning-Making Cycle builds meaning through a sequence of phases, students return to a phase when doing so supports them in building their understanding of science.

Resources for teaching and learning: Students use a wide range of resources to support the cycles of inquiry. These include hands-on investigation, science readings, published scientific data and reports, additional reports on the Internet, and a multimedia DVD presentation on global warming, *An Inconvenient Truth.*

Twenty-first-century outcomes: The box lists some specific unit outcomes for the "Understanding Climate Change" unit in terms of each of the major twenty-first-century competencies emphasized in the Supported Literacy framework.

These outcomes articulate with National Science Standards (National Research Council, 2006): Content Standard A (9–12), Science as Inquiry, which includes abilities necessary to do scientific inquiry and understandings about scientific inquiry; Content Standard B (9–12), Earth and Space Science, such as energy in the earth system, geochemical cycles, origin and evolution of earth system; Content Standard F (9–12), Science in Personal and Social Perspectives, such as environmental quality, natural and human-induced hazards, and science and technology in local, national, and global challenges; and Content Standard G (9–12), History and Nature of Science, which includes science as human endeavor and the nature of scientific knowledge.

OUTCOMES FOR "UNDERSTANDING CLIMATE CHANGE"

Multiliteracies:

- Understand how to use digital and multimedia resources to view scientific data and scientific processes, and use Internet search engines such as Google to find appropriate Web sites for finding data and reports on climate change.
- Use reading comprehension strategies, particularly writing and drawing, to visualize complex scientific processes.
- Synthesize data and concepts related to climate change through writing, discussion, and multimedia presentations to peers and adults.

Conceptual Understanding:

- Understand terms and concepts such as *climate, greenhouse gases, greenhouse effect,* and the *carbon cycle*.
- Understand natural versus human influences on the greenhouse effect and the contribution of carbon dioxide emissions to global warming.

Critical Thinking:

- Understand how to interpret climate change data.
- Compare and evaluate different information sources on global climate change.
- Explain the carbon cycle and its relationship to global climate change.
- Describe the human influences on climate change.
- Analyze personal carbon footprints.
- Reason logically about factors that influence global warming.

Creative Thinking:

- Imagine how the opportunities and threats of climate change might show up in daily life in the future.
- Represent solutions to global warming to a particular audience (teens, adults, policymakers, neighborhoods) through print and multimedia modes of communication.

Collaboration and Communication:

- Carry out a cooperative investigation of climate data with peers.
- Collaboratively research and present the impact of climate change in other parts of the world.

Assessment: In the Classroom Close-Ups, we illustrate two of the three kinds of assessments of student understanding described in Chapter Two. Ms. Robbins selects a variety of methods to monitor her students' progress in understanding the greenhouse effect and our human contribution to global warming. She examines entries in students' science notebooks, their poster presentations on climate data, their lab reports, and their presentations on regional impacts. She also listens to their discussions. For a culminating assessment, her students prepare sections of a podcast presentation to inform others in the school and community about the science of climate change and the actions their community can take. They invite other faculty, students, and their parents to a presentation of their posters and a demonstration of their podcast.

LESSON OUTLINE

The unit is organized around eight lesson topics (see box), each of which might take two or more class periods (see Appendix A for a description of the eight lessons). This chapter's Classroom Close-Ups highlight five of these lessons (1, 3, 5, 7, and 8) to show in detail how multiliteracy tools, integrated into an inquiry cycle, can support a diverse group of students in understanding key concepts related to climate change.

In the Close-Ups, we present several lessons from the flow of Ms. Robbins's teaching that highlight how multiliteracy tools support cycles of science inquiry to build understanding. One lesson relates to the first essential question ("What climate changes are taking place? What is the evidence?"), two lessons relate to the second essential question ("What causes climate change? How do humans contribute?"), one lesson to the third question ("What are the impacts of climate change?"), and one lesson to the fourth question ("What can be done about climate change?"). Ms. Robbins chooses literacy tools for teaching these lessons that help students with what they are trying to learn. Her role in an activity shifts depending on whether students will learn through independent study, collaborative learning, critical analysis of their group products, or direct and explicit teaching of a science inquiry tool.

LESSON OUTLINE FOR CLIMATE CHANGE UNIT

Essential Question 1. What climate changes are taking place? What is the evidence?

Lesson 1: What do we know about the big picture of climate change?
Lesson 2: How do we interpret climate change data?

Essential Question 2. What causes climate change? How do humans contribute?

Lesson 3: What makes Earth habitable?
Lesson 4: How does the greenhouse effect influence climate?
Lesson 5: Who is to blame? What are the natural versus human contributions?
Lesson 6: How can we evaluate what we read about global warming?

Essential Question 3. What are the impacts of climate change?

Lesson 7: How is climate change affecting different regions of the world?

Essential Question 4. What can be done about climate change?

Lesson 8: How can we limit our contributions to the greenhouse effect?

Ms. Robbins Prepares to Use the Framework

"Teaching climate change won't be a slam dunk," Ms. Robbins says of a class that includes not only Eva and Ted, but also twenty-four other students with "really fuzzy ideas—if any at all—about global warming." After her students answer the three questions about climate change in their science notebooks (see opening of this chapter), Ms. Robbins has three concerns. First, how can she motivate her students to learn the science of climate change? Students like Eva find the topic compelling, but they would rather organize a political action group than look at climate data. Students like Ted are not sufficiently uneasy about what is happening to want to dig into the hard work of understanding science. Ms. Robbins's concerns are justified given that studies of adolescents' attitudes find that only half of eleven- to seventeen-year-olds are worried about global warming, and most say they feel powerless to affect climate change (U.K. Department of Environment, Food, and Rural Affairs, 2006).

Ms. Robbins is also concerned that while her students have limited backgrounds in Earth science, they also have very deeply rooted misconceptions. She observes, "They just don't know what they don't know." Her third concern is the wide variation in her students' ability to read and understand the reports and articles that, in addition to lab experiments they do with carbon dioxide, will be important sources of information in the course.

With these concerns in mind, Ms. Robbins plans to integrate a number of literacy tools for science inquiry. She will use a multimedia presentation to try to captivate her students' interest and create a sense of urgency about the topic, as well as to begin building their background knowledge about the global warming effects of climate change. She will have her students write, draw, and construct charts in their science notebooks throughout the unit to help think through what they are learning and reflect on new information. She will teach critical reading skills for analyzing science texts and use various discussion formats that have students working collaboratively to interpret climate data and results of their own experiments. These multiliteracy tools will help students who know very little about climate science participate in the Meaning-Making Cycles that form the core of the unit and investigate the evidence for and causes of the current climate change.

Organizing the climate lessons around this seamless inquiry process—*engage, respond, elaborate, revisit,* and *represent*—pushes every student to think, exposes students to others' ideas, and makes their thinking visible in both writing and talk so that Ms. Robbins can use the whole-class discussions to surface misconceptions and identify areas of confusion. As we noted in Chapter Two, Meaning-Making Cycles build conceptual understanding as students work with concepts in many representations—print, visual images, writing and drawing, talk, digital texts, and multimedia experiences. Ms. Robbins does not always organize the inquiry phases in a strict linear sequence, however, as lessons may move back and forth between several rounds of the engage and respond phases, for example, before moving on to the phase in which students elaborate on their learning. In the early lessons (see the

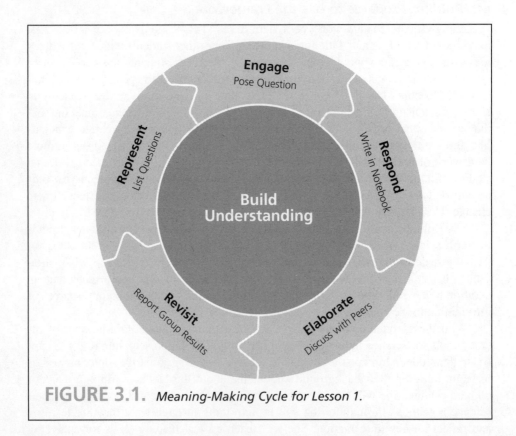

FIGURE 3.1. *Meaning-Making Cycle for Lesson 1.*

full lesson descriptions in Appendix A), she creates a series of multimedia activities to ensure that her students engage with the material and to motivate them to learn complex science related to climate change. When they get to the end of the unit and plan an exhibition for their class blog and for parents and community representatives, her students spend more time on representing their ideas to other students and to parents with images, video footage, and text. In the Close-Up that follows, Ms. Robbins uses a multimedia presentation, supported by peer discussion, notebook writing, and group writing, to engage students in the unit and to establish the groundwork for her to achieve her goals. Figure 3.1 shows how these multiliteracy tools are distributed across the phases of the Meaning-Making Cycle in Lesson 1.

> *Essential Question 1*
> *What climate changes are taking place? What is the evidence?*
> *Lesson 1: What do we know about the "big picture"*
> *of climate change?*
> *Lesson 2: How do we interpret climate change data?*

CLASSROOM CLOSE-UP

Using Digital and Multimedia to Engage Students (Essential Question 1, Lesson 1)

Ms. Robbins's first goal is to fuel her students' interest in climate science. As she thinks about this challenge, she reflects, "It's hard. I can't be preachy. I have to let them see the evidence of a problem. I want them to see how complex it is without turning them off. And I want them to see that it's urgent, but I have to balance hope and disaster. We can all do something." Her second goal is to familiarize her students with analyzing climate data that provide evidence of climate change.

Engage

Ms. Robbins begins by telling her students, "Your questionnaires and our conversations show that you each know something about climate. Not all of it is accurate, however. Your science notebook will be a record of how you change your understanding—really change your mind—over the next weeks. And if you get confused, that's progress."

(Continued)

The climate change questionnaire has stirred up students' thinking. To drive them further into the topic and pique their curiosity, Ms. Robbins projects onto the wall pairs of pictures of glaciers in Italy, South America, and the United States that show glacial melting over time. "Wow," Ted comments on pictures of melting in Montana, "No more skiing." "Is anyone else having thoughts about these same pictures?" Ms. Robbins asks, and another student adds, "These areas aren't as beautiful now." Ms. Robbins encourages these varied and candid comments, wanting students to begin to distinguish visual data from their varied interpretations of them.

Her students ask questions that show they are paying attention, "Is it a problem to lose glaciers, I mean, if you're not a skier or tourist?" "Most of these are far away. Does this melting hurt us?" To build interest and background knowledge, Ms. Robbins shows a segment of Al Gore's *An Inconvenient Truth* (Guggenheim, 2006) that shows similar pictures of melting. Gore narrates background information about some of the consequences of glacial melting. He explains that the Himalayas contain a hundred times as much ice as the Alps and provide more than half of the drinking water for 40 percent of the world's population. "That 40 percent of humans will face a shortage if warming continues at the same rate."

Ms. Robbins shows additional segments of the DVD to add to this shared overview. The students view animated images of the coast of Florida and parts of Manhattan disappearing under water—projections of what will happen if the sea level rises by twenty feet worldwide—and images of polar bears unable to climb up on thinning slabs of ice. The DVD chapters explain some basic science concepts related to global warming, some of its current impacts, why and how scientists are collecting carbon dioxide data, and how glacial ice cores can reveal climate history.

The DVD captures students' attention with its stark contrasts of physical beauty and devastation, and with the data explaining warming trends. Ms. Robbins wants students to feel the pictures tug at their minds and emotions, hear each other's questions, and want to know more.

LITERACY NOTE

Multimedia Messages

An important skill in reading multimedia texts and thinking critically about what they contain is being aware of the messages they communicate through sound and image. Ms. Robbins focuses on students' visceral and emotional reactions to the DVD as well as the information it contains, so that their reactions will be accessible for discussion.

Respond

After the class watches the video, Ms. Robbins says, "Write in your science notebooks one thing that grabbed you, one thing you learned about climate change, and one question you'd like to have answered. Write fairly quickly and don't be concerned about sentence form and punctuation." Then she adds, "This kind of writing, remember? It's a *tool,* a multiliteracy tool to pull out when you're trying to make something of a reading." She has her students generate their own questions, rather than answer study questions at this point, so that they will be aware of their own thinking (metacognition) and own the questions they will investigate over several weeks. If they personally engage with the topic, they will comprehend what they read and see more fully. These exploratory notes (Thier, 2002) give her students material to bring to a subsequent discussion of the DVD in peer discussion groups.

Elaborate

Ms. Robbins assigns her students to get into their discussion circles to read and talk about what they wrote about the DVD in their science notebooks and then compile a set of questions from their group. Students are visibly excited, and they chat about the DVD with each other as they move into their groups. In each group, one student assumes the role of facilitator and another student serves as recorder, participation roles essential to accountable talk that they learned earlier in the year. The facilitator keeps the group focused on the task and ensures that each person participates and is heard. The recorder notes group members' ideas in print or visual form (some students develop a chart or diagram of the group work) and summarizes them briefly to the class after the discussion.

Ms. Robbins walks around observing students talk about different aspects of Gore's presentation, and listening for how much information they have actually absorbed. Students' vigorous participation in their discussion circles is evidence for Ms. Robbins that the DVD has created a sense of urgency about understanding climate change, the topic of the unit. She also hears a great deal of confusion in their talk. Many students express Ted's and Eva's misconception that the hole in the ozone layer is causing global warming. She makes a note to herself to talk about this misconception in an upcoming lesson. Like Eva and Ted, most of the class has confused ideas about how, exactly, climate and weather differ. Ms. Robbins's observations serve as an informal assessment of students' work and cue her to what to highlight as she helps students revisit their conversations.

Revisit

When students report out the results of their peer discussions, they notice that some groups are focusing on the breakup of Antarctica's ice fields while other groups are intrigued with the ways scientists bore ice cores from glaciers to study temperatures from thousands of years ago. From these varied reactions, students generate a composite list of twenty-five questions from the class that include "How did they drill down in

(Continued)

LITERACY NOTE

Peer Discussion

Research on middle and high school teachers (Langer, 2001) finds that effective teachers create situations in their classrooms that lead to extended student discussions of content. "At least 96 percent of these teachers helped students engage in the thoughtful discussion we call shared cognition. Teachers expected their students to not merely work together, but to sharpen their understandings with, against, and from each other" (p. 872).

the ice?" "How can scientists work in the cold?" "What else can scientists read in ice cores?" "Could polar bears adapt to the changing environment?" "How do we know Al Gore isn't a fake?" (That one was Ted's.) This step plants students' questions at the center of the investigation; all of them link to the unit's first essential question.

As an ongoing homework assignment, Ms. Robbins asks students to use a section of their science notebooks for news articles, pictures, and readings; they will find and clip them and look for patterns and themes in the reported items. A student suggests that they set up a blog for the unit and post their questions and what they find out. That student has set up other blogs, and tells students, "We can post our conversations, graphs, pictures, and we can do a podcast." Ted says he will help design the blog because more kids might believe there is a climate problem if they read about it in a student Web site.

LITERACY NOTE

Using Blogs and Podcasts to Learn Content

A class blog allows students to showcase their essays, images, data, and podcasts. Blogs give young people a chance to tune their thinking and writing to a larger audience, and some teachers find that their students' writing skills improve when they edit a peer discussion for a podcast (Dlott, 2007). For a teacher's discussion of the benefits of blogs and podcasting in several content areas, see "Web Pulls World into Classroom," an article in the *Christian Science Monitor* by Mark Franek (2007).

Progress Monitoring

Each phase of the Meaning-Making Cycle during Lesson 1 yields assessment information about students' progress toward understanding climate change. Ms. Robbins has some rough baseline information on her students' understanding of climate change from the questionnaires they completed (engage). From their science notebook writings (respond) and peer discussions (elaborate), she observes their growing level of engagement and can further identify what they know as well as pinpoint their misconceptions. These observations help her discern that so far her students have acquired only beginning background knowledge, and certainly not a common body of knowledge—each one took something different from Gore's presentation (engage). Yet the combination of the multimedia presentation and students' reflections in writing and discussion generated many relevant science questions (represent). Ms. Robbins's students are taking some responsibility for understanding this complex topic.

CLASSROOM CONNECTIONS

Motivations and Misconceptions

How do you motivate your students to study a complex topic in science or another content area? How do you find out what they already know and think they know about the topic? Which student misconceptions of history, science, literature, and other subjects have surprised you most? Which have been the most difficult to change, and why have they been so challenging?

The four lessons related to the second essential question focus mainly on engaging students in learning about the greenhouse effect and how humans are contributing to the rising temperature of Earth's atmosphere. Ms. Robbins has an opportunity to surface and discuss their misconceptions about the cause of global warming during this lesson. The Close-Up of Lesson 3 shows Ms. Robbins teaching students to use several multiliteracies to help them comprehend technical readings about the greenhouse effect and the human contributions to carbon dioxide production. In Lesson 3, they use drawing—a visual comprehension strategy—to portray the processes described in the article. They make individual drawings and then compare and revise them in peer groups.

Essential Question 2
What causes climate change?
How do humans contribute?
Lesson 3: What makes Earth habitable?

CLASSROOM CLOSE-UP

VISUALIZING A READING ABOUT THE GREENHOUSE EFFECT
(ESSENTIAL QUESTION 2, LESSON 3)

Engage

Ms. Robbins asks her class, "So how cold is it outside Earth's atmosphere?" Some students say they don't know, and one guesses that it is 100 degrees below zero. "Put on your parkas, it's minus *454 degrees* Fahrenheit," Ms. Robbins says, as the class groans loudly and fakes shivering, "yet, on Earth we have life—us, trees, flowers, animals that need warmth. How can this be?"

Ms. Robbins's opening question pushes her students to visualize a verdant Earth in a cold universe. She recognizes that her students need multiliteracy tools like visualizing to help them understand dense and technical science texts. "They have to visualize and interpret complex processes. I want them to see how complex the science of global warming is. It's work—necessary work—to understand it." To this end, she focuses this lesson on teaching and using writing and drawing, along with discussion of the students' visualizations, to help her class understand difficult scientific readings.

Respond

Ms. Robbins adds her question to the class list: "If the temperature is minus 454 degrees outside Earth's atmosphere, how can we survive?" She passes out a reading about what happens to light energy from the Sun (see box). She explains that the description of the path of light energy is simplified in the reading, since the percentages of light energy units given are averages and vary from one part of the globe to another and through time. They will explore two factors that influence how much of the Sun's light energy is absorbed by Earth's surface and transformed into heat energy. The first factor is how much light energy gets trapped by Earth's atmosphere—the greenhouse effect—and the second factor is how much light energy is reflected back into space, the albedo effect. Ms. Robbins guides her students to use drawings to help them build and express the meaning of these two factors: "After you read the article once or twice, draw a diagram in pencil in your science notebooks that shows what happens to the light energy that is transmitted to Earth from the Sun, based on the information in the reading"

FOLLOWING THE PATH OF LIGHT ENERGY

The temperature of space outside Earth's atmosphere is minus 454 degrees Fahrenheit. And yet the atmosphere near Earth's surface is a much more comfortable average temperature of 59 degrees Fahrenheit. It seems remarkable that the atmosphere could be so effective in protecting Earthlings from the deep cold of space, especially since Earth's atmosphere is very thin. In fact, compared to the diameter of Earth, the atmosphere's thickness is like the peel on an apple. Although its thickness may seem insignificant relative to the size of Earth, the atmosphere has so successfully regulated Earth's surface temperature that for nearly four billion years Earth has remained the only planet known to have had liquid water continuously at its surface and to have supported life.

How does the atmosphere regulate Earth's temperature? The Sun delivers energy to Earth in the form of light, or electromagnetic radiation. The atmosphere controls the amount of energy that is absorbed by Earth and warms it, and the amount that is radiated back into space.

On average, scientists have determined that for every 100 units of light energy falling on Earth, approximately 25 units (25 percent) are reflected by clouds back into space. Another 25 units (25 percent) of this light energy are absorbed by the atmosphere. The remaining 50 percent travels to the surface of Earth. Approximately 5 percent of the light energy striking Earth's surface is reflected off the ground, polar ice, or ocean surface directly back into space. Most of the light energy that reaches the surface, however (45 of the original 100 units), is absorbed into the water or ground. This energy absorbed by Earth's surface is key to the greenhouse effect, which you will learn about in the next reading.

Draw a diagram that shows what happens to the light energy that is transmitted to Earth from the Sun, based on the information in this reading.

Source: Adapted from *Foundation Science: Earth Science Curriculum Project* (EDC, 2006)

To help her students understand the reading, Ms. Robbins gives a brief mini-lesson on using visualizing as a comprehension strategy. She tells them, "Try to see in your mind the process that the author is describing, just as you would if you heard someone describe a winning soccer play. Close your eyes and see the play as I talk it through." They practice visualizing players passing the ball back and forth until the final kick results in a goal. As her students practice, Ms. Robbins comments, "Drawing is another multiliteracy tool for

(Continued)

your tool kit, a way to visualize and capture what you see as you read. Science texts tend to condense a complex process into a paragraph. Making a diagram about what you are reading will help you unpack and clarify that process. We'll use drawing a lot in this unit." Students read and draw individually.

LITERACY NOTE

Using Visualization to Comprehend a Science Reading

Visualizing what is being described in a text is a valuable comprehension strategy (NICHD, 2000). Drawing is a particularly helpful science comprehension strategy because it makes the student's interpretation of a complex phenomenon visible to others and available for comparison, discussion, and revision. "Visual representations in science can also help students recognize relationships between concepts and data, help them solve problems, and draw conclusions" (Douglas, Klentschy, & Worth, 2006, p. 239).

Elaborate

Students go into discussion circles to talk about their drawings. Comparing drawings in small groups helps highlight information that students might have missed in their first reading of the article. Figure 3.2 shows the drawing Eva made.

Eva asks one of her group members, "Where's something to show the light energy bouncing back from the clouds?" Her group decides to reread that part of the article to make sure no information is missing from their drawing. One student reads the paragraph about the pathway of light aloud while the others look to make sure each part of the 100 units of energy falling on Earth is represented in a new group drawing. Thus drawing leads them into rereading, a valuable comprehension strategy that many students do not think to use. Ms. Robbins walks by and congratulates the group for digging back into the articles, speaking loud enough that the other students will hear.

After Eva's group looks at their drawings, one student says, "I don't think it's true that the same amount, 5 percent of light energy, is reflected from land and water. Think about the glare off of the water when you're in a boat!" Other students agree. They write a question about reflection in their notebooks and decide to bring it up in the full class discussion. The drawings stimulate this interplay of talking, rereading, and generating ideas, which takes students beyond their initial, fragmented understanding of the article.

(Continued)

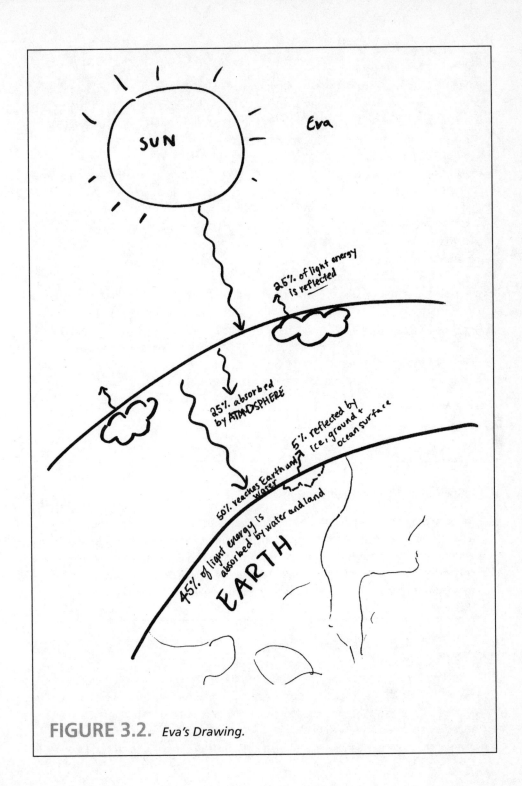

FIGURE 3.2. *Eva's Drawing.*

Revisit

When students reassemble to present what they think was the clearest drawing from their group or a new group drawing, Eva's group brings up their question about the difference in light reflection from land and water. "If you look at the light reflecting off of water compared to a blacktop street, there's a big difference," says one student. "That's a great observation," says Ms. Robbins. "Remember this article is a generalization about the pathway of light, and the 5 percent reflection is an average. In reality, different surfaces reflect the light's energy differently." She returns to the term *albedo,* which is a measure in percentage of how much light energy is reflected of the total light that hits a surface. After considering this term, the class decides that snow, ice, and water reflect the most and soil, volcanoes, streets, and city buildings absorb the most. "But that reflection would change. In winter there would be more reflection from snow than in summer," comments one student.

"Good point," says Ms. Robbins. "But let's look more closely at the albedo of oceans." She projects a satellite image of Earth in natural light. Students are surprised to see how dark the oceans look from space. "So oceans reflect less light than we thought," muses Ted. "Yes," says Ms. Robbins. "They actually have a relatively low albedo; they absorb light energy." She asks students to think about how this differing reflectivity of surfaces might affect temperatures in different parts of the world as they read another article about the greenhouse effect. "This is more complicated than I thought," adds Ted.

SCIENCE NOTE

Influences on Regional Temperatures

Albedo, the percentage of the total incoming light energy that is reflected by a particular surface, is one factor that affects climate in different regions of the world. Another factor is *latitude,* our closeness to the equator, where the sun's rays strike Earth most directly. Other factors are the circulating currents of air that transfer heat from the equator toward the poles, and ocean currents.

Elaborate

Ms. Robbins gives students a second reading on the greenhouse effect that introduces the heat trapping effect of carbon dioxide (see box). It explains the difference in wavelengths of light energy that come into our atmosphere from the sun and the heat energy that bounces back out. She asks students to read the new article and work together on revising and adding this additional information to their drawing about the pathway of light and heat energy. She notices that several of the groups are rereading parts of the article together to make sure they understand it. Occasionally, Ms. Robbins intervenes to clarify a concept or help students connect it with their drawings. She prompts, "Ask yourself, 'What does this reading on wavelengths add to my understanding?' Show that new thinking in your drawing." She asks students to choose the clearest drawing from their group—or design a drawing together—to present to the class. Ms. Robbins listens as Eva shows Ted her revised drawing and explains, "I get it now; see, this line shows the heat energy rising up and being trapped by greenhouse gases in the atmosphere. *That's the greenhouse effect.*"

(Continued)

THE GREENHOUSE EFFECT

To understand what keeps Earth warm, you must focus on the light energy that is absorbed by Earth's surface. Light energy has a relatively short wavelength, which can pass easily (back and forth) through Earth's atmosphere. However, most of the light energy that is absorbed into Earth's surface is transformed into longer-wavelength heat energy, which we can feel but not see. Have you tried to walk barefoot on black asphalt that has been in the bright sunlight for several hours on a summer day? The light energy from the Sun is absorbed by the asphalt and transformed into heat energy, which warms the surface, sometimes making it very hot.

According to a basic law of physics, heat naturally flows from warmer areas to cooler areas. Therefore, the heat energy warming the surface of the asphalt begins to rise into the air (you can feel this happening as you stand on the asphalt). This longer-wavelength heat energy rises into the atmosphere, and this time, instead of passing easily through the atmosphere and back into space, some of it is trapped. This is because certain gases in the atmosphere, primarily water and carbon dioxide, allow shorter-wavelength light energy to pass through toward the surface easily, but tend to trap some of the longer-wavelength heat energy and reradiate it back toward Earth.

These heat-trapping gases are known as *greenhouse gases,* and without them Earth would be too cold for life to survive. The amount of reradiated heat that is trapped by the atmosphere depends on the concentration of greenhouse gases in the atmosphere. As the concentration of these gases increases, more heat is trapped and the temperature of Earth's atmosphere rises. This is known as the *greenhouse effect.*

Source: Adapted from *Foundation Science: Earth Science Curriculum Project* (EDC, 2006)

LITERACY NOTE

Rereading

Rereading with a purpose is a vital strategy for promoting both fluency and deep understanding of texts in every discipline (Perkins-Gough, 2002; p. 92 in Schmoker, 2006). Other useful comprehension tools that help students read science texts are distinguishing important ideas from less important ones, summarizing a passage, connecting what they read to what they already know, and "reading between the lines" to make inferences (Block, Gambrell, & Pressley, 2002).

Revisit

After each group presents a drawing, Ms. Robbins has the class post all the drawings, and she helps them compare and evaluate them. She adds to their explanations of what makes Earth habitable, and she explains the role of greenhouse gases, particularly carbon dioxide, in trapping the heat from the sun in the greenhouse effect. Ms. Robbins hears Ted comment, "I guess it's not about a hole in the ozone layer." Students realize that not all pollutants are greenhouse gases.

Represent

The drawings reflect what students understand about the greenhouse effect at this point in their inquiry. Over the next couple of weeks, students will continue to examine and talk about the drawings.

The class moves on to Lesson 4, in which they do a laboratory investigation to compare the absorption of heat energy by pure carbon dioxide to that by air, and they look at natural and human contributions of greenhouse gases. After they have gained an understanding of the role of carbon dioxide in warming, they take up Lesson 5, in which they inquire into the human role in producing that carbon dioxide. In Lesson 5, they use writing and drawing in other ways as they organize information in a chart and then construct, as a class, a visual model of the inflow and outflow of Earth's carbon into the atmosphere.

Essential Question 2
What causes climate change?
How do humans contribute?
Lesson 4: How does the greenhouse effect influence climate?
Lesson 5: Who is to blame?
Lesson 6: How can we evaluate what we read about
global warming?

CLASSROOM CLOSE-UP

USING ACCOUNTABLE TALK AND GRAPHICS TO INTERPRET DATA
(ESSENTIAL QUESTION 2, LESSON 5)

Engage

As the class settles in, Ms. Robbins reengages them in the topic of climate change: "The greenhouse effect makes our planet habitable. Yet if we add *too much* of a greenhouse gas such as carbon dioxide, the warmth is trapped and builds up. You saw evidence of that in last week's lab investigation. You saw the warming trend in the climate data. So what's our human role in this warming trend?"

Respond

Ms. Robbins asks students to speculate in their science notebooks about where they think the carbon dioxide in Earth's atmosphere comes from and to hold onto their notes until later in the class. Once again, the students use writing as a multiliteracy tool to advance their own critical thinking about an interrelated set of concepts. In quickly reading some of the entries and hearing them discussed in peer groups, Ms. Robbins is able to connect her teaching with students' thinking. She sees in several entries that most students connect carbon dioxide to car exhaust, but few make the connection to respiration and photosynthesis, processes she knows they learned about in their biology course the preceding year.

Elaborate

Ms. Robbins uses a cooperative learning strategy to have students build a visual model of the various natural and man-made sources of carbon dioxide in Earth's atmosphere. She shows students a list of six natural or human processes that affect the inflow and outflow of carbon dioxide in the global atmosphere: chemical weathering of rocks; formation of fossil

(Continued)

fuels; combustion of fossil fuels; photosynthesis, respiration, and decomposition; volcanoes, seafloor spreading, subduction, and volcanism; and diffusion of carbon dioxide into and out of the ocean. She gives each discussion circle a different card with a brief description of one of these carbon flux processes and a list of science Web sites where they can locate additional information about their source of carbon flux. (The box provides a couple of sample cards.) Students go to available computers to research more about their process and then discuss the flux process with their groups to try to figure out its role in the carbon cycle.

SAMPLE CARBON FLUX PROCESS CARDS

Combustion of Fossil Fuels and Other Organic Matter

Net effect: CO_2 that was stored is added to the atmosphere
Carbon flux: 5 billion metric tons/year

When fuels such as oil, natural gas, and coal are extracted from the earth and burned (combusted), carbon and hydrogen in the fuel reacts with oxygen from the air to form carbon dioxide, water, and heat. The heat may be transformed to electricity and transported to people's homes and businesses for power, or may be transformed to mechanical energy in cars, trucks, or other vehicles. When wood or other organic material is burned, it also releases CO_2. The net effect of the combustion of fossil fuels and other organic materials is to release CO_2 to the atmosphere.

Formation of Fossil Fuels

Net effect: CO_2 is removed from the atmosphere and incorporated into rocks
Carbon flux: <1 billion metric tons/year

When living things die, they usually decompose, releasing the carbon from which they are built into the atmosphere. In some (rare) cases, these organic remains are instead preserved in an oxygen-poor environment such as the bottom of certain ocean basins or in stagnant swamps. These remains accumulate and, over millions of years, are buried and incorporated into rock. Heat and pressure transform the preserved organic material into oil, natural gas, and coal. Oil and natural gas form primarily from the remains of microscopic marine organisms. Coal forms from land plants. It is estimated that approximately 100 tons of ancient life is converted to one gallon of gasoline. The net effect is to store carbon in the rocks of the earth.

Source: Adapted from *Foundation Science: Earth Science Curriculum Project* (EDC, 2006)

SCIENCE NOTE

Carbon Flux

Carbon is an essential component of every living cell, and has been around since before Earth formed 4.6 billion years ago. Soil, rocks, oceans, living things, and the atmosphere are all "carbon reservoirs." Sediment and rock (coal, for example) hold the most carbon by far and store it for a very long time. *Carbon flux* refers to the amount of carbon that is transferred from one reservoir to another during a given time period (EDC, 2006).

Revisit

Students reconvene so that each group can teach the rest of the class what they learned about their carbon flux process. Before they begin, Ms. Robbins creates a graphic organizer like the example shown here on the board to help students organize what they will be hearing and to make explicit what this science multiliteracy tool can do. "Graphic organizers are helpful for sorting out and comparing information. They are a valuable strategy to use when you read complex science articles. Think about using them whenever you have a lot of information to sort out."

Process	Description	CO_2 Added to or Subtracted from Atmosphere?	Carbon Flux

Source: From *Foundation Science: Earth Science Curriculum Project* (EDC, 2006)

Ms. Robbins asks students to copy this chart into their science notebooks and to use it to capture what they learn from each group's presentation. Ms. Robbins tries this strategy as a way to keep students focused during the presentations and accountable for understanding the information. "Don't let a group sit down until you really understand their carbon flux process."

Represent

Ms. Robbins tapes two large sheets of chart paper onto the wall and, with her students, talks through a drawing of the carbon cycle that shows how each carbon flux process

(Continued)

affects the flow of carbon into and out of the atmosphere. "This will be our model, as best we understand it, of how carbon enters into the carbon cycle. This is another way to use drawing to understand what you read," Ms. Robbins points out. "This is our current group view about how we're putting a lot of carbon into our atmosphere, and contributing to a higher rate of warming than at any time in history." Students add up all the inflows and outflows of carbon dioxide to determine the net flow of atmospheric carbon dioxide. Ms. Robbins's commentaries about the multiliteracy tools students are using weave through her questions and comments about the scientific processes they are working on. In calling attention to their science literacy tools this way, she encourages them to adopt the tools and to be able to use them intentionally and independently in other science inquiries.

Revisit Again

Students continue analyzing and synthesizing information in this way through another class period, where they look at scientific evidence that the levels of carbon dioxide in Earth's atmosphere relate to warming patterns. First, Ms. Robbins shows them a graph

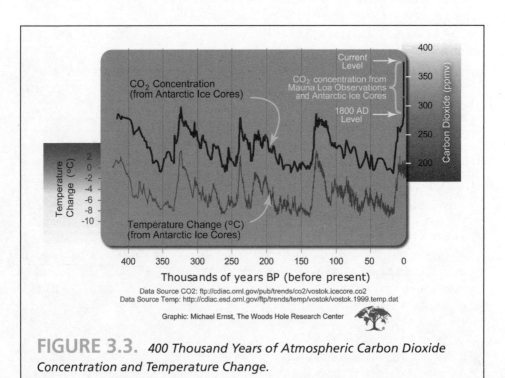

FIGURE 3.3. *400 Thousand Years of Atmospheric Carbon Dioxide Concentration and Temperature Change.*

of CO_2 concentration and temperature over the past 400,000 years. Undisputed in the scientific community, the reported data result from studying ice cores from Antarctica and carbon dioxide emission data from Mauna Loa Observatory (see Figure 3.3).

"What do you see here?" Ms. Robbins has given her students practice analyzing climate data in an earlier lesson, and she wants them to apply the skill to new data. She's going to try having them use an accountable talk multiliteracy tool to grasp the meaning of the graph; they will translate this graph into words that describe their understanding. One student will start, and another student can build on that explanation by adding "and" to expand the explanation, or "but" to disagree with it, or the student can ask a clarifying question, as Ms. Robbins does in this exchange.

Laura: After a big warming it gets very cold. I read those are ice ages.

Eva: They're, the lines are like, a kind of copy of each other. The carbon dioxide and temperature trends are like mirrors of each other.

Ms. Robbins: Does carbon dioxide have an effect on temperature? Or the opposite? Do you have any evidence about this? Think about our lab investigation (Lesson 4) where we measured and compared heat absorption in air and pure carbon dioxide.

Emanuel: When we did the lab, the pure carbon dioxide absorbed heat from the lamp at a faster rate than the air did.

Ms. Robbins: Well, so then how does that finding relate to this graph?

Jared: Well, carbon dioxide absorbs heat energy at a faster rate than air, so if the carbon dioxide concentration in air goes higher, I would expect the air temperature to go up. This graph shows that pattern exactly, that's why the temperature and carbon dioxide data trends are matched.

Ms. Robbins hears her students begin to connect the various concepts that help explain global warming. They are seeing connections between their lab experiment and the professional scientific data. She notes, "This is good group work. It's not easy to synthesize these various kinds of data from your own experiments and from scientists."

Pushing them to further critical thinking, Ms. Robbins shows her students a second graph with detail between 1880 and 2006 (see Figure 3.4) and asks what might have caused the jump in carbon dioxide and temperature from 1880 to present times. Shifting from synthesizing to conjecturing, students call out possibilities: factories, the industrial age, cars, logging and burning forests, combustion of fossil fuels. One of the students connects more of the group's conceptual work by saying, suddenly, "It's the human-related carbon flux processes we just studied. It's, wow, all that carbon dioxide." Ms. Robbins comments, "Good connections."

(Continued)

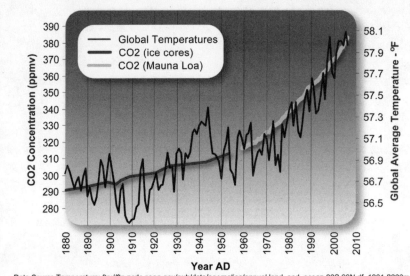

FIGURE 3.4. *Global Average Temperature and Carbon Dioxide Concentrations, 1880–2006.*

LITERACY NOTE

Making Inferences from Data

Students use clues in the graph and its upward trend, along with their background knowledge about carbon flux processes and the history of that time period, to infer the cause of the trend. The graph gives them a common visual text around which to connect and synthesize the other concepts they have been struggling with. In this instance, the graph is a multiliteracy tool for synthesizing information and deepening their understanding of global warming.

Ted continues the conversation, still skeptical: "But look, the temperature and carbon dioxide have gone up and down over hundreds of thousands of years. Aren't we maybe just in an up time?" Ms. Robbins asks students to try to answer Ted's question by looking at the graphs again. She prompts, "Compare present levels of carbon dioxide to the past." Laura notices how the concentration of CO_2 in 2006, 379 ppm, is much higher than the range over the last 400,000 years (180–300 ppm) (Woods Hole Research Center, 2007). Ms. Robbins asks, "If you were to project a trend of CO_2 emissions for the next hundred years, what would it look like?" One student remembers what Al Gore looked like standing on the ladder pointing out the trend. "It doesn't look good; it looks like a straight shot up." "But," Ms. Robbins points out, "that's only if we don't change how much carbon dioxide we are putting into the atmosphere." She replays the section of *An Inconvenient Truth* that discusses this carbon dioxide emission and temperature data to reinforce their learning visually. "So is the world going to end?" Ted asks. "There's hope. Let's keep going and see how to answer that big question," Ms. Robbins ends the class.

LITERACY NOTE

Synthesizing Reading

Science reading involves not just collecting discrete pieces of information but also synthesizing those pieces into a complete, deep, and personally meaningful understanding (Thier, 2002). Summarizing individual readings, using charts and graphics to organize data, engaging in multiple rounds of reading and analysis, and participating in well-facilitated discussion are all multiliteracy tools for synthesizing science information from print and nonprint sources.

Progress Monitoring

Ms. Robbins has been accumulating evidence from students' drawings of the pathway of light and heat energy (respond, elaborate) from which students are building their understanding about the greenhouse effect. Their lab reports display their interpretation of evidence about the warming effects of increased carbon dioxide in the atmosphere. Students are taking ownership of teaching their classmates about carbon flux (elaborate, revisit) and developing a class drawing (represent) describing the carbon cycle. The most important indication of their progress is their thoughtful synthesis, through listening to and building on each other's comments, of their lab investigation findings, their readings, and their study of the carbon flux to interpret a complex graph displaying the relationship between carbon dioxide emissions and global warming.

(Continued)

CLASSROOM CONNECTIONS

Synthesizing Content

When do you use visual strategies to help your students learn information or concepts in your particular content area? Ms. Robbins usually has students use discussion in conjunction with visualizing tools. What does discussion of readings add to the visualizing process? How do you know whether students understand particular information and concepts well enough to begin connecting and synthesizing it?

As most of her students have grasped some causes of global warming, Ms. Robbins shifts her class to evaluating the impact of climate changes in the United States and globally. This application will indicate how well they truly understand the science of climate change. Because articles about the impact of climate change vary widely in their accuracy and intent, Ms. Robbins helps students use a set of critical reading criteria in Lesson 6 to evaluate the accuracy of articles about the impact of global warming—including articles that might attempt to obfuscate or contradict peer-reviewed scientific research findings.

After they complete Lesson 6, the students continue to use these criteria in Lesson 7 as they work in discussion circles to gather information from reports and from Web sites about the global impact of climate change. The Close-Up of Lesson 7 shows students using a combination of multiliteracy science tools for inquiry, including applying their critical reading tool, writing summaries of reports in their notebooks, using peer discussions to think critically about evidence of impact and to synthesize their findings, and using digital and media tools to gather information and to communicate what they learn to the class. The Close-Up attempts to show how these multiliteracy tools interweave, seamlessly, to assist students in understanding the impact of climate changes.

Essential Question 3
What are the impacts of climate change?
Lesson 7: How is climate change affecting different regions of the world?

CLASSROOM CLOSE-UP

BECOMING CRITICAL CONSUMERS OF INTERNET DATA ON CLIMATE CHANGE (ESSENTIAL QUESTION 3, LESSON 7)

Engage

Ms. Robbins points to the long list of class questions about climate change. She reminds students, "Our class question list has a lot of questions about whether our rising CO_2 and temperature levels really make a difference. Eva noticed a freaky hailstorm at camp. Ted didn't think Katrina had anything to do with it. Are there effects now?" Ted asks, "Didn't they say something about it melting the ice? The warming affects how the world works. Some animals really need a comfortable climate."

To help students think further about possible impacts of climate change, Ms. Robbins gives them a list of Bogus or Believe? it statements about the impacts of global warming (see box), and she has them circle *Bogus* or *Believe It.*

(Continued)

SAMPLE BOGUS OR BELIEVE IT? STATEMENT

If the Global Temperature Continues to Rise, What Could Happen?

Is It Bogus, or Do You Believe It?

Consequence: more droughts, heat waves, and wildfires
Warmer temperatures could increase the probability in certain areas of drought and the risk of wildfires. *Bogus* or *Believe* It?

Consequence: the spread of disease
Increasing global temperatures could affect human health by increasing the spread of mosquito-borne illnesses such as malaria and dengue fever. *Bogus* or *Believe* It?

Source: From Foundation Science Curriculum Project (EDC, 2006)

Then Ms. Robbins asks students to do a class *value line* for several of the statements. They position themselves on a line that she forms with string across the room, with *Strongly Agree* written on a sign at one end and *Strongly Disagree* at the other. Students express a lot of disagreement. As students stand at various points on the line, Ms. Robbins has them explain their position. Jared says, "I agree that there will more droughts, heat waves, and wildfires. Look at what's happening in California and Greece this year. Wildfires around LA and San Diego have wiped out houses, and in Greece, they've killed people and threatened the site of the ancient Olympics." Eva counters, "Yes, but remember when we learned about the difference between climate and weather. You can't just look at what is happening right now and decide that it's related to global warming. Climate happens over a long period of time, like thirty years." As students discuss their positions on the line, they move to another location if they are convinced to change their position or if they feel their position is closer to another person's.

LITERACY NOTE

Active Forms of Accountable Talk

Although this fairly boisterous kind of discussion format is not often used with high school students, if done well, it creates an effective form of accountable talk. Having to speak up for their positions requires that students listen to others' arguments and build from them to formulate their own. Talking through their arguments teaches them key features of a supported argument essay, which the history teacher taught in Chapter Two.

Respond and Elaborate

"Now let's look at the actual data about possible impacts of climate change. Choose a region." Ms. Robbins has listed ten different regions of the world where climate change data has been compiled, including the U.S. West Coast. Ms. Robbins has each discussion circle choose one of the regions and conduct Internet research on the current evidence of climate change impact. She encourages them to gather information across at least three sectors of their region, which can include health, agriculture, water supply, economics, and biodiversity. They are to be alert to positive as well as negative effects. For example, while cereal crop production will go down in some areas that become too hot, it will increase in some areas that have been too cold.

Ms. Robbins reminds students to evaluate their sources using a format called the "Critical Reading Tool," which they created together in Lesson 6.

Criteria	Reading 1	Reading 2
Credible Source		
Peer-reviewed		
Current Information (Date)		
Evidence Included		

Ms. Robbins invites an Earth sciences professor from a local college, Dr. Banes, to be a resource for them during two class periods, and she and Ms. Robbins suggest addresses for objective Web sites that provide access to the latest evidence, including the IPCC reports, the UCS regional reports, and the U.S. Global Change Research Program's U.S. National Assessment of the Potential Consequences of Climate Variability and Change Web site.

Groups divide up the work once they see what is available on the different Web sites, pairing up to read and summarize reports over the next week. They meet periodically to connect and relate their findings, and to organize findings by sectors—for example, health and agriculture. With Ms. Robbins and Dr. Banes as their resources, students work on their own and collaboratively to summarize their findings in writing and then design a multimedia presentation, using PowerPoint to communicate their findings and evidence. Ms. Robbins reflects, "Did I wish that they would see how complex climate change is? I thought they'd be overwhelmed. The local basketball court is their thing, not Senegal and India." Yet her students dug into the data.

Revisit, Represent

Before the presentations begin, students have the idea of drawing a graphic organizer to chart the global effects they've found. As groups present, Dr. Banes and Ms. Robbins help the class track and summarize the impacts the groups find across sectors across the regions. They also look across regions to see if temperatures differ—the hot and cold spots they hypothesized about earlier. In presenting and comparing their findings, students see the complexity of climate effects in different parts of the world.

Working on California, Ted's discussion circle shows the class photos of the Sierra Nevada they've gotten from the Internet and explains that Californians rely on this water supply in dry months. Members of Ted's group explain that if carbon dioxide emissions continue at the current rate, statewide annual temperatures are expected to rise into a higher warming range (8–10.5 degrees Fahrenheit). These higher temperatures could

(Continued)

result in more rain and less snow and reduce the Sierra snow pack by 90 percent, causing water shortages. "So it's like dominos," Ted shows their photos and diagram. "Heating leads to water shortage that affects industry and eliminates skiing and other fun snow activities." The group explains that fruit crops of almonds, cherries, and apricots depend on a minimum number of hours per year of temperatures below 45 degrees in order to set the buds. These "chill hours" are already rapidly decreasing in many areas and will likely eliminate certain fruit crops there (UCS, 2006a).

Students decide to post their presentations and the class summary chart on their blog. To their total astonishment, later in the week they hear from students in a classroom in Northern California, who have also been looking at warming effects on the Sierra Nevada. Ted's group members continue a discussion with the California students.

In the next week, to broaden their discussion of impact beyond current effects, students view the segments of *An Inconvenient Truth* that focus on predicted long-term unintended consequences if current trends continue at the same rate. Students comment on the part of the DVD that shows that the relative U.S. contribution to global warming from greenhouse gases is 30.3 percent in contrast with that of Southeast Asia, India, and China combined, at 12.2 percent.

Progress Monitoring

During the *Bogus or Believe It?* value line activities (engage), Ms. Robbins hears students articulating their ideas and can assess the depth of their thinking (respond). She sees progress in how students think and challenge each other's assumptions, asking for more evidence. She monitors students' research on impacts and sees that some groups have more trouble than others working through the Internet options and need more instruction from other students and from her on how to work with a scientific site. They need a lot of support from her in finding information that they can compare across regions and add to their matrix (elaborate). Nevertheless, she observes that they are able to ask good questions about the impact data across regions and to use the chart to summarize the data (represent). She feels that her students now have an adequate knowledge base and some critical thinking skills for considering possible solutions.

Essential Question 4
What can be done about climate change?
Lesson 8: How can we limit our contributions to the
greenhouse effect?

CLASSROOM CLOSE-UP

**Using Multiliteracies to Evaluate Solutions to Global Warming
(Essential Question 4, Lesson 8)**

More than in any science unit she has taught, Ms. Robbins feels compelled to end this final lesson with a practical conversation about action and social change. She observes, "Too many people go from denial or ignorance straight to hopelessness, and the science suggests that there is time to prevent the worst consequences." Her goal for the final lesson, which extends over several class periods, is for her students to apply their critical reading and analysis skills to identify a range of solutions and to be able to use scientific information and other credible sources to present and defend their solutions.

Ms. Robbins has no difficulty engaging students in discussing solutions to global warming. More equipped with knowledge, Eva is in her element:

> Things that are eco-friendly aren't cheap. Not everyone can buy a Prius. The reason that companies don't do things the other way is because it's not in their best interests because our country runs solely on money. Essentially, in my opinion. And so the only way to stop global warming from becoming an issue is to change a lot more than just like your lifestyle because only a very small minority of people can support that and they are rich people.

Another student comments, "We need to put suggestions on our blog, or kids will get hopeless."

In the first Meaning-Making Cycle in this lesson, Ms. Robbins gives students an opportunity to immerse themselves in information about possible solutions to global warming—the processes and actions that could slow this global problem. She gives them a Union of Concerned Scientists article about "the human fingerprint" on global warming (UCS, 2006b), and they view the last sections of Gore's presentation. She instructs her class, "Read and view all sources critically, using your Critical Reading Tool, including Gore's multimedia material." Working individually and together, students see a comparison of fuel emission standards that shows the U.S. at the very bottom, Japan at the top, and photos of renewable energy sources other than gas, oil, and coal (respond, elaborate). As a group they review (revisit) their peer conversations, and they talk about Eva's idea that many solutions are "inconvenient" for companies that are invested in practices that threaten Earth's livability.

Ms. Robbins wants students to understand their own contributions to carbon emissions before identifying solutions. For the second activity cycle, she shows students how to use an online calculator from the Environmental Protection Agency (2007) to assess

(Continued)

their personal carbon footprints by looking at their energy use at home and from driving (engage, respond). Then students work together to determine the class impact on carbon dioxide emissions that contribute to global warming (elaborate). Students are amazed when they calculate the magnitude of auto emissions from their state alone. Eva gets particularly excited by this activity because it highlights personal responsibility and raises questions about the kinds of legislation needed for manufacturing cars: "You know it's all about profit, profit, profit. I'm just a teenager, obviously I can be like called naive or whatever, but I think that it's really important for people not to be selfish in times like this. It's not about making me an extra million dollars. It's like, will your grandkids be able to, like breathe."

Next, Ms. Robbins assigns students to each read, think about, and come prepared to the next class with at least ten possible solutions that relate to the carbon flux processes they studied that influence global warming (respond). As an example, she points out that promoting residential and commercial solar energy use would decrease combustion of fossil fuels. In their discussion circles, students create criteria for sorting and prioritizing their set of solutions (elaborate). When students present their sorting criteria and solutions to the class as a whole, they agree on the categories local, state, national, and international as one way to sort and code solutions, and they decide that another way to sort solutions is by likely impact (minor, moderate, major) on reducing carbon dioxide in the atmosphere (revisit).

With a background of possible solutions, students write individual essays arguing for two solutions that teenagers can do and two that the U.S. government must undertake. They illustrate their solutions with poster presentations, a visual kind of scientific representation they learned about in Lesson 2 (represent). Ms. Robbins uses the scientific term *claim* to talk about their solutions. "We don't know for a fact that they will work; you are making a claim and need to support it with evidence." Students are careful to include the scientific evidence that links their claims to their conclusions.

LITERACY NOTE

Supporting a Claim in Science Inquiry

This essay format in science is related to the supported argument essay that students learn in their world history and literature class, described in Chapter Two. A *claim*, in technical science language, is "a statement of one's understanding about a phenomenon, about the results of an investigation or experiment, or about other data" (Sutherland, McNeill, Krajcik, & Colson, 2006, p. 166).

Supporting a claim in science includes stating a claim or position in a sentence, providing several pieces of detailed evidence that support that claim, and using clear reasoning to explain how that evidence supports the claim. "The discourse of science is . . . about organizing claims and evidence into arguments expressed in a scientific way of 'talking' or 'writing'" (Douglas et al., 2006, p. 237).

In their discussion circles (elaborate, represent) students prepare sections of a podcast presentation to inform others about the science of climate change and actions that their community can take. As a culminating performance of their understanding about climate change science, Ms. Robbins's students invite other faculty, students, and their parents to a presentation of their posters and demonstration of their podcast. Ted takes on the role of emcee at their public presentation, somewhat nervous about his father seeing him in the role. His group's poster presents their "family footprints" and advocates that most of their families change to more fuel-efficient cars. He watches his father talk with great animation to other parents and Ms. Robbins afterward, and he is relieved when his dad gives him a big smile and "thumbs up" from across the room.

CLASSROOM CONNECTIONS

Considering Social Action

In Chapter One, we defined *critical inquiry* as active and social, as well as intellectual, going beyond simply gathering inert knowledge. How appropriate do you think it is for Ms. Robbins to end the course by focusing on solutions to global warming? Where in your teaching do you connect students' conceptual understanding with social action or social responsibility? Is this a part of teaching or do you think it is overreaching your job?

THE BENEFITS OF USING MULTILITERACIES FOR SCIENCE INQUIRY

In Ms. Robbins's Earth science class, literacy has not taken the place of science. Instead, Ms. Robbins uses multiliteracies to enhance students' understanding of important science content. The Meaning-Making Cycle provides the engine of inquiry, and the use of multiliteracy tools fits naturally and seamlessly within that engine to develop students' deep conceptual understanding, critical and creative thinking, and collaboration around and communication about the complex science of climate change.

What is unique about this Supported Literacy framework is that Ms. Robbins takes the time to explicitly explain multiliteracy tools, and she refers to them as she is teaching to make the tools more transparent to students. If they understand the tools, they might be able to use them beyond this unit and classroom for further scientific learning. She explains how the essential questions focus their learning, and she helps students become aware of the inquiry process within the Meaning-Making Cycle. She helps students become aware of their own thinking and identify where they need more information and how to get it so that they can monitor their own learning. Ms. Robbins supports students' efforts to become critical consumers of Internet research, and she helps them design and use graphic organizers to summarize and synthesize their findings. They learn how to create scientific arguments supported by credible evidence. By knowing what they are doing, students can, increasingly, steer their own learning.

Ms. Robbins provides scaffolding to support diverse students in the collaborative nature of the discussion circles, increasingly giving them more responsibility for their own learning. She also provides them with practice articulating and communicating their thinking. Students' science notebooks are an evolutionary record of their deepening understanding of the science concepts; although they have much to learn and climate change is a continually evolving science, Ms. Robbins's students can look back and reflect on how they have deepened their knowledge since the first questionnaire.

All this inquiry is focused on the ultimate purpose of helping students gain the underpinnings of climate science so that they can be scientifically literate participants in the dialogue to address the twenty-first-century challenge of global warming. Ms. Robbins feels that her students can now participate more fully as part of the solution. They have gone from a black-and-white, superficial, and often inaccurate understanding to a deeper, more knowledge-based scientific understanding of the complexities of climate change. Along the way, they have begun to master literacy tools for learning that will stand them in good stead throughout their schooling and prepare them to work and live successfully in the twenty-first century.

CHAPTER

4

TEACHING WRITING TO UNDERSTAND TEXT

A Fiction Unit

CLASSROOM CLOSE-UP

"How Far Would You Go to Fit In?"

Mark Stein's eighth-grade students are trying to understand the character Maleeka in Sharon Flake's (1998) novel *The Skin I'm In*. Maleeka goes to an inner-city middle school; she is African American and gets teased for getting good grades and wearing home-sewn clothes. She lets another character—Charlese—control her and get her into trouble because Charlese gives her good clothes and promises to stick by her. Mr. Stein's students are planning to write essays about whether Maleeka is changing and more able to stand up for herself, and right now they are discussing how the author shows Maleeka's change.

Mike: I wrote that I don't think Maleeka has changed. The book says here she's still smoking in the girls' room and going with Char.

Ilia: She's not doing Char's homework anymore, though. In Chapter Twenty-Three, Maleeka says, "I ain't been doing Char's homework like I was, neither. Lately, I been making up excuses." I wrote that she decided not to get in trouble.

(Continued)

Mike: But look, on this page, it says "Char asked me to come over. Her sister's got some new things. I was going to say no. Then she mentioned something about a black-and-gold skirt set." She's still hooked on Charlese.

Mr. Stein: Which of these events happened first? Keep rereading and writing with our questions in mind: "Does Maleeka learn to stand up for herself?" and "How does the author show you?"

The novel is the main text of a six-week unit on understanding fiction, titled "How Far Would You Go to Fit In?" The novel is narrated in Maleeka's voice; in this way, the author reveals the character's inner struggle to stand up for herself and for what she thinks is right.

Mr. Stein is excited about the unit and the core book. "My students care about Maleeka's dilemmas and want to read, talk, and write about every scene in the book. They think they don't like to write, but they're writing about Maleeka several times in a class period." Mr. Stein's first goal for his students in this unit is, in fact, that they get comfortable with and more skilled in writing. Many of his students write so little that he has no idea whether they have actually read the book and, if they have, what they are thinking. Even when they are bursting with ideas about a literature selection, many lack confidence that they can express those ideas in writing. He wants them to be more fluent in getting ideas on paper and eventually to be able to express their interpretations of literature clearly in varied genres. He cares about their writing—and not just because of their state tests, which now require essays for the mathematics and the reading exam, but because he thinks that "writing gets you thinking and gives you ideas to bring to discussion."

Mr. Stein has two challenges: writing is hard for his students, but it is also hard for him to teach. Despite all the importance he gives writing, he knows it is probably his weakest teaching area. Having been through a Supported Literacy seminar series (see Chapter Seven) where he had to write so frequently that he stopped being anxious, he wants to give his students the same opportunity for development.

His second goal is for his students to read the book as though they were writers, looking for how the author creates main characters and shows their development. "Does Maleeka really change? How does the author show that?" He wants the class to understand the special feature of fiction—authors invent characters and make innumerable decisions about what will happen to them. "I want them to read the novel, thinking about it as a set of decisions by a writer, about what the character is facing, how they react inside and in their actions, and how to show us."

Mr. Stein's third goal is for students to deeply explore the theme of the unit in their reading and writing about the novel. He wants them to understand that "literature is about human dilemmas and offers readers a chance to learn about being human." He hopes these goals will work together—that the theme and the way Flake develops Maleeka's struggles will captivate students' interest and motivate them to express and build their ideas in writing.

SUPPORTED LITERACY AND WRITING DEVELOPMENT

Perhaps you, like Mr. Stein and many of his colleagues, are concerned about students' writing ability across the curriculum. If so, you are not alone. Throughout the United States, many teachers are talking about their students' difficulty in expressing their ideas clearly in writing. They are looking for tools and strategies to build more writing into their content area teaching, "not to be writing teachers, mind you," they often say, but to help students learn science and social studies. Together, teachers, their principals, and business and government leaders who need workers with stronger writing skills form a national movement to revitalize "the neglected R."

As Table 4.1 shows, Supported Literacy reflects the features of effective writing instruction that two policy reports, *Writing and School Reform* (National Commission on Writing, 2006) and *Writing Next* (Graham & Perin, 2007), identify as effective practice in writing instruction. Table 4.1 synthesizes the recommendations from both reports.

While we focus on a language arts unit in this chapter, the opportunities we present for using and building multiliteracies in writing are relevant to every middle and high school content area. Writing, in various forms, can support students in every phase of the Meaning-Making Cycle. For example, you might use writing to engage your students in an essential question in your content area and to motivate them to investigate in depth, as Ms. Robbins does in teaching about climate change in Chapter Three. Writing about what they know and think they know at the beginning of an inquiry can surface your students' background knowledge and misconceptions and help guide your instruction.

When your students respond to a text by writing a journal or science notebook entry, they become aware of their thinking. Journaling can also be a way to bring their personal and family histories to their reading and into the class discussion. One of the most effective ways to get students to take responsibility for their own interpretations of a text or observations in a science investigation is to have them respond in writing with their initial ideas. These responses give them material to share in peer discussions, where they can further elaborate their ideas. In peer groups, students can use group writing—a group summary or a synthesis of members' findings—to organize their ideas and bring them to a reporting session with the whole class. You can use group writing again when you want students to revisit and evaluate their claims. Putting up a summary of group work, or coding or categorizing findings, gives your class a new common text and reflects deeper thinking than usually happens through an individual's first reading or analysis. This group work represents the community thinking at that stage of the inquiry. At later stages, posters, reports, essays, or dramatizations prepared by individual students, working on their own, become the representation of each student's well-developed thinking.

TABLE 4.1. Features of Effective Writing Instruction in Supported Literacy.

Effective Practices in Teaching Writing	Writing Practices in Supported Literacy
Encourage students to bring their home language and experiences into the classroom.	Curriculum units and writing activities encourage students to connect content with their experiences and home cultures.
Position students and teachers as co-inquirers and co-learners.	Through the use of essential questions and the Meaning-Making Cycle, the framework positions students and teachers as co-inquirers and co-learners.
Encourage students to use writing to collect, analyze, synthesize, and communicate information and opinions.	Students use writing to collect, analyze, synthesize, and discuss important content.
Ask students to write for varied purposes and audiences.	Teachers explicitly teach a variety of formal writing genres and engage students in drafting and revising to meet writing standards.
Require students to use listening, speaking, reading, writing, and thinking together.	Students integrate reading for deep understanding, writing to build and express meaning, accountable talk, and digital and media fluency to support inquiry.
Explicitly teach writing strategies.	Units guide teachers in explicit teaching of writing tools and strategies.
Encourage collaborative student writing (pairs, small groups, whole class).	Students generate and discuss writing in pairs and peer groups and use group writing to summarize and synthesize work.
Use word processing and other technology tools.	Integrates a wide variety of technology tools that support inquiry.

Source: "Effective Practices" list adapted from National Commission on Writing (May 2006) and Graham & Perin (2007).

These cycles of inquiry can create authentic opportunities for you to teach explicitly these literacy tools in the very contexts where they make sense, and where students can experience their value. Students learn comprehension strategies by writing in response to a text, and they master the features of supported argument when they are ready to express a well-formed claim or interpretation.

In the Supported Literacy approach, writing flows naturally throughout the inquiry process, enhancing students' critical thinking and building understanding for individual students and the entire community of inquiry. A mark of students' intellectual involvement in inquiry is that they reach for their keyboard, pen, pencil, or drawing tools to help them think and communicate. Another characteristic is that the more students journal, summarize, group write, and chart their results, the more fluent they become, and the more writing becomes a helpful tool for them to express themselves in many situations.

You might find that you already use many of these Supported Literacy features and multiliteracy tools. If so, we hope that this chapter gives you additional ideas for how to build on what you are doing and reach even more of your students so that you will deepen your approach to teaching writing.

The next section gives you an outline of the design of the curriculum unit, "How Far Would You Go to Fit In?" Following that, we present three Classroom Close-Ups of lessons that illustrate how Mr. Stein works to achieve his goals to improve students' writing and teach them about the craft of fiction. As students investigate the overarching thematic question of how far someone might go to fit into a group,

CLASSROOM CONNECTIONS

Teaching Writing

Whatever your content area is, what role does writing play in your students' content learning? Do you view writing as a form of summative evaluation? Do you see writing mainly as a basis for grading your students? What do your students think is the purpose of writing? Have you asked them? Many students cringe at writing assignments because they assume you are testing them and evaluating their ideas. Have you given them a chance to experience the power and mystery of using writing to explore their ideas and to find their voice? What writing skills do they have? Do your students know how to use writing and drawing to help them make sense of a difficult text? Can they use writing to think critically about information, summarize it, and synthesize it? Do they use it to help them talk about their ideas? Do they know the value of a written argument?

Mr. Stein uses the Meaning-Making Cycle to structure their inquiry and has them use varied kinds of writing to support meaning making. We conclude this chapter by summarizing the benefits of Supported Literacy for building students' writing.

TEACHING WRITING TO UNDERSTAND CHARACTER DEVELOPMENT

"How Far Would You Go to Fit In?" offers an example of a Supported Literacy unit on fiction for students in Grades 7 through 9. We developed the first version of the unit in collaboration with teachers in an urban school district in Massachusetts. An overview of the unit's six components—vision, essential questions, Meaning-Making Cycles, resources for teaching and learning, twenty-first-century outcomes, and assessment approaches follows.

A vision of adolescent learning: The unit envisions adolescents as active readers and generative writers, whose imaginations thrive when they think about human dilemmas that are relevant to their lives. Adolescents can take responsibility for investigating complex themes and are capable of making valuable interpretations. They thrive in a learning community where each student's ideas and experiences are treated with respect.

Essential questions: Unlike the science unit in Chapter Three, three sets of essential questions weave together throughout this unit because they are interconnected. Any session can work with one or more of the questions:

- Why can it be hard for an individual to fit in? What choices do people have when they are being harassed? (Focus: The overall theme of the unit.)

- What writing craft can an author use to create characters and show character development? (Focus: Key elements of fiction.)

- How can writing help us understand fiction? (Focus: How a reader can use writing to understand literature.)

Mr. Stein and his students investigate these questions together, rather than in sequence, as Ms. Robbins' students did in the Chapter Three unit on climate change. Each lesson usually foregrounds one of the three questions. The final lessons integrate answers to the three questions as students synthesize their learning in a written essay.

Meaning-Making Cycles: Students use a number of multiliteracy tools to help them understand fiction—strategic reading, writing to understand and think critically about a novel and communicate their interpretations, peer discussions to support deep reading, and using digital and media composing tools that help them make meaning from a novel. Mr. Stein explicitly teaches several writing skills within Meaning-Making Cycles to help students make sense of Maleeka's dilemmas about fitting in.

Resources for teaching and learning: The core book for the unit is Sharon Flake's *The Skin I'm In,* an acclaimed novel for adolescents. The unit also includes informational readings about bullying—a problem for characters in the core novel—for Mr. Stein and his students. For independent reading, students select from a collection of short stories edited by Donald R. Gallo (2004). The stories broaden the theme of fitting in to the special challenges of immigrant students. Finally, to support the creation of a classroom blog, so students can write for audiences beyond the school, the unit draws on material on blogging from Linda W. Braun's book on new technologies, *Teens, Technology, and Literacy: Or Why Bad Grammar Isn't Always Bad* (2007).

Twenty-first-century outcomes: The box lists some specific unit outcomes for the "How Far Would You Go to Fit In?" unit in terms of each of the major twenty-first-century competencies in the Supported Literacy framework.

OUTCOMES FOR "HOW FAR WOULD YOU GO TO FIT IN?"

Multiliteracies:
- Read strategically and think critically about a text.
- Write to build and express meaning, including using writing and drawing to comprehend texts.
- Use writing to think critically about content and write clearly for many purposes.
- Engage in critical or creative thinking through discussion (accountable talk).
- Read and write blogs to explore the social theme of fitting in (digital and media fluency).

Conceptual Understanding:
- Understand the concept of character development and how an author reveals it in fiction.

Critical Thinking:
- Engage in textual analysis of a character's choices and their consequences.
- Compare and contrast two characters.

Creative Thinking:
- Develop monologues to take the role of a character.

Collaboration and Communication:
- Use collaborative learning to understand a novel and to provide feedback on writing.

These outcomes align with national language arts standards published by the International Reading Association and National Council of Teachers of English (1996) and adopted by most state assessment systems. Relevant standards include Standard 3, applying a wide range of strategies to comprehend, interpret, evaluate, and appreciate texts; Standard 4, adjusting the use of spoken, written, and visual language—such as conventions, style, and vocabulary—to communicate with varied audiences for varied purposes; and Standard 6, applying knowledge of language structure, language conventions such as spelling and punctuation, media techniques, figurative language, and genre to create, critique, and discuss print and nonprint texts.

Assessment: The progress monitoring and final unit assessment notes at the end of the second and third Close-Ups describe how Mr. Stein uses informal assessments from various phases of the Meaning-Making Cycle, and particularly from students' writing, to measure his students' writing skills and their understanding of the novel. Assessments of students' ability to plan and write a supported argument at the beginning and end of the unit provide him with data for monitoring student progress in understanding this genre and for judging his success in teaching this form. The unit also offers other assessment opportunities. For example, Mr. Stein could draw upon standardized reading assessments to see the range of comprehension and vocabulary levels in the class. He could also communicate with other content teachers and with a reading specialist about accommodations that would enable struggling readers to participate in the unit.

LESSON OUTLINE

The unit is organized around fourteen lesson topics (a pre-assessment, a pre-lesson, and twelve lessons), each of which might take two or more class periods (see Appendix B for an overview). The chapter's Classroom Close-Ups highlight three lessons, 1, 4, and 11.

LESSON OUTLINE FOR "HOW FAR WOULD YOU GO TO FIT IN?"

Essential Questions:

Why can it be hard for an individual to fit in? What choices do people have when they are being harassed?

What writing craft can an author use to create characters and show character development?

How can writing help us understand fiction?

Lesson Topics:

Pre-assessment: Writing a Supported Argument About Fiction

Pre-lesson: How do we see ourselves?

Lesson 1. How does Maleeka see herself? (Chapter 1 of *The Skin I'm In*)

Lesson 2. What are Maleeka's relationships like? How does the author show us? (Chapters 2–4)

Lesson 3. How can dramatizing characters help us understand them? (Chapters 5–8)

Lesson 4. What dilemmas about fitting in does the author portray? (Chapters 9–10)

Lesson 5. What are Maleeka's possible choices? (Chapters 11–12)

Lesson 6. What choices do we have when someone we know is being bullied? (Reading)

Lesson 7. How do characters differ in the ways they cope with fitting in? (Chapters 13–14).

Lesson 8. How can writing help us resolve a dilemma? (Chapters 18–19)

Lesson 9. How can adults help students with dilemmas of fitting in? (Chapters 20–23)

Lesson 10. Why does Maleeka engage in vandalism? What clues does the author give us? (Chapters 24–26)

Lesson 11. How can we support an interpretation in writing? (Full book)

Lesson 12. How do authors show character change in fiction? (Full book; independent reading)

As you read about how Mr. Stein prepares his students for the unit and presents several of these lessons, you will see that his teaching draws from the unit guidelines but reflects his own decisions about what to include, omit, or expand with his students. The unit is not a script but an example or model of how to connect the multiliteracy tools, and particularly with teaching writing, in the context of making meaning of fiction.

CLASSROOM CONNECTIONS

Structuring a Curriculum Unit

How does this Supported Literacy unit design relate to how you organize your teaching? Which if any of the six components are simply what you already do? If you are a social studies or science teacher, you probably already organize your teaching around modules or units. As a language arts teacher, you might be more accustomed to using a genre-by-genre or thematic organization. What do you see as the advantages of this kind of design? How might it make your teaching more challenging? What aspects of this particular unit are most appealing for you?

Mr. Stein Prepares Students for Inquiry into Fiction

"I think my students will love *The Skin I'm In* and this focus on fitting in, but will they put effort into reading it closely and writing about it? Can I teach them the writing skills they need for building and expressing their interpretations?" Mr. Stein knows that many of his students are unused to the kind of active and extensive inquiry that the Supported Literacy approach requires. Many students will expect and hope there is a right interpretation of *The Skin I'm In,* and they will assume that Mr. Stein will give them the answers. Taking responsibility for developing and defending their own well-reasoned interpretations of a novel in writing will be new to many of them.

As a pre-assessment of his students' skills in this challenging kind of writing, Mr. Stein devotes a class period before they begin the novel to an assessment of their supported argument writing. He gives them an unfamiliar piece of text—an excerpt from Richard Wright's novel *Black Boy* (1998 [1945])—in which a mother bars her young son from the house until he confronts some bullies who have been stealing their grocery money from him when he goes alone to the grocery store. "You just stay right where you are," she says in a deadly tone. "I'm going to teach you this night to stand up and fight for yourself." Mr. Stein explains that he is interested in their ideas about the passage, and he gives them the assignment shown in the box to complete on their own.

PRE-ASSESSMENT
WRITING ASSIGNMENT

Write a 2–4 paragraph essay in the space below to describe and support your position on this question: *Was it right for the boy's mother to tell/teach him to fight? Why or why not?*

1. State your position in response to this question.
2. Give at least three reasons to support your position.
3. For each reason, give at least one example from the story and say why it explains or supports the reason.
4. Also, support one reason with an example from your own experience.

He explains how he will assess and grade students' work in the unit. "I expect you to learn how to do this kind of writing, and it's my job to prepare you. Because you will need to use your mind actively to learn all of your lives, I expect you to be always listening and thinking in this classroom. And I expect you to read each other's work and to listen to each other, because you have ideas." He explains that their grades for the unit will be based on four points: writing something for every journal prompt, completing all assignments, participating actively in discussions, and improving their writing.

In a pre-lesson, Mr. Stein connects his students personally to an idea that Sharon Flake develops in *The Skin I'm In:* we have images and beliefs about ourselves that affect how we interact with others. He asks them to each think about the question, "Through my own eyes, what do I see when I look in the mirror?" Then he asks them to make collages from a variety of paper, cloth, and paint materials to create visual images of their faces. Before they talk about these images in discussion circles, Mr. Stein begins a discussion of guidelines that will help students express their ideas in groups. After they create these norms, they talk in their groups about the qualities they tried to represent in their collages.

Mr. Stein introduces the idea of students using a class blog to share their ideas about the unit's theme of fitting in, and he mentions that they can also read blogs from other classrooms. Because about half of his students have read blogs on the Internet and three have their own blogs, he asks two students to help him set up a blog for the class. "This is new to me but not to many of you." He is somewhat awkward as the students take him through the steps of setting up a free account. The students pick "Teens Fitting In" as the name for their blog.

They decide to post some of their self-image collages on the blog by photographing them with a digital camera. With the collages, they post the essential questions of the unit, and several students write some initial ideas about fitting in to post on the blog. Two student volunteers offer to work with the school librarian to look for blogs that relate to the essential questions and recommend them to the class. The students are enthusiastic, and Mr. Stein thinks that their interest in the blog indicates that the unit has taken hold and his class is ready to meet Maleeka and ask how she sees herself and thinks about fitting in.

CLASSROOM CONNECTIONS

Does Blogging Build Literacy?

Linda W. Braun (2007) shares Mr. Stein's view that blogs can build students' literacy skills. "When setting up and maintaining a blog, when writing posts on the blog, and when replying to comments, a teen blogger needs to think about the audience" (p. 33). Braun also believes that "by giving teens the chance to write about what they are interested in at a particular moment in time, to link with other sites and information that connects with their interests, and then to comment on their own writing blogs give teens an enormous opportunity to discover who they are" (p. 31).

In the following Classroom Close-Ups, we show Mr. Stein's classroom at three points, allowing you to observe how he uses Meaning-Making Cycles to structure students' inquiry into the novel. In Lesson 1, he teaches students to use exploratory journal writing to raise questions about the reading and to reflect on how the author reveals the characters' dilemmas. In Lesson 4, he teaches them to write monologues to understand the idea of point of view and to express their inferences about various characters' relationships with Maleeka. He also makes them aware of the value of "group writing"—working collaboratively to summarize interpretations and to develop composite lists that synthesize ideas from the class. In Lesson 11, over several class periods, he introduces the purpose and format of a formal supported argument and engages students in peer review sessions to assist their drafting and revision of supported arguments. For assessment purposes, he compares their arguments with the writing samples they produced in the pre-assessment. In all three lessons, you will notice that we spotlight one student's work. Christina, a bilingual student, recently immigrated to the United States from Venezuela. Even in small groups, she is shy about speaking, yet her writing shows the depth of her engagement with the novel. The Close-Ups track Christina's thinking about the novel and follow Mr. Stein's teaching decisions about how to help her bring her excellent ideas and writing to the class.

CLASSROOM CLOSE-UP

Using Journaling to Comprehend a Reading (Lesson 1, Chapter 1)

Mr. Stein introduces *The Skin I'm In* to his class by saying, "Focus first on the outside of the book, the front and back covers. Write what you predict this book will be about." Students turn the book over in their hands, look at the picture on the front, read the back cover, and write predictions in their journals about what they think Maleeka is like (engage). Some students, although not Christina, volunteer to read what they wrote. Christina writes:

> I think the story is about the girl, Maleeka, and she will go to a school and find out people make fun of her and don't like her. The school may have students and teachers of a different culture. I do think she will make a friend sometime.

While Christina writes fairly fluently—that is, quickly and accurately—many students write just one line, and some keep erasing and fiddling with punctuation. "So, why do I ask you to write about your predictions?" Mr. Stein asks. Several students answer: "Like a game." "To get us excited." He teaches a ten-minute mini-lesson to demonstrate how writing about their responses to a book gets their thinking going and will help them comprehend a reading. Standing at an overhead projector, he thinks aloud while he looks at the cover of a book of short stories that he plans to assign students for independent reading. He starts skimming through stories, and predicting what the stories might be about.

"Okay, this overhead is, like, my journal. I'm looking at this—" [Mr. Stein lowers his head to write] "—this book, *First Crossing*. It has a subtitle *Stories About Teen Immigrants* and I wonder what countries they represent."

[Mr. Stein is writing]

"I'm thinking that fitting in is hard enough in high school or middle school, and that if you come to this country as a teen, with a different language and culture, it must be even harder. This title is *Second Culture Kids*, so I predict that cultural differences—differences in customs, ways of learning—may be a thread here."

[Mr. Stein continues writing]

"*Aheen, Sopeap, Nurzhan,* I predict, from these names, that the kids come from a variety of home countries . . . names. Notice that—" [He looks up at the class for a moment] "—that I'm not worrying about making this perfect. Now, I'm thinking as I write—" [Mr. Stein lowers his head again to write] "—that several of you were born outside the United States and maybe you'll share your experiences with coming here and fitting in. What's good, what's different about being here. . . . "

[Mr. Stein lifts his head to make eye contact with students]

"So, as I've been doing this, my writing has gotten me thinking and it made me come up with some questions. That's why I'm asking you to do a lot of journaling as you read Sharon Flake's novel. The purpose of journaling in this unit is to express your thoughts and questions, not to evaluate your thinking. A journal is not private like a diary, and it is not public like a blog posting. It's a way to build and share ideas. I will read all of your journals and comment on them."

Mr. Stein ends the mini-lesson by saying that predicting what will happen in a novel, or a science or history reading, is a strategy for understanding the text. Writing about their predictions helps students focus their minds on using that strategy. "Now, read the first chapter and journal with a different strategy—*visualizing*. 'See' these characters in your mind, talking and doing and interacting with each other. What do they look like? How do they sound? What are their thoughts? And then think about how you'd answer these questions: 'How does Maleeka see herself? What might her self-portrait look like?'"

Students begin the first chapter of *The Skin I'm In*. As they read the chapter, they write in their journals. This time, most students' heads are bent over their task, and they are writing more in response to Mr. Stein's comprehension prompts (respond). Christina's entry is longer this time, too:

I think Maleeka feels discouraged and ashamed with herself. She feels like no one likes her and everyone hates her. She doesn't like her clothes, skin, and herself.

(Continued)

She may see a poor sad girl with a little life. She is probably sadder since someone of her own skin color laughs at her and sings a song. Since her teacher told about herself, she may feel less ashamed.

If Maleeka were creating a self-portrait I think she would put a picture of herself in the middle. Probably fancy clothes, friends, pretty girls with different skin and other things she wishes she had. She may put a picture of her mother and father. She would also put phrases that may be personal to her and some pictures that are also personal. And last, she may put happy thoughts of her own.

Students bring their journal entries into their discussion circles and read and talk about what they visualized (elaborate). Groups discuss how people's views of themselves can affect their relationships and predict what Maleeka's relationships might be like. Christina is quiet until Peter, the student in her circle who is serving as the discussion director, turns to her, expecting her to read her entry. She does so in almost a whisper. She is surprised to notice that the students bend forward to hear her.

When the students reassemble as a whole class to talk about their group discussions, Mr. Stein asks, "How were you able to visualize what Maleeka thinks about herself? How did the author show you?" Students are silent and mostly look blank, until Peter comments, "Maleeka. She's telling the story and we get her thoughts." Mr. Stein gives them some terms for this, "You can say that the story is all told in Maleeka's *voice*, from her *point of view*. In life, we never know exactly what's in another person's thoughts. Think of it; the fiction writer can choose to have the whole book be seen from the main character's eyes."

To connect this discussion with their journaling, Mr. Stein adds, "From Maleeka's thoughts you made a creative leap to visualizing her self-portrait. Notice how far we've gotten into this first chapter by using your journals to predict and visualize and then talking about your writing with each other. Good work."

In Lessons 2 and 3, Mr. Stein and his students continue to explore the theme of how people's images of themselves shape their relationships with others, and they talk about how the reverse is also true. That is, some students harass Maleeka because her good grades, height, unstylish clothes, and darker skin make her stand out, and that treatment deepens her negative idea of herself.

In Lesson 2, students focus on Maleeka's relationships with adults at home, at school, and with other students, and they write individual journal entries in response to the prompt, "What are Maleeka's relationships like? Who are her friends?" Working relentlessly to have his students see how they are using comprehension strategies in their writing, Mr. Stein adds, "Asking questions about what you read is another strategy for understanding anything you read. Ask your history teacher!" In their discussion circles, students use some visual comprehension strategies to summarize their ideas. These strategies can include constructing a web—a drawing and labels that connect one piece of information to another—developing charts that list a set of questions or sources of evidence, or, as students do in the climate change unit in Chapter Three, making drawings to portray a concept. In this case, students build a web of Maleeka's relationships by writing "Maleeka" in a circle in the center of a piece of chart paper and drawing other circles to represent all the people in her life. They add in notes from their journals about whether those relationships include her in the school or make her an outsider. In Lesson 3, students continue to read and talk about Maleeka's relationships, by dramatizing scenes from the book that include those characters.

CLASSROOM CLOSE-UP

Using Oral Language Activities to Build Meaning (Lesson 4, Chapters 9–10)

Today students examine Maleeka's relationships by writing monologues from other characters' viewpoints. "The book is from Maleeka's point of view, but as writers, we can choose to imagine other characters' inner thoughts." Mr. Stein demonstrates how to write a monologue, choosing Sharon Flake, the author, as his subject rather than any of the characters. He imagines her thinking as she plans the book:

> This character, I'm going to call her Maleeka, is a lot like me. Oh, I really thought I was ugly when I was her age, and it didn't help that kids thought I was weird for liking to write. I like this character Maleeka and I want to show how much she wants to belong to someone, and Charlese needs her as a buddy. I want to show how hard it is to push away trouble when you think it will help you be somebody.

Mr. Stein comments, "So a monologue is from inside another person. The book is Maleeka's monologue. But imagine writing in the inner voice of another character: Charlese, her teacher Ms. Saunders, Caleb, the boy she likes. Use what you know from a close reading of scenes with that character—what do they say and do? How do they relate to Maleeka? And use your imagination to create something in their voice" (engage).

Students work on writing a monologue in their journals. Christina writes two monologues. Her first monologue is written from the viewpoint of Ms. Saunders, an English teacher who sees Maleeka's struggles and encourages her writing. Ms. Saunders is also African American and has a noticeable birthmark that spreads a white patch across her face:

(Continued)

I am Ms. Saunders, I am a teacher at McClinton Middle School. I have a job where I help kids learn things. In the story I tell students it doesn't matter what you look like on the outside. I hear what the kids have to say and share my own ideas. I am some pounds overweight and I'm average height. I have a blotch of skin different color than the rest of my face. I have my own look.

Christina's second monologue captures Maleeka's dilemma and feelings about herself as she sits at the hairdresser.

I am Maleeka and right now I am at the Barber Shop getting a new do! I feel confident on the outside but in a way I am worried. I am afraid I will have the wrong look. Char may not like and I will get made fun of worse. I know deep inside it doesn't matter what other people really think but at my school it matters. Right now, I am being told by many people that I look good but I know tomorrow it will be different.

Students read their monologues aloud in discussion circles (elaborate). This time, the discussion director forgets to draw Christina in, and the group does not hear her monologues and clear formulation of Maleeka's conflict between expressing her individuality and "having the wrong look" to be accepted in her school. When the groups reassemble as a whole class, Mr. Stein asks them to talk about their monologues and what dilemmas Maleeka is experiencing as she tries to fit in at her school.

He defines *dilemma* for them as a special kind of problem where either solution you choose has a negative cost. "You feel caught. She's willing to wear Char's clothes that are probably stolen and do Char's homework. Char calls Maleeka an ugly geek in front of other kids and lets another girl attack Maleeka for something Char did. What's going on? How can we summarize what we know about Maleeka's dilemma?" Christina is silent but attentive as students try to put Maleeka's difficulties into words.

Andres says, and Mr. Stein writes on the board, "If she doesn't go with Char, she'll have terrible clothes and Char might harass her more. Maleeka thinks [he reads from the book], 'Bad things happen around here to people who can't keep their mouth shut.'" Ilia adds, "Ms. Saunders and Caleb think she's smart and beautiful, but if she goes with them, she won't have good clothes or Char's protection."

Mr. Stein points out that this group writing synthesizes a lot of their reading, writing, and thinking. "This wording pulls together our ideas about Maleeka's struggles. Let's see, as we read forward, how she deals with them. Is she stuck? What can she do?" Students continue to post dilemmas on the board (represent).

CLASSROOM CONNECTIONS

Oral Language Activities with Second Language Learners

Writing is always linked with discussion in classrooms that use the Supported Literacy framework. For second language learners, oral activities such as reading and talking about their writing, dramatizing a scene, reading aloud, or participating in small group discussion circles are all ways to build English listening and speaking skills for school. Discussion circles give these students time to respond orally and feel less like a performance. You can prepare these students, and other students just acquiring academic discourse skills, for small group participation by suggesting some sentence starters, such as: "I thought the character was _____ because _____" or "I wonder why the author wrote _____" (Brisk & Harrington, 2007).

Progress Monitoring

Now that students are well into the unit, Mr. Stein takes stock of where he is in meeting his first goal for the unit—to have students grow more comfortable and skilled in using writing tools for inquiry. He realizes that he is drowning in his success with an overwhelming amount to read. He divides the stack of journals into two piles and reads one pile, commenting on each student's ideas on Post-it notes rather than writing on their pages. He will read and comment on half the journals each week.

The journals Mr. Stein samples tell him that his students grasp the purpose of the different comprehension strategies. From observing them during the respond phase, he sees that most of them start journaling quickly and write without lifting their heads until he calls them—a sign of growing fluency. He notices that most of them are freely reading and talking about their writing in discussion circles. They comment on different points of view and seem to grasp that more than one prediction or visualization can be valid. Given his students' growing comfort with responsive and exploratory writing, Mr. Stein wants to move on to include more formal kinds of writing. Comparison-and-contrast writing and supported argument are two genres that will push and deepen their critical analysis of fiction and will also require Mr. Stein to provide more writing instruction.

Considering his second goal of having students read fiction with a writer's eye, he feels they are making progress. He hears students use phrases in their discussion

(Continued)

circles that show their awareness that the novel is a writer's creation. He overhears "Flake lets us know that . . ." or "I think that her [the author's] letting us read Maleeka's diary helps us see how deep she is." He also hears their personal involvement with the character's dilemmas around fitting in. In one discussion circle, participants talk about what they would do if another student taunted them with a demeaning song as one character, John John, does to Maleeka. Nicholas comments, "I would have the courage to say something to Maleeka," then notices, "I'm acting like I'm in the story!"

As for Mr. Stein's own dilemma—how to build in a great deal of writing instruction without distracting students from their inquiry—he notices that he feels more comfortable in his role of writing teacher. Demonstrating journaling and monologues seems to give students examples without directing their content. When he doesn't quite know what he's doing, students seem to realize that he's thinking, not that he's a poor teacher. And he finds an unexpected benefit of modeling writing strategies—he realizes he has become an authentic part of the inquiry. He now keeps his own journal and writes when the students are writing. When he mentions his own entries, his students don't appear distracted from listening to each other.

Still, Mr. Stein is concerned that Christina and a number of other students rarely voice their ideas out loud, even in discussion circles. Some have become more verbal as their confidence in their writing grows. But the disparity between Christina's writing and her participation in discussions persists. He sees the richness of her thinking and writing in her journal, but he worries that the other members of her group have almost forgotten her. He doubts that the issue is English language proficiency, because Christina's writing shows advanced proficiency and many students in the class have speech that is accented with another first language. He decides to attach a note to Christina's journal saying that her entries are insightful and that he wants her to share her ideas more in her discussion circle. He also plans to talk with her about how the class is going for her and find out how she feels about sharing her very good writing. Without singling out Christina, he will remind the class that the role of a discussion director is to encourage everyone to share their ideas.

CLASSROOM CONNECTIONS

Participation Challenges

The stronger the role accountable talk plays in the teaching and learning process, the more students who are quiet (for whatever reason) stand out. Many factors, including reading or writing ability, general self-confidence,

English language proficiency, newness to the school, or cultural issues, can affect students' ease in bringing their ideas to the class. For second language learners, discussion circles and other oral participation strategies will help them learn school discourse (Brisk & Harrington, 2007). In literature study, which often addresses themes of growth and identity, participation helps everyone advance; yet, students' willingness to voice their understanding is also important in other content areas because it exposes different points of view and surfaces misconceptions. What kinds of participation issues do you see in your classroom?

For the next several weeks, the class builds up to the analysis and final essay that will conclude the unit. In Lesson 5, they read and talk about Maleeka's dilemmas and her opportunities to make choices in how she responds to Charlese's bullying. In Lesson 6, they develop a time line of major scenes where Maleeka has choices to make. Each discussion circle selects one or two scenes to reread, using the chart format shown in the box to analyze whether Maleeka is changing or still vulnerable to Charlese's bullying.

Analysis of Maleeka's Choices and Consequences

Scene (page numbers)	Choices Maleeka made	Consequences (positive or negative)	Other possible actions
1. John John singing			
2. Fight with Daphne			
3. Cafeteria scene			
4. Burning a teacher's classroom			

Finally, Mr. Stein guides students in practicing informal versions of the supported argument essay in their journal entries. He asks them to take a position on an open-ended question and support it by referring to at least three specific excerpts from the novel. "We discussed what we mean by *argument*," he reminds them. "It's not like having a fight or a disagreement with a friend. It's an explanation that is reasonable, and for which there is evidence, in this case *literary* evidence." Mr. Stein engages them in comparing and contrasting how Maleeka and Char handle fitting in (Lesson 7).

The students discuss the excerpts that the author gives them from Maleeka's diary, and they talk about how personal writing can help a person resolve a dilemma (Lesson 8) and how adults can help adolescents with the challenges of fitting in (Lesson 9). Mr. Stein also introduces the idea of taking a stance and developing an argument in a *Doubters and Believers* activity (Lesson 10) in which they have to argue a position on whether Maleeka had any choice in engaging in the vandalism with Char that resulted in burning Ms. Saunders's classroom.

All this close reading and oral analysis prepares students to take a position on the question of whether or not Maleeka has changed and to construct a well-supported and well-reasoned argument. They will support their arguments with evidence from the book and from their own experience.

During these lessons, Christina speaks once or twice during each discussion circle; her discussion circle members make sure to encourage her to read her writing and contribute to the group task. Peter, in her group, recognizes how strong her ideas are and how much clearer her writing is than his own. Mr. Stein also sees Christina making eye contact in the group. Still, without encouragement, she does not volunteer her ideas in her discussion circle or in class discussions.

CLASSROOM CLOSE-UP

**Using Supported Argument Writing to Synthesize Interpretations
(Lesson 11, Full Book; Lesson 12)**

"Some of you think Maleeka has changed and is becoming more independent of Char. Some of you think she is more able to stand up for herself. Others of you disagree. In a new piece of writing, you'll get a chance to take a stand on this question and show us your reasons and your evidence from the book."

Mr. Stein approaches this culminating writing assignment with some trepidation because of the amount of thinking students need to pull together. "Have they done enough close reading for this? Can they build an argument that really takes Maleeka's development, or lack of it, into consideration?" A supported argument is a new kind of writing for them, and he knows he will need to teach them the format before they can use it to synthesize their thinking. He wonders, "Do I really understand it myself? How can I explain it?"

Mr. Stein teaches the class the structure of a formal supported argument essay so that they can use this form to synthesize their interpretations of the novel. He explains that they will also be able to use this skill in state assessments in reading and in mathematics. The general guidelines he gives them are much like the ones that Ms. Harris, the history teacher, uses to teach her students how to write an essay on the question, "What problems did Japanese families face after World War II?" (see Chapter Two). Mr. Stein translates this very general rubric to a literature context, as he models how the students can state an interpretation, formulate arguments, and draw evidence from a piece of fiction and from their own life experience.

He begins with more journaling: "First, just journal for a few minutes about the question, 'Did Maleeka change in the choices she makes about how to fit in?' What is your evidence? How does the author communicate that?" (engage). Students write in their journals, looking through the book from time to time (respond). In response to Mr. Stein's prompt, Christina writes the following journal entry. She attributes Maleeka's greater strength and confidence in herself to her keeping a diary about a girl chained in the hold of a slave ship sailing from West Africa to North America. Even in captivity, the girl that Maleeka writes about—Akeelma—has choices in how she treats others and thinks of herself.

Has Maleeka changed or not? (Christina)

I think Maleeka changed a lot in the story and grew up. She now isn't as shy and afraid to share her thoughts. She can defend herself and at times do the wrong thing and hang out with the wrong people and get herself in trouble. I think writing in her diary about Akleema (a near reversal of her name) has helped her open up [Christina's spelling].

After giving them a few minutes to write, Mr. Stein engages students in a whole-class discussion to demonstrate how to develop their initial entries into well-formed essays.

Mr. Stein: What will you do to plan this essay?"

Peter: Keep writing.

Ilia: Hmmmm . . . if we're looking at change, don't we have to see what she did before and then did at the end?

Peter: The time line!

Mr. Stein: Exactly. Our analysis of her choices and consequences only extended through Chapter 12; let's bring it up to date. See if she makes different choices, and what

(Continued)

the results are, through the last chapter of the book. You need to analyze before you can plan an essay.

For the next half hour of Lesson 11, students work together in discussion circles filling out the time lines for the later chapters of the novel (elaborate). They list important points in these chapters when Maleeka has a choice to make, and they discuss whether she makes different decisions than she would have earlier in the book. Christina's group can't agree on whether Maleeka had a choice about trashing Ms. Saunders's room, and they can't decide whether her actions show that she's backsliding. For the first time, Christina volunteers: "Maleeka lit the fire . . . that was her action on the outside. Inside she was in conflict, and then Char threatened her." Her comment takes the group back into the text:

Arturo: You're right. [He reads:] "Char grabs hold of my shoulder blade and squeezes till my knees get weak. 'Like I said, I will jack you up, girl. Do you hear me? . . . Do what I say or I'm gonna do worse yet' she says, flicking her lighter's flame close to my head."

Ilia: She might have set fire to Maleeka.

Christina: But after that, Maleeka listens to Ms. Saunders and her mother. She takes responsibility. She breaks with Char.

Groups bring their analysis back to a whole-class discussion (revisit), in which Mr. Stein demonstrates how to organize a supported argument essay. He takes a different open-ended question, "How should Maleeka be punished for her role in the vandalism?" and thinks aloud as he rereads key scenes and states his position that she should have to help restore the room but not get suspended. He thinks out loud about why Maleeka deserves another chance in the school. He writes his outline on the board and suggests that for their next step students develop their own outlines of their stances, arguments, and reasons and evidence to support their positions.

Mr. Stein posts the list of features that they first encountered in their pre-assessment writing assignment when they wrote about *Black Boy,* and now they will apply those same features in writing a supported argument about another work of fiction.

Final Unit Assessment

Over the next few days, students continue to develop their essays. They share their drafts during discussion circles and pair with peers to provide feedback on whether the essay reflects the guidelines. They also learn editing guidelines and, unlike most of their other writing in the unit, they attend carefully to spelling and punctuation and have at least two other students read and edit their essay for "mechanics." The pre-assessment is not directly comparable to this final essay because students did the pre-assessment on their own and have had much support for this one. Yet the final essay helps Mr. Stein determine whether the students are now more able to elaborate their ideas and to understand how to cite the novel as evidence in their arguments. He uses a formal rubric to assess their essays.

For his scoring guideline he draws from two different assessments—the persuasive writing assessment of the National Assessment of Education Progress (NAEP) and his state's guidelines. The NAEP Persuasive Writing Assessment seeks to influence the reader to take some action or bring about change and can contain factual information, such as reasons, examples, or comparisons. The topics in the NAEP Writing Assessment ask students to write letters to friends, newspaper editors, or prospective employers, as well as to refute arguments or take sides in a debate (National Center for Education Statistics, 2003). The limitation of the NAEP is that while it requires students to take a position, it does not involve students in analyzing a text. So Mr. Stein also uses a state assessment that is based on students' reading of a literature text, and he uses a five-point scale that he thinks will enable struggling writers and readers to show more of their understanding. The state guidelines don't, however, address the persuasive features that should be present in supported argument writing. Mr. Stein combines the best features of each assessment to make his guidelines. Other colleagues who plan to teach the unit help him. Table 4.2 shows his scoring guidelines, and the following box shows Christina's essay, to which he gave a 5.

(Continued)

TABLE 4.2. **Scoring Guideline.**

Score	Explanation
5	Includes the following items: • A statement of opinion • Several pieces of evidence from the text that are detailed, elaborated, interrelated, accurate, and relate to the opinion • Explanations for how the text supports the opinion that are consistent and clear throughout

(Continued)

TABLE 4.2. (Continued)

Score	Explanation
	The writer supports the reasoning with specific references to the text, as well as with personal experience, cause and effect, comparison and contrast, point of view, drawing conclusions.
4	Includes the following items: • A statement of opinion • Several pieces of evidence from the text that are accurate and relate to the opinion • At least one explanation for how the text supports the opinion Either the evidence or the elaboration is not well developed or consistent. The writer supports the reasoning with specific references to the text, as well as with personal experience, cause and effect, comparison and contrast, point of view, drawing conclusions.
3	Includes the following items: • A statement of opinion • At least one piece of evidence from the text that is accurate and relates to the opinion • At least one explanation that makes sense and shows how the text supports the opinion
2	Includes the following items: • A statement of opinion • At least one piece of evidence from the text that is accurate and relates to the opinion Even if the evidence is somewhat detailed, the writer's explanations for how the text supports the opinion are absent or weak.

Score	Explanation
1	Includes a statement of an opinion.
	Either there is no evidence from the text or the evidence from the text is not accurate or does not relate to the opinion.
0	There is no opinion or the author does not choose one point of view.

Source: Adapted from Morocco et al. (2001).

CHRISTINA'S ESSAY

Has Maleeka Changed? Will She Stand Up for Herself in the Future?

In *The Skin I'm In* I believe that Maleeka will take a stand, should she be put in that situation again, because she learned from her previous experiences. She's never needed people to defend her physically, and because she knew when to stick up for herself after the fire. The following essay will discuss these points in full detail.

Maleeka has never needed to depend on people to protect her, physically. In one incident, a girl from Maleeka's school thought that she had stolen her boyfriend. In reality, Char was the culprit. Instead of telling the girl that, Maleeka held it in and fought her. In yet another case, when Maleeka was being harassed by the boys in the street, she came up with the courage to fight back. Also, when the boys were beating John John, Maleeka helped defend him. These examples show that Maleeka can fight her own battles, as well as help others physically.

In most cases through the story, Maleeka knew how to defend herself, when needed. The first time this happened was in McClinton's cafeteria when Char ordered Maleeka to get another lunch for her. Although Maleeka did, she showed a significant sign of defiance by finally talking back to Char. Then, when Char and the twins made Maleeka do their homework, she refused to do so. She told them that she couldn't do it because she was too busy. Also, when Char planned to trash Ms. Saunders classroom, Maleeka voiced her opinion, saying that it was a bad idea.

However, the most prominent case of where Maleeka defended herself, was after the fire in the school. Maleeka told on Char and the girls. She also told Char she was a very loathsome person. Maleeka has obviously learned her lesson not to let people use her.

Towards the end of *The Skin I'm In,* Maleeka learned and grew from her previous experience. For example, she told on Char. After she told on Char, she was more independent and she didn't care what people thought of her. However, although she's been hurt by many people in the past, she is still willing to give people, like Caleb and John-John, who hurt her a chance. Maleeka's learned early on in the story that in order to survive, she needs to move on and forget her horrors.

Maleeka has grown a lot this year. She no longer depends or, lets them use her.

In a culminating lesson for the unit (Lesson 12), after their final assessment, Mr. Stein's students meet in "book alike" groups to talk about the teen immigrant stories they have read on their own. They talk about the dilemmas these authors portray, the choices these characters make, and how their choices affect their success or lack of success in fitting in at their new schools and communities. In summarizing the results of their conversations for the whole class, the students open up new dimensions of the concept of integrating into a peer group. Students ask Christina and Ilia—for the first time—what it is like to, as Peter put it, "helicopter into our school" from another country.

Several students post their supported argument essays, along with a personal comment on how the novel has changed their ideas about fitting in and about writing. Christina posts her final essay with this comment:

Like Maleeka, I was afraid to speak up for myself and writing was an easier way for me to communicate. Even when I was in Venezuela, I liked to write more than speak. I still and maybe always will find writing easier than discussing, but now I know that if I really think something needs to be said, I can say it.

Mr. Stein thinks about his own growth as a writing teacher and reflects that his most important role has been to actually be a writer and "put myself out there to show the process, humbling as it is." Although he would like to duck it, he makes himself do most of the assignments he gives his students—and now he can say, "Hey, I'm getting more fluent myself." In their next unit, he wants to build in other kinds of writing such as drama, poetry, and student memoirs. "They can do anything," he is sure.

TEACHING WRITING AS A TOOL FOR CONTENT INQUIRY

Over the course of this unit, you have seen Mr. Stein's students use many kinds of writing for a variety of purposes and audiences. His students are on their way to viewing writing as a many-faceted tool that supports them in conducting an inquiry. Although students' focus here is on using writing to understand fiction and character development, the writing tools they use in the Close-Ups are applicable to other content areas. They assume a broad definition of writing—that it occurs any time one's mind is engaged in choosing words to be put on paper or in a digital format. That definition includes taking notes, making lists, writing down observations, making charts, and expressing feelings, as well as "the traditional activities like writing lab reports, essay test answers, essays or stories" (Mayher et al., 1983, p. 78). The multiliteracy "writing to build and express meaning" encompasses deeper skills of writing to understand texts, to think critically and creatively about content, and to write clearly for varied purposes and audiences. The latter includes students' being able to communicate with others in their immediate environment and beyond. These three kinds of writing skills, which we summarize here, provide tools for inquiry in all content areas.

Writing to Understand Texts

Mr. Stein uses journaling to engage his students in comprehension strategies such as predicting, summarizing, visualizing, posing questions, and eliciting their own background knowledge. Students can use these same strategies in the context of a science notebook (to help them make sense of a challenging science reading) and in the context of a history journal (to understand a primary source). The purpose of the reading will be different in these other content areas, and students need to combine these strategies with building new vocabulary. But they are tools that, with translation, students can carry with them beyond the language arts classroom.

In the unit "War and People" (see Chapter Two), students journal to elicit what they know about World War II and to predict how the Kawashima family will survive in postwar Kyoto. In the unit "Understanding Climate Change" (see Chapter Three), students express their knowledge of the topic by answering questions in their science notebooks. In writing about the role of literacy in learning science, Thier (2002) calls this kind of journaling "exploratory writing"—an "essential tool for students to figure out what they have just learned and what it means to them" (p. 59).

Writing to Think Critically and Creatively About Content

In the Close-Ups, Mr. Stein's students use writing to scaffold their critical thinking when they use charts and webs to assemble their questions and diagram relationships among characters. Students use a time line to map Maleeka's major decision points and analyze her choices. The visual format of the time line and chart gives them a way to synthesize the results of their analyses. These writing strategies make students' analysis visible for discussion. Writing can help students summarize and synthesize their interpretations. Group writing—developing a summary or time line together—can involve many students in synthesizing information and ideas. Variations of those visual scaffolds for writing can help students write about their procedures and results in science and compare the information in a set of historical documents.

Creative writing activities also support critical thinking. In writing monologues to better understand characters in *The Skin I'm In,* Mr. Stein's students reread the text to make inferences about a character and then stretch their imaginations to express that character's thoughts. In a similar way, history teachers use monologue and dialogue to encourage students to consider the perspective of a historical writer or a participant. While this book has not focused on mathematics, mathematics inquiry learning uses these same writing tools—including writing to think creatively about a topic. In a middle grades unit published by EDC on concepts of ratio and proportion, students explore the ideas by reading and writing about the Lilliputians (small people) and Brobdignagians (giants) in *Gulliver's Travels* and build models of cups and pencils to fit the scale of those imaginary lands.

Writing Clearly for Varied Purposes and Audiences

Mr. Stein's students use the supported argument essay to represent well-developed interpretations of the novel for their class. When they write for the class blog, they need to think about a more distant audience. They learn the special purpose of comparing and contrasting Maleeka and Charlese to better understand the characters and Maleeka's struggle to separate from Charlese. Versions of comparison-and-contrast and supported argument writing are important in every content area, as students explain a claim in science or a varied interpretation in history. In Chapter Five, Lisa Alverez chooses to focus her students on comparison-and-contrast writing because she knows that writing genre is relevant across all of their content learning.

While these are not new writing strategies, Supported Literacy gives them added power by integrating them into a collaborative process of inquiry. Across all phases of the Meaning-Making Cycle, writing is always integrated with reading and talking with other students, with class discussions with the teacher, and, in some cases, with students beyond the classroom through blogging. Writing activates your students' minds and encourages them to take responsibility for their learning as individuals and as a learning community. Never an isolated process, writing grows out of reading and talking and contributes to further and deeper discussions that build understanding.

Finally, the most important quality of writing is its transparency. Writing in all the forms and variations we discuss in this chapter can make your students' thinking *visible.* As their teacher, you have a window into their thinking and their confusion, and you can provide meaningful and timely feedback to advance their understanding. In talking with peers about their own and others' writing, your students can see the power of bringing different ideas to the investigation of a challenging question and issue. In seeing the results of collaboration in a group chart, summary, or set of blog postings, they might realize the value of collaborating to investigate complex issues beyond bullying, global warming, or immigration to the whole range of questions they will need to face as adults in the twenty-first century.

The next three chapters focus on key aspects of adapting, augmenting, and implementing the framework to meet the needs of all. In Chapter Five, we introduce you to the students in Ms. Alverez's special education classroom, and we show you how Ms. Alverez modifies "How Far Would You Go to Fit In?" to support the learning of young adolescents with significant disabilities. In Chapter Six, we describe how you can use the Supported Literacy framework to respond to some basic reading difficulties. We also discuss the Supported Literacy Intensive tutorials that your school's reading specialists can use to address students' more complex reading difficulties. Finally, in Chapter Seven, we provide in-depth information about the steps your school's leaders, specialists, and teachers need to take to launch and sustain a Supported Literacy initiative.

CHAPTER

5

MEANING MAKING WITH SPECIAL EDUCATION STUDENTS

ALISA HINDIN

CLASSROOM CLOSE-UP

"How Far Would You Go to Fit In?"

For the first time, Lisa Alverez does not arrange her classroom's chairs in rows. Her students face one another in groups of three with their journals out in front of them. In each group, one student acts as the recorder and makes a cumulative list that includes each group member's comparisons of Maleeka and Charlese, the two main characters from Sharon Flake's young adult novel *The Skin I'm In*. Rob scans his list and says, "[Maleeka's] mom makes [her] clothes." Karen chimes in, "Doesn't Charlese steal them?"

Rob and Karen are deeply involved in a discussion that is part of "How Far Would You Go to Fit In?" The two students in Ms. Alverez's self-contained eighth-grade classroom have moderate learning disabilities that many educators might assume would prevent them from engaging in accountable talk. Yet Ms. Alverez's participation in a Supported Literacy group—a learning community within her school that meets to plan and carry out the Supported Literacy framework—enables her to use the unit with her students.

As EDC researchers, several of us participate in Ms. Alverez's Supported Literacy group, as do all of her school's seventh- and eighth-grade language arts teachers, special education teachers, and reading teachers. Our team of teachers and researchers works together to design the unit (see Chapter Four), to teach it to students in many classrooms, and to evaluate the results. All across the school, typical students, honors students, and students with disabilities are reading *The Skin I'm In,* discussing Maleeka and Charlese, and talking about how Maleeka struggles with difficult adolescent choices. From the design through the final evaluation, our group meets almost weekly after school to plan and to focus on the outcomes of the unit by looking at students' work, discussing and resolving teaching challenges, and viewing videotapes that we make of some of their classes. In all our work, we seek to take into account diverse learning needs so that all the teachers will be able to adapt the unit for their own students.

While most of the language arts teachers have several students with learning disabilities in their classrooms, Ms. Alverez teaches nine students with more substantial learning disabilities—and, in some cases, cognitive delay—all of their subjects. As with other students with mild or moderate cognitive disabilities, her students struggle with almost every area of literacy instruction including decoding, reading comprehension, and expressing what they understand, both orally and in writing. Ms. Alverez is well aware that after years of difficulty with reading and writing, her students have little confidence in their ideas. Early on, when we design the unit, she voices her doubts about using it with her students:

> They [the students] aren't sure enough of themselves. A lot of them have the same thoughts [as other students], but they aren't willing to share them because they don't think they are good enough. They don't think that their own thoughts are good enough, but once they hear someone say something, they say, "Oh yeah, that's this and that's that." So it's hard for them to put their thoughts down on paper. In some instances, it's even hard for them to vocalize their thoughts.

Much like you, Ms. Alverez worries that highly challenging academic work will further discourage her struggling learners. However, the other teachers in her group persuade her to try the Supported Literacy approach with her students and express great interest in how she might adapt the unit activities to meet her students' needs. With their urging and ongoing support, Ms. Alverez takes the leap and, for the first time, she teaches her students the same novel that typically achieving students across the school are studying. She scaffolds students' learning through every phase of the Meaning-Making Cycle, drawing on support strategies from her own experience as a special education teacher and inventing new ones.

In this chapter, we provide a window into Ms. Alverez's classroom and describe how she adapts "How Far Would You Go to Fit In?" for young adolescents with moderate disabilities. A Classroom Close-Up illustrates how she uses the Meaning-Making Cycle to support her students in learning how to compare and contrast two characters in the book, a cognitively demanding strategy. The interactions between Ms. Alverez and her students show how she teaches them this valuable reading, writing, and critical thinking strategy and how her instruction benefits her students.

CLASSROOM CONNECTIONS

Teaching a Novel with Students with Cognitive Disabilities

What are your expectations for students with cognitive disabilities with regard to reading fiction? In your school, do these students learn how to use analytic tools such as comparison and contrast to make sense of literature or nonfiction texts? What opportunities do your school's special education teachers, language arts teachers, and content area teachers have to talk with each other about how to teach these students multiliteracy tools for reading for deep understanding? What opportunities could you create?

TRANSFORMING MS. ALVEREZ'S TEACHING

In a meeting of her Supported Literacy group, Ms. Alverez explains that she has never before taught her students by using a whole trade book. She is skeptical that her students could read for deep understanding or use any of the multiliteracy tools that might help them. She definitely does not think of critical inquiry as something her students could do, and she has never used daily journals with them. When her group members ask her what her instruction is generally like, she says, "We would never do a unit like this. I do not use the literature book very frequently. What we work on, and what I used to think was more important, is grammar, sentence structure, and getting the kids ready to write."

She describes her typical reading and writing instruction as skill-based with a focus on decoding and the mechanics of writing; she never connects her writing assignments to what her students are reading. The idea of the Meaning-Making Cycle—that students integrate reading, writing, discussion, and even digital and media tools to explore a question about a literary text—is totally new to her, and it's formidable.

Ms. Alverez's approach to teaching students with learning disabilities is not surprising. Research on literacy instruction shows that many students who struggle receive mostly skill-based instruction and have the fewest opportunities to engage in higher-level comprehension processes and inquiry learning (Allington, 1977, 1983, 2000). Students with disabilities are less likely than typically achieving students to engage in peer-led discussions, despite the finding that smaller groups are helpful for students with learning disabilities (Englert & Palincsar, 1991; Gersten, Fuchs, Williams, & Baker, 2001), who often find it difficult to respond during whole-class discussions (Goatley, 1997).

Group Planning to Support Change

Despite her reservations, Ms. Alverez is intrigued by the possibility of trying a new approach to teaching literature and literacy skills. As her Supported Literacy group designs the unit, she finds that her peers give her the support she needs to make a change. One after-school professional development meeting with her group is especially pivotal. During this meeting, Ms. Alverez and two other teachers gather, fishbowl style, in the center of the teacher group to discuss the difficulties and the value of peer-led discussions. Ms. Alverez, who often looks to the group for guidance and advice, asks how best to manage student-led discussions. A language arts teacher explains how she sets up discussion circles so that students can manage them independently and how she observes them. The continuing support of the other teachers enables Ms. Alverez to teach her students in entirely new ways (Hindin et al., 2007).

Ms. Alverez is buoyed by the possibility that her students can help each other learn in literacy discussion groups. She predicts that her students will easily connect with the characters and dilemmas in the book and hopes that their great interest in Maleeka will motivate them to tackle new skills of analysis, writing, and talking about literature. She decides to focus several lessons on teaching her students the compare-and-contrast strategy and to support them in applying the strategy effectively in their reading and writing (Kos, 1991). Many students find it hard to understand that different kinds of reading—expository texts, historical fiction, narratives, personal essays, arguments, and directions—vary in their features and organization (Englert & Thomas, 1987; Pearson & Camperell, 1994). Teaching students with learning disabilities to use comparison and contrast helps them gain an understanding of the organization of different genres, elaborate their writing, and produce a better quality of writing (Montague, Graves, & Leavell, 1991; Wong, Wong, & Blenkinshop, 1989).

Although the approach and focus of the unit is new for Ms. Alverez, she takes on the goal of creating a deeper level of learning in her classroom. She uses the weekly support from her colleagues to find new instructional strategies and tailors the unit to meet her particular students' needs. She comments, "I find it helpful to sit in on the teacher meetings, because the other teachers are so willing to share ideas." She is eager to try the unit with her students.

CLASSROOM CONNECTIONS

Building a Professional Community

How different is the Supported Literacy approach from your current ways of teaching? Could you get support from other teachers to change your approach? Ms. Alverez's Supported Literacy group became a support team for language arts and special education teachers as they used the framework to design curriculum units. What opportunities do you have to expand your teaching repertoire in collaboration with other teachers? Do special education teachers with more significantly disabled students participate in these professional development opportunities?

Preparing Students for Inquiry into Fiction

In an early lesson, to help her students connect to Maleeka, Ms. Alverez guides them in thinking, writing, and talking about the question, "What makes a good friend?" With their own friendships as a reference, Ms. Alverez has them think and write about the question, "Who are Maleeka's friends?" She asks them to draw and label a web of Maleeka's friends and family, and instructs them to add notes to this web throughout their reading of the book. Then she asks each student to select one of Maleeka's friends and to consider how the friend treats Maleeka, why Maleeka chooses to be around the person, and what Maleeka seems to get from this friendship.

One of her students, Anna, decided to write a monologue to express what Maleeka might have been thinking after a bad experience with Charlese in the lunchroom. Anna writes in her journal, "Why did she [Charlese] pick me for? She always tells me to do her stuff. [Her homework.] Why do I have to do her stuff? I'm not doing that for her."

Continuing her focus on the characters, Ms. Alverez builds toward her central strategy, compare-and-contrast. To introduce the strategy, she has her students connect compare-and-contrast with events from their own lives. In one class, she asks her students to compare their experience in sixth grade and eighth grade; as part of their planning, they organize their comparisons in two columns in their notebooks that represent the two grade levels. In another class session, she has her students compare a conversation they participated in at home with a conversation in school. Using graphic organizers, she has her students draw two webs in their notebooks, identifying the main features of the context of each conversation—the people there, the topic for their conversation, their tone of voice, and the purpose of the talk. To introduce comparison and contrast in relation to the text, Ms. Alverez simplifies the process by asking students to reflect just on the similarities between Maleeka and Charlese. In a whole class format, she coaches her students as they generate a list of characteristics the two characters share.

These lessons accomplish several of Ms. Alverez's teaching goals. One is to motivate her students to read a whole book and to connect sections of the book around the question of how Maleeka and Char are similar. She hears evidence of success while listening to her students talking about Maleeka and Charlese as though they are real people. She also hears them compare the characters to other students in their own school ("She's a Charlese"). Ms. Alverez explains to the Supported Literacy teachers in a meeting after school, "I have one boy who is so quiet. He looked up at me today and said, 'I *like* that Charlese.'" She also hears her students begin to meet her second goal—to connect their prior knowledge, the strategy, and the text. And she finds evidence of progress toward her third goal—to have her students develop peer discussion skills. During these early lessons, Ms. Alverez teaches her students to focus on a task, to make sure each member contributes, and to master the role of recorder to make notes on the discussion.

The following Classroom Close-Up draws on a videotape that expert EDC videographers made of this class, a verbatim transcript of Ms. Alverez's interactions with her students, and copies of students' written work during the class. In the Close-Up, Ms. Alverez encourages her students to work individually, in discussion circles, and as a whole class to contrast the characters of Maleeka and Charlese. Building on these prior lessons, she scaffolds students' work through each phase of the Meaning-Making Cycle.

CLASSROOM CLOSE-UP

USING THE MEANING-MAKING CYCLE TO TEACH COMPARISON AND CONTRAST

Engage

"Yesterday we did how Maleeka and Charlese are alike. Today, we'll think about how they are different." Ms. Alverez believes that hearing her intentions helps her students begin to organize their thinking. She reminds students of their preceding day's work and explains her plan for today; they will make a list of all the ways they can think of that Maleeka and Charlese are different, and she expects they will each bring a wide range of ideas from the reading. Because retaining and connecting ideas might be difficult for students with learning disabilities, Ms. Alverez gives her students clear directions and procedures.

"I'm going to give you a few minutes to work on your lists alone, and then I'm going to put you into groups of three. In your groups, you are going to combine on the back side of a piece of paper all of the differences you had. Next, as groups, you are going to tell me what you said, and we're going to put your ideas on the charts on the board so that we can use them when we write our big paper."

Ms. Alverez always strives to make her expectations clear to her students, regardless of the focus of the class. In this case, she wants her students to support their statements

(Continued)

about how the two girls are different with information from the text. She introduces the idea that statements of comparison or contrast require evidence: "When you put down something, how they are different, you have got to be able to prove it. If I say to you, 'Where in the book does it say that?' you have to be able to provide it to me." She wants to make sure her students verify that their impressions about the characters actually have some basis in the novel. This is a challenging task for her students, particularly because they are going to work on their own at first. Almost literally, Ms. Alverez holds her breath to see whether they are intrigued enough with Maleeka and Charlese to take up the analytic challenge she has given them.

Respond

Anticipating that many of her students will find this initial task difficult, she walks around the room observing who needs help generating contrasts between Maleeka and Charlese. While typical students often engage in this reading and journaling phase of the Meaning-Making Cycle on their own, Ms. Alverez's students need help with rereading the novel, finding appropriate material, and writing ideas in a list.

One of the ways she supports students is by asking them questions that prompt them to think of categories for the comparisons, an approach that is often used in a compare-and-contrast strategy. She walks over to John and asks, "Do they both like Ms. Saunders? [one of the teachers in the characters' school]. What kind of kid would you say Maleeka is?"

Karen seems to be struggling, so Ms. Alverez models how to generate a category for comparison. Karen is interested in discussing the characters' physical appearance, and Ms. Alverez prompts her to focus on clothing.

> *Ms. Alverez:* When Char comes to school, how is she dressed?
> *Karen:* In these dirty clothes.
> *Ms. Alverez:* Char is?
> *Karen:* No, Maleeka.
> *Ms. Alverez:* Not so much dirty, but . . .
> *Karen:* No, like ...
> *Ms. Alverez:* Not very stylish?
> *Karen:* Yeah.
> *Ms. Alverez:* What kind of clothes does Char come to school with?
> *Karen:* Nice?
> *Ms. Alverez:* 'Cause where does her sister get them?
> *Karen:* She steals them.
> *Ms. Alverez:* We *think*. We think she steals them, right?
> *Karen:* Yeah.

Ms. Alverez builds on Karen's responses by modeling an answer if Karen is unsure how to proceed ("Not very stylish"), or extending the comparison by asking a follow-up question ("'Cause where does her sister get them?"). Prompting Karen to consider the evidence that Charlese's sister is stealing clothes, she reminds Karen of an earlier class conversation in which the class decided that the text implied but did not directly state that Char's sister stole clothes for Char. Ms. Alverez also helps students recall details from the text. She prompts Justine to remember that Charlese's sister's name is Juju. Ms. Alverez asks, "What's her sister's name?" and gives a clue, "It's like a candy I used to buy in the movies." Because many of her students have writing difficulties, Ms. Alverez simplifies this writing task by telling her students to focus on their ideas. ("Spelling doesn't count.")

Ms. Alverez differentiates her support depending on what each of her students needs. Jim has extreme difficulty generating ideas either in speaking or in writing. When she sees Jim sitting, without writing or looking at the book, she asks him how he thinks the girls differ and urges him, "Just give me a *word*, Jim, and I'll work from there with you."

(Continued)

Table 5.1 summarizes the verbal scaffolding strategies Ms. Alverez uses during this phase of meaning making to help students generate contrasts between the two characters. This "interactive scaffolding," which is spontaneous and responsive to each student's needs as they work (Morocco & Zorfass, 1996), is critical for Ms. Alverez's students; they could not do the task without this support.

TABLE 5.1. Ms. Alverez's Verbal, Interactive Scaffolding During the Respond Phase.

How Ms. Alverez Supports Students	Examples of What Ms. Alverez Says
Repeats or restates directions and maintains a focus on the task	How are the two kids, the two girls different?
Monitors student progress	What are you doing, Anna?
Elicits or provides categories for contrast	When Char comes to school, how is she dressed? Do they both like Ms. Saunders? What kind of kid would you say Maleeka is?

(Continued)

TABLE 5.1. (Continued)

How Ms. Alverez Supports Students	Examples of What Ms. Alverez Says
Prompts students to recall the text or the class's prior discussions of the text to elaborate a contrast	'Cause where does her sister get them?
Models syntax of a contrast statement	One is really dolled up. The other is just in regular clothes.
Asks student to elaborate or clarify	So which one is the popular one? OK, what else?
Provides correct information from the text	No, she [Charlese] doesn't like her [Ms. Saunders]. Maleeka likes her now.
Elicits meaning or explains vocabulary	Do you know what a bully is?
Differentiates level of support	Elicits minimal response: Just give me a *word*, Jim, and I'll work from there with you.
Makes the category or criterion for comparison explicit	What they have is a difference in *where* they're working and the *jobs* they are doing.
Acknowledges and praises student work	Beautiful! That's a perfect one!

CLASSROOM CONNECTIONS

Supporting Struggling Students

Are some of Ms. Alverez's support strategies relevant to the students you teach? She uses these strategies in teaching fiction, but could you use them in your subject area to help students inquire into challenging content area questions? She also uses these strategies as students are working in contexts that require individual or small group work. How do you help students with learning difficulties work independently and with other students?

Elaborate

When Ms. Alverez's students complete their independent lists of contrasts between the two characters, they move into three groups of three students. Ms. Alverez's goal for this phase (elaborate) is for her students to collaborate so that all group members share their own thinking. Ms. Alverez knows that because some of her students are not confident enough to voice their ideas even with two or three other students, the stronger students will tend to do all the talking. She comments later to the Supported Literacy group, "I found that the same kids did all of the work and some kids weren't doing anything." She uses several strategies to encourage each student to participate. She divides students into three structured groups by considering students' literacy strengths and their personalities. So that writing difficulties do not hamper their group discussions, she selects a student in each group who has an easier time with writing to be the group's recorder. Finally, she asks students to compile a list of contrasts that includes all of the group members' ideas, even if some ideas appear more than once.

In moving among the groups, Ms. Alverez sees evidence that her students' peer collaboration skills are growing. One group, with Anna, Rob, and Karen, demonstrates her vision of true collaboration; each student shares ideas and also takes responsibility for helping the group work productively. As the recorder, Anna fosters this collaboration by asking the other members to contribute their contrasts before she reads her own. Since Anna has many more contrasts on her list, this invitation to Rob and Karen ensures that all members of the group have an opportunity to contribute. Anna, Rob, and Karen engage in accountable talk by building upon one another's ideas. When Anna says "[Maleeka's] mom makes [her] clothes," and Karen asks, "Doesn't Charlese steal them?" Anna and Rob respond to her question by recalling a section of the text that implies that Charlese's sister is the one who steals the clothes.

A second group shows that they can negotiate disagreements as they work to integrate their contrasts into one group list. This group interprets Ms. Alverez's directions to mean that the list should not include similar items. In this excerpt they discuss whether two items have the same meaning.

Aaron: [Reads from his list] Maleeka is a slave and she [Charlese] isn't a slave.

Justine: Maleeka is. Yeah but that's—

Aaron: She's *like* a slave.

Jim: A slave.

Justine: Yeah, but that's kinda like [what] we wrote over here. [Reads another item on the composite list.] Maleeka works for free and she works for money.

Aaron: Char makes her do everything.

Justine: It's the same thing.

(Continued)

Aaron: Like Char makes her do work for her.

Justine: That's the same thing. So, let's just say she eats her own lunch, Char eats school lunch.

When Aaron proposes a new contrast (Maleeka is a slave), Justine compares this contrast with one they discussed earlier and decides that the two contrasts are too similar. Aaron adds several clarifications to strengthen his contribution. He notes that he is comparing Maleeka to a slave and that Charlese makes her do things as a slave master would—that is, the relationship is based on coercion. These language distinctions express Aaron's understanding of the characters' relationships. The discussion shows that the students not only can argue constructively about the similarity in meaning of the contrast statements but that some of them are building a deep understanding of the novel. In the story, Maleeka keeps a journal in which she depicts herself as a slave, and the students in this group are connecting this idea metaphorically in characterizing Maleeka as a slave because of the way Charlese treats her.

The third small group shows evidence of close reading and listening when one group member, Kevin, asks John how he arrived at his understanding that Charlese does not have parents. This conversation shows close comprehension of the text because the author describes Charlese as living with her sister, not with her parents.

Kevin: She lives with her sister Juju, right, Alice?

Alice: Yeah, she lives with her sister.

John: She doesn't have a mom or dad.

Kevin: She lives with her mom. How [do] you know Char doesn't have a mom?

John: It said in the book and her sister was home. . . .

As she walks around, Ms. Alverez models how to state a contrast so that it makes the difference between the two characters explicit. "If you just say, 'Maleeka is thirteen,' that's not enough, because we need to know how old Charlese is and whether that's a difference. Say, 'Maleeka is thirteen and Charlese is fourteen.'"

In all three groups, students work together to share ideas and to develop a list that represents all of the group members' thoughts. Their success in this phase of the Meaning-Making Cycle demonstrates their ability to apply the contrast strategy to help them comprehend the novel.

Revisit

During the revisit phase, the class comes back together and Ms. Alverez facilitates a discussion of their lists of contrasts. To make sure each group has several chances to share ideas, Ms. Alverez asks the first group to give only one contrast statement from their list—such as "Maleeka packs her lunch and Char gets a school lunch"—and then she calls on a second group to give one contrast that is different from that of the first group, and so forth. She writes the students' responses on the board in a chart with a column for each character. To make sure the contrast is explicit, she occasionally rephrases responses or asks for clarification. The class continues this reporting process until they have one composite list. The chart lists the fifteen contrasts that the students report to Ms. Alverez.

Character Contrasts the Students Identify

Maleeka	Charlese
Maleeka packs her lunch	Char gets school lunch
Maleeka lives with her mom	Charlese lives with her sister Juju
Maleeka doesn't get her way with Charlese	Charlese gets her way, she's bossy
Maleeka don't [doesn't smoke]	Charlese smokes
Maleeka is not popular	Charlese is
Maleeka is 13 years old	Charlese is 14 years old
Maleeka has short hair	Charlese has long hair
Maleeka has a little mouth	Char has a big mouth
[Maleeka's] mom makes [her] clothes	Charlese steals clothes
Maleeka goes to class	Charlese skips class
Maleeka does [get made fun of]	Charlese doesn't get made fun of
Maleeka hangs out with John John or by herself	Charlese hangs out with the twins and the gangs in school
Maleeka likes Ms. Saunders	Charlese doesn't like Ms. Saunders
Maleeka works for the office	Char doesn't work for the office
This story is based on Maleeka	This story doesn't talk about Charlese much

This revisit phase requires students to express their ideas to the whole class. As students take turns reporting out their contrasts, Ms. Alverez again uses interactive verbal scaffolding to help students clarify their statements. When John says, "She gets her way, Charlese. She don't, Maleeka," this statement could refer to a number of incidents in the text, so Ms. Alverez asks John to specify the context for clarification. John then responds, "At home, like when Juju [Charlese's sister] let her [Charlese] do anything she wants." This new statement shows that John understands the text and is able to apply the contrast strategy.

During this phase, Ms. Alverez keeps pushing toward her goal of having students point to evidence for their statements. When Alice says, "Maleeka is thirteen years old

(Continued)

and Charlese is fourteen years old," Ms. Alverez asks, "Are you going to be able to prove that?" She maintains her focus on evidence and also indicates that she is not the only expert on the meaning of the book by replying "Okay, I'm going to put it down. I'm not sure on this one myself."

Represent

The students' composite list represents what they collectively understand about the differences between Maleeka and Charlese at this point in the unit. Some of the contrasts reflect their attention to physical descriptions in the book (Maleeka has short hair and Charlese has long hair). Other contrasts reflect their interpretations of the characters' behaviors (Charlese is bossy and Maleeka is not bossy). The contrasts also reflect some understanding of the book as a whole and the difference between a main character and a supporting character, as when Alice says, "This story is based on Maleeka. This story doesn't talk about Charlese that much."

Throughout the represent phase, Ms. Alverez shows her students how much she values their thinking. She affirms their contrasts as she writes them on the list. She knows her students so well that she is able to consider their individual needs in acknowledging their contributions. Alice is the student who independently generated the most contrasts during the respond phase of the cycle. Alice is proud of her list and Ms. Alverez gives Alice credit for her work by stating, "Well, I know you have tons of them [contrasts] on there [her paper]."

Ms. Alverez's students draw on this representation and their earlier discussions of the similarities between Maleeka and Charlese in writing a comparison-and-contrast essay. They write the essay at the midpoint of the unit, and each student drafts, revises, and edits the essay before typing it up in "publishable" form. The first box displays Anna's essay, which includes one contrast from the class-created list (Maleeka goes to class and Charlese skips class) and one additional contrast (Maleeka has a chance to go to another school and Charlese has no brains to go to another school). The second box displays Kevin's essay. He lists one contrast from the class list (Maleeka wears the clothes that her mother made and some are not that stylish, while Charlese has her sister's clothes that her sister stole), and he adds a description of Charlese's clothes as "stylish."

ANNA'S COMPARE AND CONTRAST ESSAY

Maleeka/Charlese

This paper is about two characters from the book "Skin I'm In" named Maleeka and Charlese.

Maleeka and Charlese are different in these ways. Maleeka don't smoke and on the other hand Charlese skips classes to have a cig. Maleeka has a chance to go another school because she passed the test. Right now Charlese has no brains to go to another school.

Here are two ways that they are the same. They both get bossed around by their mom and her sister. Charlese gets bossed around by her sister because at parties JuJu bosses her around. Maleeka has to wear the clothes that her mom makes to school.

These two girls are friends and that means opposites attract.

KEVIN'S COMPARE AND CONTRAST ESSAY

Maleeka and Charlese

This paper is about two characters from the Skin I'm In named Maleeka and Charlese One is popular and one is not.

This is one way Maleeka and Char are different. Maleeka wears the clothes that her mother made and some are not that stylish. Charlese has her sister's clothes that her sister stole. Her clothes are stylish.

This is how they are the same. They both have a loud mouth and get into trouble because they are loud, yelling at the teacher and in the classroom and out of the class also.

That's how Maleeka and Char are alike and different.

CLASSROOM CONNECTIONS

Fostering Critical Thinking in Every Classroom

What surprises you about the teaching and learning taking place in this classroom? What aspects of Ms. Alverez's teaching are particularly helpful to these students? How could she build on this work when she is teaching these students science or social studies? Members of Ms. Alverez's Supported Literacy group found that her approach helped them use the Meaning-Making Cycle with their more academically able students. What do you take from her teaching?

BENEFITS FOR STUDENTS WITH MODERATE DISABILITIES

In adapting "How Far Would You Go to Fit In?" for her class, Ms. Alverez helped us all learn that students with significant disabilities can also participate in inquiry and develop multiliteracy skills in the process. Although her students took longer than students in the regular classrooms to learn the compare-and-contrast strategy, they were able to use the strategy to better understand the novel. Every student, albeit with various forms of assistance from Ms. Alverez, responded by generating contrasts between the characters and brought these responses to the discussion circles. Their success in the elaborate phase is evidenced by their joint product, which included responses from each group member. Moreover, they succeeded in managing the peer-led group and made certain each group member had a voice in the conversation. The students' composite list, the culminating representation of the group thinking, demonstrated that they understood the strategy and could use it to organize their thinking about the text.

Further, some students were able to apply the compare-and-contrast strategy to a new context—Maleeka's character over time—across several situations. Ms. Alverez told us that Kevin reflected, "You know, at the beginning of the story, Maleeka was really against Ms. Saunders and Caleb. And throughout the story, those are the people who she really does want to be friends with."

The students' sense of connection to Maleeka's struggles motivated them to read the entire novel, a first for most of them. Despite their lack of confidence in their learning abilities, they participated fully and, as Ms. Alverez reflected, began to see that they had good ideas: "I think more and more of them joined in the discussions. I think that they realized that their words were as valuable as anybody else's."

Several factors contributed to the success of Ms. Alverez and her students. One factor was Ms. Alverez's willingness to try a new approach that involved connecting the literacies. She was frank about her hopes and difficulties with her peers, and she was willing to accept their help. Another factor was Ms. Alverez's ability to transform the curriculum unit that our group developed into instructional plans that would work in her classroom. Ms. Alverez broke down each lesson into smaller parts to help her students learn one of the most cognitively demanding reading and writing strategies. Because she knew her students very well as individuals, Ms. Alverez could anticipate the level of support each needed to participate in the phases of the Meaning-Making Cycle. An avid learner, she was open to changing her teaching and seeing her students with new eyes. "I learned that the kids can do more than I think they can. I think you just have to present it to them and try it, fly with it, and see how it works." Ms. Alverez's extraordinary expertise allowed her to scaffold her students' learning at multiple levels. This expertise, joined with a new approach to instruction, a well-designed unit, supportive colleagues, and a compelling novel, enabled her students to make meaning from fiction.

CHAPTER

6

RESPONDING TO ADOLESCENT READING DIFFICULTIES

ANDREA WINOKUR KOTULA

Meet Edward

A few months ago, Hayes Middle School science, social studies, and language arts teachers began to use the Supported Literacy framework. Today several eighth-grade teachers are meeting to discuss their progress and challenges so far. They spend the first half of the meeting excitedly sharing success stories about how the units they have designed are enriching and extending their students' learning. Then, as they discuss Edward, the conversation slows down.

Edward is a puzzle to his teachers. On one hand, he is very much like other adolescents. He demonstrates good thinking and reasoning skills, finds girls intriguing but confusing, and enjoys playing video games and baseball. He is also a talented artist who loves to draw cartoon characters. But when it comes to reading and writing assignments, Edward often seems disengaged from the class and does not appear to be working to his full potential. Social studies teacher Laura Michaels, science teacher Margaret Austin, and language arts teacher Richard Jacobs share their pieces of the "Edward puzzle."

(Continued)

Ms. Michaels: Edward jumps right into the small group discussions. He speaks up, makes great points, and keeps the conversation going. He seems really interested in history and current affairs. But he doesn't complete the readings I assign, he tries to avoid researching topics online or in books, and he's really struggling with the essay and journaling activities.

Mr. Jacobs: I've noticed the same sorts of things in language arts. When other students are busy reading, Edward rifles through the pages of the book or doodles in his notebook. He shares his opinions about topics but hardly ever reads about them, and he avoids doing research. When he writes something, he really struggles to communicate his ideas. His ideas are good, but it's hard to tell that.

Ms. Austin: Yes, I know just what you mean. Misspelled words and missing punctuation make Edward's lab reports and notes difficult to decipher. He's eager to dissect lab specimens and to work on experiments with his small group—and he really does well in our discussions after the experiments. But I often wonder whether Edward understands the articles I assign. His answers to study questions are vague and incomplete. He seems capable of doing much more. So we agree there's a problem here. What are we going to do?

Do you have students in your class who are a mystery, as Edward is to his teachers? Do you find that these students are bright, sometimes respond exceptionally well in oral discussions, but do not achieve well because they do not or cannot read the required materials? And do you ever wonder about the comprehension abilities of other students who often surprise you by missing the point of online and print materials?

It is probable that, like Edward, some of your students experience reading difficulties that challenge their ability to master the content you teach. If you use the Supported Literacy framework in your classroom, you will find that you can investigate, identify, and meet the reading needs of most of your students. The framework offers a good deal of assistance for reading because you introduce and integrate into lessons multiliteracy tools that help many kinds of learners read, write, and talk about challenging texts. Yet some of your students will require diagnostic assessments and interventions, and you will need to partner with reading specialists and school leaders to meet their needs.

In this chapter we help you distinguish between reading problems that you can address in your classroom and needs that go beyond most content teachers' expertise. We begin with an overview of reading difficulties and a summary of indicators that signal that your students are struggling with reading. Drawing on examples from preceding chapters, we explore how you can use the Supported Literacy framework to respond to some reading weaknesses. Next we describe more complex reading needs that specialists can remediate using short-term small group supplementary instruction—sometimes in your classroom with the help of an inclusion or English language learner (ELL) teacher and sometimes at a different time outside your classroom. We conclude this chapter by describing the Supported Literacy Intensive tutorials. During these small-group tutorials, students participate in basic reading skills instruction that accelerates their reading ability as quickly as possible and enables them to benefit from your content area instruction.

As you read the pages that follow, you might find yourself wondering, "Why do I need to know about instruction that will occur outside my classroom? Isn't that the reading specialist's responsibility?" When using the Supported Literacy framework, it might be valuable for you to glimpse what the additional instruction entails and to understand the kinds of changes it might bring about in your students' classroom work. The solution to the puzzle students like Edward present will only emerge as you, your colleagues in other content areas, and the reading specialist confer. Knowing what specialists do might help you plan the best classroom support for your students and also give you a sense of relief that the solution is not all in your hands. Moreover, if your struggling students know that you understand and value their additional out-of-classroom work, they will be more motivated to make the effort and sacrifice that it requires.

READING DIFFICULTIES

In earlier chapters we described many ways that you can use the Supported Literacy framework to engage your students and motivate them to investigate challenging questions. However, even motivated students can struggle to understand online and print materials because of the following reading difficulties:

- Weak comprehension, including background knowledge and the application of comprehension strategies

- Limited basic and discipline-related vocabulary

- Dysfluent reading—reading slowly and haltingly, hesitating, repeating, and self-correcting (often with poor phrasing or intonation)

- Weak foundation reading skills, including *sight word vocabulary* (quickly and automatically reading high-frequency words that appear regularly in classroom reading materials), *phonics skills* (decoding or sounding out unfamiliar words), and *phonemic awareness* (knowing that words are made up of parts that can be manipulated in different ways and performing those manipulations)

Some of your students might experience more than one of these difficulties at the same time. In Table 6.1, we list some indicators that you can watch for in your classroom.

TABLE 6.1. Indicators of Students' Reading Difficulties.

Reading Difficulties	Indicators
1. Weak comprehension (including background knowledge and the application of comprehension strategies)	Students' comments in preliminary discussions of topics reveal lack of knowledge or misconceptions; students read straight through texts without pausing to reflect on the meaning and cannot describe their reading process.
2. Limited vocabulary	Students misuse words; students' oral or written vocabularies (or both) are very basic.
3. Dysfluent reading	Students are slow to finish work; students do not read in meaningful phrases.
4. Weak foundation reading skills (including sight word vocabulary, phonics skills, and phonemic awareness)	Students substitute words for other words and mispronounce words; students read slowly and haltingly; students make spelling errors when they write.

Older readers can have diverse instructional needs because their growth is uneven across the components of reading (Buly & Valencia, 2002; Leach, Scarborough, & Rescorla, 2003). Because struggling readers often have strengths in one or more areas but deficits in others, it is important that you note your students' areas of strength as well as their weaknesses.

In this chapter, we discuss each of the areas of reading difficulty from Table 6.1 by defining the difficulty, suggesting indicators that you might watch for in your classroom, and identifying some ways that you can respond within a Supported Literacy unit. You are likely to spot indicators of most of these reading problems, and there are ways that you can help a student in your classroom with mild reading difficulties in comprehension, vocabulary, and fluency. However, the fourth area, weak foundation reading skills, is usually beyond the expertise of content area teachers. Students with limited sight word vocabulary, phonics, and phonemic awareness generally require more diagnostic assessment from a reading specialist and may need additional instruction beyond your classroom. In the section that follows this one, we discuss the roles that specialized staff—a reading specialist and reading teachers—play in responding to weak foundation reading skills.

Weak Comprehension

Your students might not understand what they read because they lack the comprehension strategies they need to complete reading assignments. They might also need additional background knowledge to fully understand texts.

Comprehension Strategies. Applying comprehension strategies leads to improved comprehension (NICHD, 2000). Some of your students might have difficulty comprehending because they read text from beginning to end rather than approaching it strategically. Students who use comprehension strategies actively ask themselves what they know about the topic, predict what might happen next, pose and respond to questions about the text, summarize what they understand so far, and sometimes visualize what the author is describing. One way to determine whether your students are strategic readers is to ask them to think aloud as they make sense of text and to explain how they are trying to figure out the meaning as they are reading. You will find that some students are quite adept at describing what they do, but others do not know how they process written material. While his students are reading difficult articles on immigration and history, Mr. Howard (see Chapter One) can ask one or two students with reading difficulties to sit with him one at a time and think aloud about the history article as they read it. If you use this technique, you can look for indications that your students are asking themselves questions about the article or summarizing the main points as they read.

In addition to using think-alouds to observe students while they read, you can informally talk with them right after they read a text. Ask them if they pondered any questions about the text as they read. Ask if there were parts they did not understand and what they did at that point. If they say they went back and reread sections of the text or they asked you about the reading, their responses indicate that they have developed some metacognitive awareness. If they report that they just kept reading, they probably need to learn metacognitive strategies.

Because of their sensitive nature, these kinds of informal assessment "interviews" need to take place out of the range of hearing of classmates. Although they are not a complete source of data, they are worth the effort; you might be surprised at how much you will learn about a struggling student's areas of need from these conversations.

As noted earlier, directly teaching comprehension strategies and giving students opportunities to practice them in meaningful contexts are an important part of the Supported Literacy framework. Ms. Harris teaches her students the genre features of a supported argument in the "War and People" unit (see Chapter Two); Ms. Robbins asks students to generate questions about climate change to guide their thinking as they investigate global warming (see Chapter Three).

Background Knowledge. Many students lack even basic background knowledge or have misconceptions about a topic. While reading can and does expand a person's knowledge base, it is very difficult to comprehend ideas that are completely unfamiliar. Readers need to bring some knowledge to the topic, and this is as true for highly skilled adult readers as it is for your students. Think about what it would be like if you were handed something to read about a topic you knew little or nothing about. The concepts and vocabulary would be so unfamiliar that understanding could be out of your reach. In the unit on climate change (see Chapter Three), Ms. Robbins faces the double challenge that the little knowledge her students have of climate change is mostly incorrect.

You can often anticipate which unit topics will be unfamiliar to most of your students and plan ways to build a common core of knowledge throughout the Meaning-Making Cycles. In the Meaning-Making Cycle process, you build your students' knowledge as you pose a question (engage) and give students resources such as trade books, videos, Internet sites, or multimedia presentations to study individually or to explore with another student (respond). You structure peer discussion groups in which students talk about new information (elaborate). After the peer discussions, you help students reflect on what they have learned and correct their misconceptions (revisit). You also present students with opportunities to express their new knowledge in charts, summaries, blog entries, drawings, and journal summaries and give them feedback on their work (represent). As you build your students' background knowledge, you will begin to notice their misconceptions and to gather information about how well they understand what they read. The earliest discussions in a unit—such as the first lessons of the "War and People" and "Understanding Climate Change" units discussed in Chapters Two and Three—can be some of the most helpful to you in terms of gauging students' knowledge and needs.

Limited Vocabulary

To comprehend text, your students need to understand what most of the words mean. Although sounding out words enables students to pronounce them, this activity is useless if the words lack meaning. Many native English speakers have limited knowledge of word meanings, but this area of need can be particularly troublesome for English language learners, who might know the meanings in their native language but not in the language of instruction. For English language learners, academic vocabulary— words such as *assume, response,* and *procedure*—are critical to school success because they have an impact on all school subjects (Francis, Rivera, Lesaux, Kieffer, & Rivera, 2006). Words such as *criteria, synthesize,* and *evidence* in Ms. Harris's class (see Chapter Two) are additional examples of academic vocabulary.

As a content area teacher, you will quite naturally notice when your students do not know technical words that are specific to your discipline. This lack of mastery almost always denotes poor conceptual knowledge because you teach these words within a discipline-specific concept. For example, if Ms. Harris's students have little understanding of words such as *refugee, economic,* and *political,* it might reflect their lack of content knowledge rather than a general vocabulary problem. On the other hand, when students lack knowledge of words that are *not* specific to a content area—words such as *interrupt, worst,* or *underneath* that recur often in oral and in written grade-appropriate materials—they might need to work on vocabulary.

To identify limited vocabularies, you can observe your class to see if they use words correctly when they are speaking or writing. Sometimes it is easiest to spot problems by comparing students. Do some consistently overuse very basic words? This is a possible sign that they are not aware of alternative words with similar meanings. Are there students who ask about the meanings of words more often? Have you noticed that a few students frequently misuse words or know a little about a word but do not understand when it is taken out of the familiar context? Discussion circles during Meaning-Making Cycles provide opportunities for you to listen to how your class uses words and to notice when students do not seem to understand ordinary as well as technical content language. If you notice students who seem to have a very limited vocabulary, you can refer them to a specialist for follow-up diagnostic testing.

You need not be concerned if your students do not know words that appear infrequently in reading and conversation; you can simply define these words and move on. Moreover, many students will not be familiar with the technical vocabulary related to scientific, historical, or literary concepts. They will learn about these as they engage in inquiry with other students over the course of the unit. It is the higher-frequency words that you expect students to know and that might require more of your attention.

As a science or social studies teacher, you are not likely to systematically teach strategies for learning new words, yet you can show students how to use context clues to get at the meaning of a word when the text is rich enough to supply adequate information. Also, look for opportunities to show your students how to attend to roots, base words, prefixes, and suffixes, particularly when they are part of your discipline. Base and root words are the core of the word, without any prefixes or suffixes. Root words originate from other languages, primarily from Latin or Greek, and usually need a prefix or suffix for completion. For example, *migrate* and *historic* are base words. *Tract* and *vis* are root words.

Dysfluent Reading

Fluency is "the ability to read text quickly, accurately, and with proper expression" (NICHD, 2000, pp. 3–5). Although a lack of fluency can impair comprehension, it can also be a result of poor comprehension. In other words, some of your students might read dysfluently because they do not understand what they are reading.

Other factors can affect fluency, such as weaknesses in vocabulary, prior knowledge, content area knowledge, reasoning, motivation, or engagement. Also, an inaccurate reader—one who has not mastered foundation reading skills—cannot be expected to read fluently. Clearly, many factors can contribute to a student's lack of fluency.

What can you look for to identify dysfluent readers? You can observe which students are consistently the last to finish reading assignments or who rarely seem to have enough time to finish. Reading rate is dependent on the purpose for reading and on the type of text, so you can expect all your students to read more slowly than usual at times. In fact, we do not know yet how fluent an older student must be to be able to comprehend; it probably depends on the individual student and on the specific task (Torgesen et al., 2007). Nevertheless, you might be able to detect slow readers by comparing them to other readers in their peer group. In addition to observing your students' reading rates, observe their expressiveness when they read aloud. Are they reading in meaningful phrases? Do they pause at commas, semicolons, and end punctuation? Are they reading smoothly?

Throughout the Meaning-Making Cycle process, students build fluency by reading and rereading print and online sources of text. This helps them increase fluency in two ways. First, it exposes them to a variety of new words that are repeated over time so that they begin to recognize them quickly. Second, when you supply feedback about inaccuracies in a trusting environment, it helps students read more fluently.

You can create additional support for your dysfluent readers, particularly in middle-grades classes, by sometimes asking them to reread texts with more accuracy and expression, by modeling fluent reading and then asking them to "echo read" the section afterward, or by having them read together with you (choral reading). However, it is important to remember that dysfluent reading can be caused by poor comprehension, poor foundation reading skills, or both.

CLASSROOM CONNECTIONS

Observing Reading Difficulties

Which of these indicators of reading difficulties do you see in students in your classes? What do they tell you? Which reading difficulties are most prevalent? What opportunities do you have to investigate these difficulties further and to discuss them with your students? Students themselves are sometimes quite aware of these and have interesting insights about their reading. Some have experienced reading difficulties for so long that they are discouraged; it is important for them to know that their challenges are not insurmountable.

Weak Foundation Reading Skills

Do you struggle to reach some of the students in your classrooms? If so, you are not alone. In secondary classrooms across the United States, millions of students cannot read the words in their texts. Because they lack foundation reading skills—sight word vocabulary, phonics skills, and phonemic awareness—they do not understand what they read and they fall behind in their subjects. Not all students master these key skills in the primary grades, and they need them to comprehend what they read.

Reading specialists conduct the diagnostic testing of students who lack foundation reading skills. However, with some knowledge of each of these skills, you can help identify your students' needs and refer students for testing.

CLASSROOM CONNECTIONS

Incidence of Poor Foundation Reading Skills

Curtis and Longo (1999) report that about 10 percent of older adolescents at the Boys Town Reading Center still have difficulty decoding words, and this figure is often cited in the literature (Biancarosa & Snow, 2006). However, this figure is not derived from a formal research study and Boys Town students might not represent the national population. If the 10 percent figure is accurate, it would encompass a great many students. In the year 2004, 33,241,707 fourth- to twelfth-grade students were enrolled in public schools (NCES, 2006); 10 percent of that figure yields about 3.32 million students.

Sight Word Vocabulary. To read fluently, your students must be able to identify most words rapidly and automatically. A weak sight word vocabulary contributes to poor fluency (Jenkins, Fuchs, van den Broek, Espin, & Deno, 2003). Torgesen (2006) suggests that the reason that it is so difficult to improve fluency in poor readers is that most of them have read much less than their peers over time—perhaps for many years—and as a result have been exposed to fewer words. A fifth-grade student with average reading ability generally reads about twelve times as many written words a year outside of school as a student who reads at the tenth percentile on a reading achievement test (Anderson, Wilson, & Fielding, 1988). It is extremely important that struggling readers with limited sight word vocabularies receive the instruction they need to catch up in this area.

To get an idea of whether sight word vocabulary is a problem for one of your students, you can create an opportunity for reading aloud (to you, another student, or a younger student). You might notice whether the reader mispronounces high-frequency words, substitutes incorrect words, or hesitates at individual words.

Phonics Skills. Because of difficulty with phonics, some students read slowly and haltingly; they correct themselves frequently and do not chunk words into meaningful phrases. They read dysfluently because they still need to figure out how to sound out the individual words. Conversely, some poor decoders read extremely quickly to get through the process, to avoid having their mistakes noticed, or both.

You are not likely to miss the poor decoders when your students read aloud in class. Students with weak decoding skills substitute or mispronounce words. In a large class it is sometimes difficult to decide without additional testing whether students have limited phonics skills or lack age-appropriate sight word vocabulary because many are weak in both areas. The poor decoder tends to misread the same letter pattern in different words and mispronounce words rather than substitute one word for another. However, these two areas have so much overlap that you should not be too concerned about distinguishing one from the other. It is enough to realize that one of your students is experiencing difficulty reading single words. In that case, you might need to involve a specialist.

Phonemic Awareness. This area might be the most difficult for you to identify during daily instruction. One indicator is weak spelling because spelling requires two essential components of phonemic awareness—the ability to separate, or segment, letter sounds and the ability to blend them together to form words. While poor spelling does not necessarily indicate a lack of phonemic awareness, spellings that display little to no relationship to the letter sounds can signal difficulty in this area.

A student with weak foundation reading skills might escape your notice by being very good at masking them. By the time students who have difficulty reading single words reach the middle or high school grades, they have usually developed strategies for saving face with their peers. They might act out, refuse to participate, or engage in other avoidance behaviors. Sadly, teachers often label these students as unmotivated and noncompliant. While many really have become unmotivated or noncompliant after years of failure, beneath the bravado is usually a frightened young person who would desperately like to be a better reader.

You can provide some support for the first three areas of reading difficulties listed in Table 6.1, but weak foundation reading skills require assistance beyond your classroom. In the next section, we describe the varied levels of support students can receive and how reading specialists and teachers work with your struggling readers.

WHEN STUDENTS NEED MORE: THE SUPPORTED LITERACY INTENSIVE

As shown in Figure 6.1, schools often use a three-tier model to differentiate the levels of reading support students need. Good core instruction for all students makes up the first tier, and supplementary and intensive interventions comprise the second and third tiers. In a tiered model of instruction, students with greater needs receive additional time for explicit instruction, a lower student-to-teacher ratio, or both.

Supported Literacy provides a strong context for building reading skills within the content areas. The rigorous curriculum units you use the framework to design fit in the first tier of the model. Some students for whom Supported Literacy is not enough also need Tier 2 instruction, a second level of support that generally takes place outside of the classroom. These students benefit from small group teaching

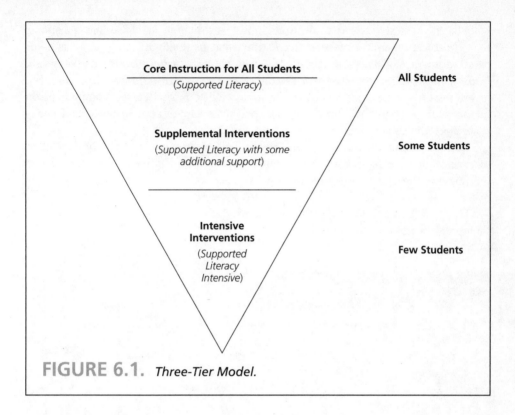

FIGURE 6.1. *Three-Tier Model.*

and practice in comprehension strategies, vocabulary, or fluency. A specialist could come into your classroom to do this, particularly if you are a middle school teacher, or might work with your students outside class at a time that does not conflict with your teaching period.

Tier 3 provides intensive and accelerated instruction to allow the poorest readers to catch up to their peers. This level of intensity is often necessary for students with weak foundation reading skills. We developed the Supported Literacy Intensive as a way to provide this level of reading instruction in small group tutorials.

Reading specialists play a key role in the system; they evaluate students' reading ability, determine what they know and need to learn, and place them in the intervention that is most appropriate for them. Diagnostic assessment provides detailed information to pinpoint a student's reading strengths and needs. It is really an inquiry process as the reading specialist uses standardized and nonstandardized tests (see Appendix C) to tease out the causes of poor comprehension. A *standardized test* is a test that is administered and scored in exactly the same way for all students, under uniform conditions. These conditions are the same ones that the test publisher used when it gave the test to a national sample of students. For example, everyone who takes the test has the same time limits, instructions, and sample questions. Standardized tests are *norm-referenced,* which means that a student's score is compared to students of the same age or grade who were in the national normative group. *Nonstandardized tests* allow more flexibility in the administration and scoring, but they do not compare the student to peers across the country. Because comprehension might break down for so many reasons, specialists cannot address individual needs without a detailed assessment.

In the section that follows, we present a Classroom Close-Up of a student receiving intensive instruction in a small group tutorial. Earlier in this chapter you met Edward through the eyes of his worried teachers. Now you will be an invisible observer as his teachers learn about Edward's specific reading difficulties and how they can make accommodations to meet his needs. Then you will follow him into his Supported Literacy Intensive tutorial.

CLASSROOM CLOSE-UP

Inside a Supported Literacy Intensive Tutorial

Edward is continuing to struggle with his reading and writing assignments. After discussing him and sharing their observations, his teachers decided to bring him to the attention of Dora Chase, the school's reading specialist, for additional assessment. Together they discuss the results.

Ms. Chase: Your observations were absolutely correct. I know you all agreed that Edward has good background knowledge and were pretty sure that his difficulties went beyond that. You were right—Edward will need some extra help.

Ms. Michaels: That's good to know. Edward's bright, and I'd like to be able to do more for him in my social studies class. When I asked him about comprehension, he said, "I just don't get it," but he couldn't explain further. He's also very anxious about reading out loud in class—he doesn't want to be laughed at—but he did read a bit one-on-one with me. Reading is a real struggle for him.

Ms. Austin: Yes—we were talking about that. He read aloud one-on-one with me in science class too. He reads very slowly and uncertainly, and I think we found that he has a lot of trouble identifying some of the words, right?

Mr. Jacobs: Right. When I did some one-on-one reading with Edward in language arts, I found that he couldn't recognize some of the words. But then when I read the words aloud to him, he knew what they meant.

Ms. Chase: All of this fits with what I found. When I tested Edward, I found that he reads at a third- to fourth-grade level. Right now he's way below age- and grade-level expectations, and he has very weak basic reading skills. I'm glad you caught the signs and called me because now we can help Edward. There are some things you can do, and a whole lot that a reading teacher and I can do.

Once they understand Edward's difficulty, his teachers draw on a number of accommodations to support him. Sometimes they give him audiotapes of the material to use at home or at a learning station in the classroom. Or they supply text-to-speech programs that enable him to see the text on a computer screen while he listens to it read aloud to him or to highlight specific words or phrases and have the computer read them aloud. In this way, Edward can access the text in books as well as on Web pages and in online articles. These devices, which he generally uses with headphones, help Edward get exposure to reading for his classes, but they do not strengthen his weak skills. He needs to learn to read independently, without the need for accommodations.

CLASSROOM CONNECTIONS

E-Book Technology

An electronic book, or *e-book,* is the digital media equivalent of a conventional printed book. Personal computers can read these documents, or they can be read on hardware called *e-book readers* or *e-book devices.* The e-book reader is a dedicated hardware device that is designed just for reading books and has an appropriate screen size, battery lifespan, and lighting for this purpose. Students can use the read-aloud feature to follow the text as the device reads it aloud, or they can activate the read-aloud feature as they need it.

For Edward, it is not a matter of either participating in Supported Literacy classroom activities or receiving intensive instruction in foundation reading skills. Rather, the reality is that he needs both. He needs opportunities to catch up to his classmates, and that means accelerating his reading skills so that he can read at grade level. Even the best teachers cannot address these needs in a class of twenty-five to thirty students. The kind of intensive instruction that Edward needs is undertaken individually or in a very small group with teachers who have received specialized training. Therefore, during the same school day in which he uses his listening and reasoning skills to participate in Meaning-Making Cycles to build his content knowledge, Edward also takes part in a tutorial to build his foundation reading skills. Here is a profile of his strengths and areas of need in

(Continued)

reading, along with the reading specialist's recommendations for his tutorial teacher and content area teachers.

Edward's Individual Reading Profile

Edward's test results on the *Diagnostic Assessments of Reading-2* (DAR-2) indicate that he can recognize words in isolation at the third-grade level and in context at the fourth-grade level. A significant drop in reading rate (forty-six words per minute) between the fourth- and fifth-grade passages indicates his difficulty with processing the text. Edward's rate is at the bottom of the below-average range and his accuracy is in the poor range for his age on the *Gray Oral Reading Tests* (GORT-4); the difference in the two scores is not significant. He has weak phonemic awareness and very weak phonics skills. His limited foundation reading skills (phonemic awareness, phonics, and sight word vocabulary) make it difficult for him to recognize printed words rapidly and automatically. This, in turn, adversely affects his reading comprehension, which is at a fourth-grade level. Moreover, even at the fourth-grade level, Edward needs to look back at the text to respond to the questions. His weak knowledge of word meanings, at a second-grade level, also contributes to his poor reading comprehension. In addition, Edward appears to process information slowly and requires a great deal of prompting and cueing.

EDWARD'S GRADE LEVELS
FOR SEVERAL AREAS OF READING

Word Recognition	Oral Reading	Comprehension	Vocabulary
3	4	4	2

Recommendations to Reading Teacher

1. Teach all areas of phonemic awareness.
2. Fill in gaps in phonics skills: soft/hard c, tw-, -nk, ph, -dge, short vowels, vowel-consonant-e (VCE) pattern, ir, er, or, common endings, vowel teams, open/closed syllables, syllabication, and later, advanced sounds.
3. Build sight word vocabulary beginning at the fourth-grade level.
4. Practice phonics and sight word vocabulary in isolation and in connected oral reading with (a) decodable text, and (b) informational text beginning at a fifth-grade level, with support for comprehension.

5. Build knowledge of word meanings beginning at the third-grade level.
6. Build fluency with oral reading.
7. Emphasize that reading is for meaning but reserve intensive comprehension instruction until Edward's basic skills are stronger.
8. Update Edward's content area teachers on his progress.

Recommendations to Content Area Teachers

1. Meet with the reading specialist to gain insight into Edward's reading difficulties.
2. Identify ways to use the Supported Literacy framework to meet Edward's reading needs.
3. As appropriate, provide aids—such as e-books, audiotapes, and text-to-speech programs.
4. Use the Meaning-Making Cycle to determine if Edward has misconceptions and, if so, to clarify them. Determine how well he understands what he reads and provide support as needed.
5. Discuss Edward in group planning time.
6. Share observation data with Edward's reading tutorial teacher and request that the teacher keep you updated about Edward's progress.

The profile summarizes both the standardized and nonstandardized test results but displays only the informal tests in the chart because they are easier for most teachers to understand. Ms. Chase, the reading specialist, gave a copy of the profile to Ella Northrup, Edward's reading teacher, and to Ms. Michaels, Ms. Austin, and Mr. Jacobs. Ms. Northrup used the Recommendations section of the profile to develop Edward's instructional plan, and the content area teachers used this section to design classroom accommodations for him. The other members of Edward's tutorial group had similar but not identical profiles.

(Continued)

CLASSROOM CONNECTIONS

Conferring with Other Teachers

When you spot reading difficulties in your students, do you have opportunities to confirm and talk about them with other classroom teachers? Does the student show a pattern of difficulties across the various settings, or do strengths and difficulties show up differently in science, social studies, or language arts? What might account for differences? What mechanisms does your school have for conferencing about students' reading needs?

Edward and the Tutorial

Ms. Chase, the reading specialist, tested Edward and assigned him to his reading group, but she does not have time to teach the tutorials. Instead, Ms. Northrup, who was specially trained for Supported Literacy Intensive tutorials, is Edward's reading teacher. She explicitly teaches and guides students' practice in phonemic awareness, phonics, and sight word vocabulary. Ms. Northrup's goal is for Edward to make enough progress in reading to comprehend close to grade level by the end of eighth grade and then move into high school almost caught-up. He can complete the catch-up process in a ninth-grade tutorial.

Today Edward sits at a table at the beginning of eighth grade with four other students and Ms. Northrup. Each student has similar reading strengths and needs; even so, these older readers display a diversity of skills. Ms. Northrup's instruction is teacher-directed with frequent interactions between her and students but limited interaction among students. Instruction moves at a quick pace, a very different approach from the Meaning-Making Cycle process.

Ms. Northrup's students understand her expectations and routines very well because she spent the first few weeks teaching them the behaviors she expects, arranging optimal seating, and building the same atmosphere of trust and risk taking that Edward is used to in his other classes. It is important that he feels comfortable because the tutorials focus on the very difficulties students have worked to avoid or mask in the past and that can cause embarrassment. In fact, it has taken awhile for Edward to get used to this class. At first he said that he felt dumb and complained that this was "baby work" for a middle school student. Over time Ms. Northrup has managed to convey to her students that having reading difficulties has nothing to do with their intelligence and that she will support them as they learn to read better.

Phonemic awareness lesson segment (10 minutes)

During the first part of the lesson, Edward's group works on separating orally presented words into individual letter sounds. Ms. Northrup asks Edward to segment the word *mock* by placing a plastic chip into a row of squares as he says each segment. He says "/m/ /u/ /k/."

Ms. Northrup responds, "Edward, you really did a terrific job on the first and last sound. The word is 'mock.' What sound do you hear after the /m/?"

Edward again responds "/u/."

"That sound is very close, Edward," Ms. Northrup says. "Look at my lips as I say the word and listen carefully." She says *mock* again, enunciating each sound clearly but in a natural voice. "Now you repeat the word 'mock.'" Edward repeats it as the other students watch and listen.

"That was good, Edward," Ms. Northrup continues, ascertaining that he is attempting to segment the correct word. "Now I want you to say it one more time, but this time, look at the shape of your mouth in the mirror when you say the middle sound." Edward repeats the word, peering at his mouth in a small mirror that he picks up from the table. "Good," Ms. Northrup says. "Do you see the round circle your lips make? Do you remember what sound we make when our lips are in that position?"

"Ah?" Edward says.

"Absolutely correct," Ms. Northrup replies. "Good job! You were saying /u/ before. Now look in the mirror and say /u/." Edward repeats the sound.

"That's right. When we say /u/," Ms. Northrup says, holding her cheeks with thumb and forefinger on either side of her lips, "our mouth is puckered a little. Can you hear the difference? /o/ /u/. Let me hear you say them both." Edward responds appropriately, more confident now. "Okay, let's move on," Ms. Northrup says, jotting down a note to herself to call on him again the next time she comes to a word with a short o or short u sound.

The other students smile, and Ricky, who is sitting next to Edward, whispers, "All right," and gives him a high-five.

Phonics lesson segment (20–30 minutes)

Ms. Northrup begins the phonics segment by reviewing the most recently taught elements. She spends extra time discussing areas that students had difficulty with the day before. Then she introduces a new phonics element. After the direct instruction, students take turns reading sentences and lists of real and made-up words while Ms. Northrup provides corrective feedback and modeling as needed. She uses made-up words, or *pseudowords,* because older students have often memorized many real words and reading them does not help them practice their phonics skills. For example, to practice reading words with the vowel-consonant-e pattern, students might read the pseudowords *yape* or *wame.* The practice is cumulative; the words are a review of previously taught concepts as well as the newly taught element. Students also read a passage of text that is largely "decodable." That is, the text contains phonics patterns that Ms. Northrup previously taught, words that the students have learned as sight word vocabulary, or words that Ms. Northrup reads aloud to students. In that way, they do not read the passage on a trial-and-error basis. Instead, reading the connected text reinforces Ms. Northrup's instruction and builds fluency.

In the nurturing environment of the tutorial, Edward is capable of and confident about reading the material. He eagerly raises his hand for a turn to read aloud and beams when Ms. Northrup praises his efforts. This eagerness is radically different from his attempts to avoid having to read aloud in his social studies, science, and language arts classes. After the first reading, students work on fluency by rereading the passage—timing, recording, and graphing their oral reading rates. Students also write words and sentences that Ms. Northrup dictates because writing reinforces decoding.

(Continued)

Sight word lesson segment (5–8 minutes)

In the third component of the lesson, students review sight word vocabulary that Ms. Northrup has already taught them, and she teaches them new words. It is essential for struggling readers to begin to make up for all the words they have missed in the years they have not been reading widely.

Concluding segment (10–12 minutes)

The session ends with the reading of a high-interest, low-vocabulary book or a game or activity to practice phonics skills or sight word vocabulary. Today students play a game of Go Fish, in which sets of cards containing words with hard and soft c replace the traditional playing cards.

In this small group tutorial, a setting tailored to fit Edward's instructional needs and based on materials appropriate for his reading level, he does not try to divert attention away from reading by acting out, leaving the room, or disrupting the class. He is engaged, although much of the work is challenging for him, and he feels safe to try new things and to learn. Students like Edward have experienced years of failure in their attempts to read; many experience success for the first time in the Supported Literacy Intensive tutorials.

Features of an Effective Tutorial

In our consultation work with schools that have piloted the Supported Literacy Intensive, we have identified several key ingredients that ensure the effectiveness of tutorials such as the one just described:

- Tutorial size, grouping, and frequency

- Emphasis on decodable text in the early stages

- Ongoing assessment of students' progress

We discuss each of these key ingredients in the following sections.

Tutorial Size, Grouping, and Frequency. Edward's tutorial is typical of Supported Literacy Intensive tutorials. They take place daily in groups of three to five students with one teacher and are as homogeneous as possible. This configuration gives struggling readers the intensity of instruction they very much need (Foorman & Torgesen, 2001; Snow, Burns, & Griffin, 1998). Without an intensive instructional intervention, poor readers become even worse over time (Stanovich, 1986). To truly bring these students up to grade level requires several years' growth in reading skills for each academic year (Torgesen et al., 2007).

In the best-case scenario, specialists first place all students within a grade who need instruction in foundation reading skills into one pool. Then, with input from other staff and teachers, they create tutorials that are as homogeneous as possible. The diversity among students—including those who are all very poor readers—makes this goal a challenge. In addition, homogeneity can be a difficult concept for staff to accept because schools have strived in recent years to achieve heterogeneous grouping; indeed, this is what we prefer for Supported Literacy. Yet students who need to catch up do it best with peers who have similar needs. The tutorial teacher can then target instruction to meet students' needs in a timely manner.

Because instruction of phonics skills occupies the most time in the tutorial, one effective criterion for placement of students is according to their mastery of phonics skills. For example, a specialist would place students who need to learn very basic single-syllable decoding together in one group. Students who know most or all of the letter-sound correspondences and the rules that govern them, but who falter when they have to read words that have more than one syllable or advanced prefixes and suffixes, would be in a different group. Grouping by phonics level tightens the type of decoding instruction and also guides the teacher's choice of the texts students will use for practice. It is desirable, although not always possible, to use sight word vocabulary knowledge as a second criterion. Because of the diversity among older students, the specialist will need to make some trade-offs in the grouping selections.

Emphasis on Decodable Text. Edward and his peers in the tutorial are primarily reading what is called *decodable text*—text that is age-appropriate in content but that follows patterns and rules that teachers have already taught students and that contains words that students learned as sight word vocabulary. Although access to non-decodable narrative and expository texts is essential to building sight word vocabulary, word meanings, and conceptual knowledge, tutorials are usually fifty minutes long—just enough time for teaching essential foundation reading skills. Also, when students are unable to correctly decode even single-syllable words, they cannot successfully read non-decodable text. However, if you use the Supported Literacy framework in your classroom, you will be able to offer students like Edward an extremely important context for accessing the content of other varied reading materials through conversations with other students, opportunities to read with the support of a partner, or the use of the accommodations we have discussed.

Ongoing Assessment of Students' Progress. Tutorial teachers need to gauge their students' progress regularly and modify instruction as needed. They are likely to monitor progress in two ways: First, during each lesson, tutorial teachers keep careful notes of each student's mastery level and needs. Ms. Northrup noted that Edward would need additional practice in distinguishing the short *o* and short *u* sounds, and she will use this knowledge to guide her in future phonemic awareness lessons. In addition to this ongoing progress monitoring of vocabulary, phonics, and phonemic awareness, tutorial teachers engage students in a nonstandardized test every ten lessons. These progress-monitoring tests are very similar in format to the usual phonics strand of the lesson except that the teachers do not give students corrective feedback. Instead, they record responses and transfer the results later to a chart so that they can easily scan its columns to see which skills have not been mastered and by whom. In this way, tutorial teachers can use the data formatively to decide whether they need to review elements, completely reteach the lessons, or otherwise modify the delivery of the instruction.

CLASSROOM CONNECTIONS

Your Perspective on Tutorials

If this inside view of the reading tutorial is new to you, what struck you as interesting about it? What surprised you? Some content area teachers are mystified by what goes on in intensive reading tutorials or feel that it is not important to know what reading teachers do. What is your view? Do you think teachers like you benefit from knowing Edward's story? What aspects are most important to your work?

Indicators of Edward's Growth

Edward receives intensive instruction in foundation reading skills during eighth grade, while his Supported Literacy content area teachers provide accommodations to help him understand important concepts and ideas from their readings. At the end of eighth grade, Edward has made significant progress in his reading ability. Ms. Northrup and Ms. Chase, the reading specialist, are pleased with the growth and believe that he will be caught up by the end of next year. Here we observe him participating in a Supported Literacy lesson at the end of eighth grade.

CLASSROOM CLOSE-UP

Demonstrating Progress

Edward is sitting with a group of students in geography class who are silently rereading an article on river pollution in the world. He has previously used the e-book reader to access the chapter from which this passage is taken. He enjoys challenging himself to see how much he can read on his own, although he occasionally still needs to click on a word to hear it spoken. If he needs to click on too many words in a passage, it affects his comprehension. Then he has to revert to having all the text read aloud.

As Edward rereads the passage at his desk in his work group, he comes to a word he does not recognize on sight and does not remember from his earlier reading of the chapter. He applies the skills he has been taught in his reading tutorial. First he scans the word for prefixes or suffixes that he knows. Next he examines the base word and chunks it into syllables. "Oh," he thinks, "I know what that means." He rereads the sentence to see if the word makes sense there, and it does. This is a skill he did not have a year ago. He continues to reread the passage so that he can discuss it with his group.

Edward has increased his self-confidence and is more willing to take risks. In his reading and writing assignments, he applies his new decoding and encoding (spelling) skills instead of skipping the difficult words or asking for help. His attempts are not always correct; words do not always follow the rules and Edward is still learning foundation reading skills. However, he is transferring what he has learned in the tutorial to his other classes, as his teachers have encouraged him to do, and he is thriving.

The Supported Literacy framework hinges upon a shared vision and concerted effort by all of your school's staff and leaders. The same is true for the Supported Literacy Intensive, in which a shared vision enhances the school's ability to respond to a range of reading difficulties that are present in making meaning. The schools that are the most successful in implementing the tutorials have already reached a state of readiness as indicated by their formation of strong leadership teams committed to literacy and faculties experienced in working collaboratively. The faculties also share a basic understanding of the reading process and the areas of reading difficulty that we outline earlier in the chapter. In the chapter that follows, we describe some of the features of a schoolwide Supported Literacy approach. (See Appendix D for the steps your school might take to launch the kind of tutorial that Edward receives.)

CHAPTER

7

ENGAGING THE WHOLE SCHOOL IN SUPPORTED LITERACY

Supported Literacy in Action

Ms. Andrews: We can't give students complete access to the Net; look what's out there.

Ms. Robbins: I disagree. It's the reality, and they might as well learn about safety and reliability issues with us.

Mr. Howard: It's not realistic to assume you can control students' access, even if parents put controls on their computers at home. It's our job to teach students the digital literacy skills that will help them make wise decisions wherever they log on.

Mr. Lane: But, you know, even when you're not trying to access inappropriate content, it pops up. I'm astounded by what shows up unexpectedly on my computer screen.

These content area teachers and coaches are participating in a value line activity where they indicate where they stand on a challenging issue by lining up along a string stretched along the floor. One end represents giving students total access to the Internet; the other end represents fully supervised access. Several participants explain their positions along the continuum. If participants change their minds as they listen to others, they are free to move. A lot of shuffling goes on.

You might recognize this professional development activity; it mirrors the *Bogus or Believe It?* value line we described in Chapter Three. After the discussion, Mr. Howard, the social studies teacher you met in Chapter One, explains some of the guidelines he gives his students for determining the quality of information on the Web. Ms. Robbins, the science teacher from Chapter Three, shares how she makes sure her students know how to find science articles that have gone through a peer review by other scientists. Together, the group of teachers and coaches comes up with a set of guidelines for conducting productive online searches.

These teachers and coaches from two high schools and three middle schools are meeting at one of the schools for a seminar on Supported Literacy. In this session, they focus on digital and media tools including the Internet, video, and DVDs that their students can use to gather information. They also discuss tools such as blogs, podcasts, PowerPoint presentations, and e-mail that students can use to communicate what they are learning within and beyond their school.

The Supported Literacy framework, which is the focus of this seminar series, provides a potentially powerful way to prepare students for success in the twenty-first century. Understanding and integrating the various multiliteracy tools for content learning—reading for deep understanding, writing to build and express meaning, accountable talk, and digital and media fluency—is a big agenda. To apply these tools in a content-rich, inquiry-oriented curriculum, you and other teachers may find that you need opportunities to engage in new learning, apply what you learn to your practice, and reflect on your results.

Successful middle schools often use a "signature practice . . . a way of teaching and learning that pervades every subject area, grade level, and classroom" (Morocco et al., 2006). As we describe throughout this book, Supported Literacy can provide that unifying schoolwide approach; its integrated set of practices can improve learning motivation and outcomes for all your students. The framework can provide your school with a vision of prepared adolescents, a common language and orientation to teaching and learning, and opportunities for professional collaboration. You can adapt to your particular discipline a common set of practices, such as organizing learning around essential questions, engaging students in inquiry learning, and using literacy tools to support students in that inquiry.

This shared approach to teaching and learning has a significant impact on students. As they use multiliteracy tools for critical inquiry in your content area and in others, they come to understand that skills in strategic reading, writing to understand a text, peer discussions, and digital and media fluency can help them understand challenging content.

Classroom Close-Ups in earlier chapters show individual teachers successfully implementing Supported Literacy in their classrooms. How do these teachers learn to teach within the Supported Literacy framework? What supports do they need to do this well?

In this chapter, which we've written for content teachers, literacy coaches, and principals, we describe two pillars that are essential for successful implementation of Supported Literacy across the curriculum in your school. One is creating a *professional learning community* that can support you and other teachers in implementing Supported Literacy in your classrooms in ways that meet your students' needs. The other is *shared leadership* that supports schoolwide implementation of the Supported Literacy framework. These two pillars are both essential for a successful implementation.

Throughout the chapter, we provide you with a Supported Literacy road map to help you consider how your school might implement a schoolwide approach:

- A description of what you, as a content teacher or coach, need to know and be able to do in order to apply the Supported Literacy framework in your classroom

- A two-phase approach to building a learning community around Supported Literacy:

  1. A seminar series that builds awareness of the approach

  2. Curriculum design workshops within content areas

- Critical elements of leadership for effective schoolwide implementation of the Supported Literacy framework

Supported Literacy's own research and development and many studies of effective school leadership argue for strong, committed, and distributed leadership where key individuals take responsibility for the schoolwide change process. Professional learning communities flourish with the nurturing of principals and coaches, as well as teachers who understand the Supported Literacy framework and take on new leadership roles in building a professional community around twenty-first-century literacy and learning.

IMPLEMENTING SUPPORTED LITERACY SCHOOLWIDE

As a content teacher or coach, you need several kinds of professional knowledge and skill to integrate Supported Literacy into your practice. You already have some of the areas of expertise we outline below, and your colleagues will have other areas. Together, you and your colleagues need to form a teaching community in which you engage in a cycle of planning, experimenting, and learning:

1. *Develop a shared vision* of the competencies that students need to be prepared to work and live in the twenty-first century—conceptual knowledge in the various content areas, critical and creative thinking, and collaboration and communication.

2. *Understand the four areas of multiliteracy skills* that support students in developing these competencies, the role these literacies play in teaching your content area, and how to use the Supported Literacy framework to adapt and design curricula and lessons in your content area.

3. *Apply this knowledge in your teaching* by identifying the essential questions and the critical content knowledge for your discipline, identifying the appropriate instructional strategies to address them, and adapting your curriculum and lesson plans accordingly.

4. *Reflect on your learning and teaching* by collaborating with your colleagues to look closely at your students' work, to assess their progress in literacy and learning, and to receive guidance and feedback from colleagues and coaches.

Having structured opportunities to learn with your colleagues is the most effective way to acquire this knowledge and apply it in your classroom. Ms. Alverez, the special education teacher in Chapter Five, is able to teach challenging parts of the "How Far Would You Go to Fit In?" unit with students who have cognitive delays or moderate learning disabilities because she is part of a supportive, school-based learning community where teachers share their teaching strategies and encourage each other to try new approaches. With their help, and the structure and guidelines of the fiction unit, she teaches her students a compare-and-contrast strategy for comprehending literature and other kinds of texts. Professional learning communities also offer opportunities to address a variety of reading difficulties, as the content teachers and reading specialists do in planning reading support for Edward in Chapter Six.

In a school-based professional community, teachers focus on student learning; they talk with each other about their teaching practice, and they are comfortable having others visit their classrooms. They also collaborate in assessment and curriculum design and develop shared norms and values (Louis & Kruse, 1995). A teacher community is strongest when teachers share a common orientation toward teaching and learning and share expertise in their specialized content knowledge and their instructional approaches (Morocco & Solomon, 1999; Palincsar, Magnusson, Marano, Ford, & Brown, 1998). Having a professional learning community is a significant factor in promoting student achievement (Louis & Kruse, 1995).

All of this work on teacher communities finds that effective professional development programs have these features:

- *Set clear goals* for both teacher learning and student outcomes.

- *Focus on subject matter* so that teachers build both content and pedagogical content knowledge.

- *Build teacher community,* so that teachers support each other in changing their practice.

- *Connect with the classroom,* giving teachers ongoing opportunities to integrate their learning into their classroom practice.

- *Value teachers' expertise and experience,* making sure to build on their current knowledge and encourage collaboration.

- *Employ different strategies* that change over time to reflect a continuum of teacher learning needs.

- *Focus on results,* offering frequent opportunities for teachers to reflect on changes in their practice and in student learning.

Your school can use a two-phase strategy to build a professional learning community that has these features and that empowers you and other teachers to implement Supported Literacy across the content areas. We discuss that process here, and also provide Seminar Close-Ups and a Curriculum Design Close-Up that illustrate teacher interaction and growth during each phase.

BUILDING A LEARNING COMMUNITY AROUND SUPPORTED LITERACY

The Supported Literacy professional development approach has two phases: a seminar series followed by collaborative curriculum design. It is best to carry out these phases over the course of a multi-year professional development program. For example, your school might conduct the seminar series throughout the first year, and then adapt or design curriculum units during the summer or during year two, or both. Alternatively, the seminar series could take place in an intensive summer institute of a week to two weeks, followed by curriculum design in the fall semester. Whichever approach your school chooses, your school leaders need to provide sufficient time and resources for coaching, mentoring, and peer networking. Both the seminar and curriculum design phases engage you and your colleagues in collaborative activities such as study groups, collaborative assessment of student work, and classroom visits.

Phase 1: Seminar Series

The purpose of this first phase of professional development is for you to develop an understanding of the Supported Literacy framework and to identify ways to apply it in your content area classroom. When you participate in the seminar series, you find that building understanding is both an individual and a collective process. Together, you and your colleagues take stock of students' reading scores and results on content assessments. You develop a *shared vision* of the twenty-first-century competencies that your students need and explore how multiliteracies can support inquiry and deep understanding. You design sample activities and lessons in which students use selected multiliteracy tools to build an understanding of important concepts in your content area.

If you hold the seminar series during a school year, you have opportunities to teach these activities and lessons to your students between sessions and to share your experiences at the next seminar. Your peers, the Supported Literacy facilitator, the local literacy coach, and other content area coaches will provide ongoing feedback and, particularly if more than one school is involved, you share your reflections with a larger learning community by posting comments on a seminar blog.

The box provides a brief overview of seminar topics and activities that teachers and coaches find most helpful as an introduction to Supported Literacy. Each seminar references relevant chapters of this book that can serve as a common text for participants. The chapters include examples from science, world history and literature, social studies, and literature study. Depending on your faculty's experience and needs, you, with your facilitator, can modify this series to spend more time on some topics than others or change the order of topics.

OVERVIEW OF THE TWELVE-SESSION SEMINAR SERIES

1. **How does Supported Literacy prepare adolescents for the twenty-first century? (Chapter One).** This session focuses on the major competencies that adolescents need for learning and work: conceptual understanding in the content areas and new fields of global learning, critical thinking, creative thinking, and collaboration and communication. The session introduces participants to the Supported Literacy framework as a way to develop those competencies.

2. **What literacy tools support twenty-first-century content learning? (Chapters One and Two).** This session introduces the four multiliteracies, including reading for deep understanding, writing to build and express meaning, accountable talk, and digital and multimedia fluency. Participants have opportunities to work with each separate tool and, using an adult-level article, experience how literacy tools work together to support meaning making. Participants discuss the social studies examples in Chapters One and Two and share examples of how each literacy tool can support learning in various content areas. This seminar usually takes place over more than one meeting, depending on faculty experience and needs.

3. **How does the Meaning-Making Cycle guide inquiry? A Science Example (Chapter Three).** Drawing on examples from the climate change unit described in Chapter Three, participants look at how inquiry learning, driven by essential questions, motivates students. They consider how inquiry helps students take responsibility for their own learning. They see how the Meaning-Making Cycle structures inquiry and how multiliteracy tools can support each phase of meaning making.

Participants also examine how the multiliteracy tools work together to support meaning making in the unit. For example, students make extensive use of digital and multimedia tools as they view Al Gore's DVD, *An Inconvenient Truth*, to see powerful images of the effects of climate change, and they use the Internet to collect climate data. They use visual comprehension strategies (drawing) and writing to understand challenging science articles, and they use peer discussions throughout the science inquiry to discuss data. Participants apply their insights into the meaning-making process and these multiliteracies to their own content area teaching.

4. **How does the Meaning-Making Cycle guide inquiry? A Literature Example (Chapter Four).** This session extends the discussion of the Meaning-Making Cycle into another content area, as participants discuss Classroom Close-Ups of students investigating how an author develops a fictional character in the unit titled "How Far Would You Go to Fit In?" The session highlights writing and gives participants the opportunity to see how writing can support every phase of the meaning-making process. They view a video of a lesson from an inner-city classroom employing "How Far Would You Go to Fit In?" and they analyze how the teacher explicitly teaches the writing skills that students need for content inquiry. Then participants apply what they are learning about the Supported Literacy approach to their own content area.

5. **How do digital and multimedia tools support inquiry? (Chapters One through Three).** This session builds participants' familiarity with a variety of technology tools that can support content inquiry. Teachers try out tools for collecting information such as the Internet and podcasts, tools that represent concepts in varied ways (multimedia presentations, modeling tools, video, photography), tools that facilitate discussion and collaboration (blogging), and composing tools such as word processing, PowerPoint, and writing podcasts. They discuss how to integrate blogging into their classroom and they practice communicating through blogs.

6. **How can you design Supported Literacy lessons? (Chapters Two through Four).** In this session and the one that follows, participants use the Meaning-Making Cycle to design activity and inquiry lessons in their content areas. Participants work on a lesson together in content area groups. They identify an organizing question for the lesson, use the Meaning-Making Cycle to design lessons, and select literacy tools that will help students build meaning. When they return to their schools after this seminar session, participants try out the lesson and plan how to report their results in the subsequent seminar session.

7. **What do successful Supported Literacy lessons look like? (Chapters Two through Five).** Participants continue to explore how they can use the Meaning-Making Cycle to design inquiry lessons in different content areas. In this session, they share their Supported Literacy lessons, get feedback from colleagues,

and plan further ways to design inquiry-oriented activities and lessons using the Supported Literacy approach and literacy tools in their classrooms. They post their activities on the seminar blog.

8. **How can teachers embed assessment within the Meaning-Making Cycle? (Chapters Two through Four).** In this session, participants look at several roles of assessment in designing and teaching a Supported Literacy unit, including diagnostic data, progress monitoring, and culminating or summative assessments. They practice looking at samples of student writing and at videos of student discussion circles and summaries of group work for progress monitoring. They identify possible summative assessments and learn to use protocols for collaboratively looking at student work.

9. **How does Supported Literacy serve struggling adolescent learners? (Chapter Five).** Drawing on a case study of a separate classroom of students with moderate learning disabilities and cognitive delays, participants examine their assumptions about what these students can learn. They follow how a special education teacher who is new to inquiry learning and teaching literature teaches her students a challenging reading and writing strategy—comparison and contrast. Participants "take a microscope" to Ms. Alverez's teaching and discuss which of her scaffolding strategies could be effective in their own mainstream classrooms.

10. **How can teachers identify and respond to reading difficulties in the Supported Literacy classroom? (Chapter Six).** Participants gain an overview of adolescents' reading difficulties, and they learn how to spot those difficulties as their students engage in Supported Literacy inquiry learning. They also acquire strategies to respond to some of these difficulties within the Meaning-Making Cycle. They learn how content teachers and reading specialists collaborate to assess students' reading needs and see examples of the supplementary and intensive reading instruction that their students may need in addition to their regular classroom learning.

11. **How can teachers build and sustain a professional learning community for Supported Literacy? (Chapter Seven).** This session introduces the elements of successful professional learning communities and helps participants identify specific professional development needs, available resources, and ways schools can incorporate professional development and build learning community supports within the daily schedule.

12. **What are next steps for implementing Supported Literacy?** In this session, teachers, literacy coaches, and principals engage in action planning for classroom and schoolwide implementation and for meeting teachers' professional development goals.

A theme of the seminars is how Supported Literacy takes into account and builds on students' current proficiencies in reading, writing, oral discourse, and digital and media fluency. To take full advantage of that theme and to connect seminar material to your classroom, you will want to review your school's reading and writing assessment data. The classroom examples throughout the book are situated in heterogeneous classrooms where students have a wide range of literacy skills; the teachers explicitly teach comprehension or writing strategies and offer additional challenges to students with more advanced skills.

The two Seminar Close-Ups that follow show typical sessions. Both Close-Ups are a part of Seminar 2 ("What literacy tools support twenty-first-century content learning?") because grappling with these tools is an important foundation for implementing Supported Literacy. Together, these Close-Ups make the following points:

- Although peer discussion and writing get less attention than reading in high school and middle school, they provide vibrant tools for building understanding.

- Reading, writing, peer discussion, and digital and media tools work together and reinforce each other in a Supported Literacy classroom.

- The Meaning-Making Cycle is a powerful way to organize teacher learning as well as adolescent learning.

In addition, these Close-Ups include the stories of mathematics and foreign language teachers who tried Meaning-Making Cycles and multiliteracy tools and found them useful. These teachers' results, which they describe in blog entries, were surprising even to the facilitators.

SEMINAR CLOSE-UP

**Using the Meaning-Making Cycle to Support Professional Learning
(Seminar 2, Day 1)**

Barb Reed is not at all sold on the concept of accountable talk. Brow furrowed, she silently puzzles over how peer discussions could possibly help her students understand math texts. When Peter Lee, the seminar facilitator, asks the group to share their experiences with and expectations about peer discussions—as a first step in exploring the benefits of productive student-led discussions in their content areas (engage)—Ms. Reed, a mathematics teacher, is quick to express her concern: "It's great to have students talk together about the material, but then we have to get back to the important information and concepts. They'll get each other off track." She continues, "I pair up my students to work on difficult problems, but I've never used a small group and don't think my eighth graders can handle it." English and language arts teacher Ken Anderson counters, "I've used literature circles for years, to get students to hear each other's interpretations."

After most of the participants have spoken—many expressing reservations about peer discussion—Mr. Lee asks the group to write in their journals to the following prompt: "Do you believe that using student-led discussion circles is a productive way to engage students in meaning making?" (respond) Participants divide into two groups, Doubters and Believers, regardless of their personal viewpoint on the question (elaborate). The two groups then line up facing each other. Each person has two minutes to express a position and some arguments to the person on the opposite side of the line.

Afterward, participants work as a whole group to list the questions and issues about peer discussion groups they surfaced in this exercise (revisit). With Mr. Lee's support, they generate a set of indicators of productive peer discussions, including both the thinking and social skills they expect students to demonstrate (represent; see Table 7.1).

(Continued)

TABLE 7.1. Teacher-Generated Indicators of Productive Discussions.

Demonstrate Social Skills	Demonstrate Thinking Skills
Respect opinions and ideas of peers	Brainstorming
Listen carefully to each other	Evaluating
No cursing, name-calling	Explaining
Normal tone of voice	Analyzing
Participate	Interpreting/making inferences
Take turns; don't dominate conversation	Comparing and contrasting ideas
Show empathy	Sorting ideas
Cooperate	Using critical thinking skills
Set guidelines/norms for group	Revising own thinking
Stay on task and engaged	Giving evidence from text
Use group roles	Looking at things from others' perspectives
Take responsibility for own learning	Synthesizing
Don't disturb other groups	Asking clarifying and open-ended questions
	Probing/questioning
	Providing feedback
	Focusing on questions asked
	Engaging in role playing

Source: EDC, 2003.

Participants try out their list of indicators by using it to analyze a video of four students discussing *My Brother, My Sister, and I* (see Chapter Two). They view the videotape and then use the list of indicators to analyze the discussion in their discussion circles and decide whether it is productive. They return to a whole group follow-up discussion where Mr. Lee introduces specific tools—assigning discussion roles and having students complete self-assessments—that help adolescents structure their accountable talk (revisit).

During this discussion, Ms. Reed has a "eureka moment" that moves her past her doubts about the value of students' discussions with their peers: "I just got it! We've been using peer discussion—accountable talk—ourselves all morning." She realizes that they have been deeply engaged in accountable talk throughout the *Doubters and Believers* activity and their own discussion circles. "We've been working through the Meaning-Making Cycle, and several times we expressed our ideas with each other. The thing is, it works for us, but can our students do this?"

Ms. Reed answers this question by experimenting with using peer discussion circles in teaching her students how to multiply fractions. She describes her experience on the seminar blog, which Mr. Lee set up and demonstrated in an early seminar:

> I am using the discussion circles in my math classroom. From the very beginning, I can see results. My students have been having trouble multiplying fractions and didn't perform well on a quiz. I went back and retaught the concepts. That second time around I used the Supported Literacy approach. To engage them I gave them the prompt, "Find the correct way to multiply two given fractions and show how you solved the problem." After they responded to the question on their own, to see what they could do, I had them justify their reasoning to their peer groups. The groups then decided not only who had the right answer but also who was able to explain their thinking. As the last part of the Meaning-Making Cycle, I gave them another chance to represent their understanding. Then I gave them a second quiz with a new set of multiplication problems to solve on their own. The average test score was 40 percent higher than for the first quiz. When I asked students why they thought they had increased their understanding so significantly, they said having to explain their thinking to their classmates made them think about the problem on a higher level than if they had just listened to me lecture. The students like working in groups. They can learn from one another. They get tired of listening to me! (EDC, 2004a; Clark, 2005)

By embedding peer discussion in a cycle of meaning making, Ms. Reed pushes her students to explain their thinking with each other. Students with a fragile understanding of the content, and particularly English language learners who need to develop academic discourse, benefit from a chance to express their ideas orally; these opportunities can also enhance their reading and writing (Brisk & Harrington, 2007).

The use of analogue experiences—activities that mirror strategies for teaching students—in this session enables teachers who doubt the value of peer discussion to see how such discussions build understanding. If teachers' thinking changes by listening to their colleagues, including their mathematics colleagues, they realize that peer talk may also help their students understand complex content.

SEMINAR CLOSE-UP

Using Writing to Support Changes in Practice (Seminar 2, Day 2)

Mr. Lee welcomes the group back and immediately elicits a chorus of groans: "In our last meeting, we highlighted lots of forms of accountable peer talk. Now, we're going to use several other kinds of literacy tools to understand a challenging article." Today, even Mr. Anderson, the English and language arts teacher who rose to the defense of accountable talk on Day 1, is out of his comfort zone. "Let's not include writing," he pleads, only half joking. "Discussion circles are okay—and reading strategies. Anything but *writing!*" Other teachers laugh and nod.

Mr. Lee knows that teaching writing is difficult for many of the participants, so he has tailored this session so that participants will be writing frequently. They will use many forms of writing, together with reading strategies, accountable talk, and digital and media tools to read an evocative article. The article, "A Sudden Illness: How My Life Changed" (2003), describes how Laura Hillenbrand, author of *Seabiscuit: An American Legend* (2001), coped with a debilitating and undiagnosed chronic fatigue syndrome while she wrote the book.

Teachers plunge into reading the article. Most of them have seen the film that is based on Hillenbrand's book, and they are all intrigued by the theme of illness (engage). In their journals, they answer an open-ended question about the article: "What particularly struck you as interesting, funny, moving, or puzzling about the way the writer told her story?" (respond). Mr. Anderson writes, "I was moved by how Laura could persevere through a fearful illness to research and write such a powerful book." They read and talk about their journal responses with one other person, and then Mr. Lee asks them to extend their journal entries by writing about three new questions:

- How does having a chronic disease shape Laura's life?

- How does writing *Seabiscuit* help her?

- Have you ever faced a difficult situation like Laura's and found a way to move beyond it?

Participants share their reflections and journal writing in discussion circles of four or five other teachers and hold a personally charged discussion that often focuses

(Continued)

on the third question, relating the text to their own lives (elaborate). Afterward, they come back together to discuss the implications of their nervousness about writing (revisit). Mr. Anderson notes, "If I'm uncomfortable reading what I've written, imagine how my students feel." "Yes!" Ms. Reed nods, "I found this whole process—writing on demand—pretty intimidating." Ms. Samuels, an eighth-grade French teacher who is eager to explore ways to connect Supported Literacy practices to her teaching goals, notes, "I never thought of writing as a way of coping with illness!" Participants continue to discuss how their journal entries gave them ideas to contribute to their peer discussions and seemed to be a different kind of writing. As math teacher Ms. Reed describes it, this writing is "just to help me think, not show my terrible writing." They talk about the importance of connecting reading to personal experiences, a proven reading strategy for enhancing understanding that can be used with students and adults alike.

Realizing at a new level how their students may dread writing, participants decide to develop guidelines for creating a more comfortable environment for writing and sharing. They also talk about ways to embed writing in everyday instruction—through the use of journals and science notebooks—to build understanding and increase students' skills and confidence in writing (represent).

Participants also share what they learned from this seminar on their blog (represent). Ms. Samuels, the French teacher, wrote a blog post about using the Meaning-Making Cycle and literacy tools in making sense of a French text.

> We followed our normal procedures, went through our lesson, and then I told the kids that I was going to give them a paragraph to read in French. (We have not been doing a lot of text readings up to this point, just going over basic vocabulary and working on speaking, so this was new to them.) I had chosen a paragraph that was completely in French, but had a few words we had already learned, and also many words which were either spelled the same as in English or were very close.
>
> I conducted this very much like the [science article comprehension] exercise [we did in the Supported Literacy training]: I asked them to read individually for a few minutes, jotting down the words they knew or any ideas about the meaning that they had. Secondly, I asked them to take four minutes to write, in English, as much as possible of what they had read in French. After this, I gave them several minutes to discuss with those around them what they had read, any questions they had, and to try to figure out from others' insights what they didn't understand. After their discussion, I asked them to return to the paragraph, reread it, and change their written translations to reflect what they had learned from the others or from rereading the text. When they had completed [this], I led a group discussion and asked them about the process. Many felt that talking to their classmates had given them new insights into the words

they could not translate at first reading. This was a very successful experiment, and one which motivated my students. They realized how much they really knew (EDC, 2004a).

In sharing her results, Ms. Samuels demonstrates how several multiliteracy tools— reading to understand, writing about a text, and discussing interpretations—work together and reinforce each other. Her story also illustrates how the Meaning-Making Cycle provides a scaffold for integrating these literacy tools. Again, the Cycle is operating at two levels in this seminar—first in the organization of teacher learning, and then afterward in the classroom. Teachers experience the Meaning-Making Cycle process as participants and then engage their students in that process (Clark, 2005).

Phase 2: Collaborative Curriculum Design

Supported Literacy curriculum design is the second phase of building a professional community around the Supported Literacy framework. Curriculum design will build on everything you learn in your Supported Literacy seminars and deepen that understanding as you integrate many literacy tools into one focused unit. The purpose of the unit design is not to provide scripted lessons but to help you think through exactly how to integrate literacy tools into a content inquiry.

Your school might decide to focus on one content area first or to support teacher teams from several content areas to work concurrently on curriculum units. Middle schools that are organized around interdisciplinary teams might decide to use the Supported Literacy curriculum framework to design an interdisciplinary unit. As noted earlier, the "War and Families" unit that Ms. Harris teaches in Chapter Two was designed by a team of language arts and history teachers in collaboration with EDC consultants.

The advantage of having teachers from more than one content area engaged in design is that teams can share ideas about how to teach multiliteracy tools and how to help students understand that a particular tool may work differently in two content areas. For example, summarizing written information about World War II during the "War and Families" unit requires close reading of texts, while summarizing the results of a hands-on science investigation uses some of the same cognitive processes but requires close observation of here-and-now events. Concurrent design across two or more content areas also provides a context for identifying and discussing students' special learning needs including reading difficulties, learning disabilities, and English language proficiency.

Collaborative curriculum design can take place in a summer institute or during the school year. A summer institute is ideal, because it creates an intensive period without distractions in which you and your content area colleagues can think through a unit. Depending on the time and intensity of the summer institute, your design process might need to continue into the fall. A school literacy coach who has participated in or facilitated a Supported Literacy seminar series can facilitate the design process by managing some of the logistics of setting meeting dates, times, and places, and by facilitating design meetings. Alternatively, a Supported Literacy staff person can play that role or serve as a resource. Facilitating the conversation, summarizing design decisions, and observing lessons in several classrooms are all coaching roles that can help make the design process more productive and efficient.

The Curriculum Design Close-Up that follows draws on the actual experiences of the language arts and special education teachers and reading specialists who developed the literature unit "How Far Would You Go to Fit In?" Mr. Stein, the literature teacher in Chapter Four, and Ms. Alverez, the special education teacher in Chapter Five, were members of this design group.

Because they were early participants in the Supported Literacy work, Mr. Stein, Ms. Alverez, and their colleagues did not have the benefit of the full set of seminars and classroom examples we outline in the box at the beginning of the chapter. They did participate in a number of awareness seminars, however, and based on that foundation they developed several curriculum units for use in their school. The teachers' goal was to develop a "living model" of Supported Literacy that would benefit all of the students in their classes. Students were heterogeneously grouped in these language arts classrooms, which included students with mild learning disabilities; as we described in Chapter Five, Ms. Alverez taught the one separate class for students with moderate disabilities. EDC Supported Literacy staff member Mary Whittier, along with Allen Hood, the school's literacy coach, served as co-facilitators of the design process.

The design story that follows is organized around the six components of a Supported Literacy curriculum unit: (1) vision of adolescent learning, (2) essential questions, (3) Meaning-Making Cycles, (4) resources for teaching and learning, (5) twenty-first-century outcomes, and (6) assessments of student understanding. The actual design process was far from sequential, however. The essential questions did not finally crystallize until teachers thought through the outcomes for the unit and designed and taught some trial lessons. Far from surprising, this iterative process of formulating the guiding questions for a unit is typical of thoughtful curriculum design (Zorfass & Copel, 1998).

CURRICULUM DESIGN CLOSE-UP

DEVELOPING A "LIVING MODEL" OF SUPPORTED LITERACY

Vision of Adolescent Learning

"Are we crazy?" Mr. Stein wonders aloud. "Who can really do this inquiry learning? My honors class, yes, but I have several students with learning disabilities, and some very turned-off students!" In the opening days of their summer design workshop, the teachers and specialists voice urgent questions about designing and using a common unit. They discover that they bring different expectations for their students and different kinds of expertise. Co-facilitators Ms. Whittier and Mr. Hood encourage these conversations and offer a kind of resolution. Ms. Whittier suggests, "Let's agree on a few design goals and work together on those." The teachers agree that they will design one unit as their blueprint and adapt it along the way to meet the needs of struggling, typical, and honors students. They will keep a running list of questions and concerns that emerge and devote twenty minutes of each meeting to discussing them. Mr. Hood closes the discussion by noting, "These are *your* essential questions about teaching, to explore as we design, teach, and then evaluate this unit. And we can support each other."

Essential Questions

The work on essential questions begins with a friendly debate between English and language arts colleagues Mr. Stein and Ms. Evans about the content of the questions. Mr. Stein points out, "This is a unit on fiction. We need an essential question that focuses on what is special about fiction." Ms. Evans nods, but reminds him, "We also agreed that we want students to learn how writing can help them understand what they read. That was a big 'Aha!' for me in our orientation seminars." Facilitator Whittier keeps things moving along by pointing out that a unit can be designed around more than one question, and she suggests that they talk about the learning opportunities the novel affords. She offers some criteria for a good essential question: "It focuses you and your students on important language arts content, captivates students' interest, and reflects our state standards. They don't spring forth on our first day."

Over several days, the teachers almost forget their design task as they discuss why the main character, Maleeka, is so drawn to Charlese and lets Charlese bully her. They circle around possible essential questions: "We need to deal with this issue of bullying because it's an issue in the book and happens a lot in school." They discuss author Sharon Flake's decision to write the novel in Maleeka's voice: "They get to hear the inner thoughts of a character who is struggling. An author has choices."

Facilitator Hood suggests that three overarching questions are as much as any one class (and teacher) can handle. He suggests that they formulate one question about the craft of fiction, one about writing, and one about a big human theme that the book explores. They decide on the first two:

- "What writing craft can an author use to create characters and show character development?"

- "How can writing help us understand fiction?"

(Continued)

The third question, about the theme of the book, "wiggles around and doesn't sit still," as special education teacher Ms. Alverez puts it. It is about bullying, or fitting in, or peer pressure. The team members decide they cannot select independent readings without settling on the thematic question and keep the third essential question open while they proceed to design some possible lessons.

Meaning-Making Cycles

As the first step in the lesson design process, the teachers divide the novel into groups of chapters and identify themes and issues for each section. This "chunking" helps them anticipate how many lessons to design. It also surfaces questions about how much they expect students to read in a week, which students need reading accommodations, and whether they will let students take the books home.

Teachers reread and journal about each chunk, and they share their insights in discussion circles where they build ideas in their own "accountable talk." As they surface their own questions and identify themes, they keep track of specific scenes and passages that they consider evidence of these themes. "These notes are a mess, but we need to do this," Ms. Evans says, looking at their "group write" in which they brainstorm possible discussion and writing prompts. Table 7.2 shows some of their board notes.

TABLE 7.2. **Notes from Teacher Brainstorming Session.**

Pages/Chapters	Discussion/Writing Prompts
Pages 1–49, Chapters 1–9	How does Maleeka see herself? Quote on p. 19 How does Maleeka struggle with the idea that she wants to be treated better? How does Maleeka try to fit in? Quote on p. 48 Why is Ms. Saunders such a threat? Quote on p. 49 Can goodness in you be seen as a handicap?
Pages 50–75, Chapters 10–17	How does Maleeka's mother influence how M sees herself? Compare/contrast Charlese—Maleeka's "poor" home life Mother and relationship • depression/father's death • role reverse. M takes care of Mother Does Charlese have a better life? Does Maleeka have a choice when it comes to peer pressure?

This brainstorming session helps the teachers come to some agreement about how they will start the unit. Hearing in Maleeka's voice how she doubts herself, the teachers want to connect students in a vibrant way to the ideas that how we see ourselves affects our relationships. Because they want students to start sharing ideas with each other right away ("So they don't wait for the right interpretation from us," says Mr. Stein), they also want to plunge students into the idea of talking with each other in discussion circles. As shown in the next box, they decide that their first lesson will be a pre-lesson that connects students to the theme of self-image and prepares them for peer discussions. These decisions lead to a lesson design that is a precursor of the final unit design in Appendix B. Only later did teachers decide to develop a unit blog to encourage students to bring their work to students beyond the school.

PRE-LESSON: TALKING ABOUT HOW WE SEE OURSELVES

To prepare for reading *The Skin I'm In,* students write journal entries about how they see themselves and then create self-portrait collages. Before they write, the teacher does a mini-lesson to demonstrate the process, thinking aloud about what the self-portrait is trying to communicate, then emphasizes that the purpose of journaling is to notice our thoughts (engage, respond).

Students take their journal entries to their discussion circles, where they first list norms for participating and then try to follow those norms as they discuss their self-portraits in their circle. They talk about the characteristics they chose to focus on in their portraits (elaborate).

Someone from each group summarizes some of the positive qualities students chose to convey (revisit). The teacher facilitates conversation about how people's self-image might affect how they relate to others. The teacher works with students to set up a section of their existing class blog for their work on the unit (represent).

Participants design several more lessons around the Meaning-Making Cycle during their summer work. In the fall, they try out the pre-lesson—"to see if we're on the right track," Mr. Stein comments—while they continue to design the unit. The design-teach-evaluate process enables them to fine-tune the unit, and sometimes they jettison ideas. "If a teaching strategy doesn't work for any of us, we'll give it up!" says Ms. Alverez.

(Continued)

It's only after they try out several lessons that they settle on the wording of the third essential question. An important part of this process is revisiting the first few chunks of the novel and clearly seeing the craft Flake uses to reveal Maleeka's struggle with fitting in. Ms. Evans comments, "There it is on this page, where Charlese makes Maleeka take off the clothes Char gave her. Maleeka says to herself, 'Enough is enough. I deserve better than for people to treat me any old way they want.' Then she says, 'But saying that is one thing, making it happen is something else.' Then she struggles for months to accept herself and to stand up for herself. *There's our theme!*"

They word the third essential question this way:

- Why can it be hard for an individual to fit in? What choices do people have when they are being harassed?

Having the essential questions in place helps the team to shape the rest of the lessons and to decide on other readings.

Resources for Teaching and Learning

With the essential questions settled, the team agrees that they will add an informational reading about bullying and harassment to build students' background knowledge of this problem. They select readings for their own information and for their students that identify the roles of aggressor, target, and bystander and ways to respond to bullying (EDC, 2004b). They decide to broaden the theme of fitting in to include the experiences and perspectives of immigrant teens because of the diversity of languages and countries of origin of students in the school. They choose a short story collection, *First Crossing: Stories About Teen Immigrants* (Gallo, 2004), and they decide that students will select one story to read on their own and discuss from time to time in "book alike" discussion circles. For themselves, the teachers read articles about teaching comprehension strategies, including a research report from Supported Literacy with examples of how to embed comprehension strategies in journal prompts (Morocco et al., 2001). A summary of what they read is presented in Table 7.3.

TABLE 7.3. Embedding Comprehension Strategies in Journal Prompts.

Comprehension Strategies	Sample Journal Prompts
Ask themselves what they know about a topic.	Think of a time when you had to make an important choice. What were your possible choices? What did you choose? What were the consequences of your choices?
Predict what the story will be about.	Focus first on the outside of the book, back and front. What do you predict this book will be about?

Comprehension Strategies	Sample Journal Prompts
Summarize what they have read so far.	Char calls Maleeka an ugly geek in front of other kids and lets another girl attack Maleeka for something Char did. What's going on? How can we summarize what we know about Maleeka's dilemma?
Pose and respond to questions.	What are Maleeka's relationships like? Who are her friends? Use what you know from a close reading of scenes with that character—what do they say and do? How do they relate to Maleeka? And use your imagination to create something in their voice.
Visualize what the author is describing.	Think about what Maleeka sees in herself and visualize—see in your mind—what Maleeka's self-portrait might look like and how it might change.

Source: Adapted from Morocco et al., 2001.

At this point in their planning, they decide that it will be a good idea for classes to create blogs to broaden the audience for students' writing beyond the school. Mr. Stein knows that several of his students have their own blogs and have far more expertise than he does: "They might as well know the truth: I am totally clueless when it comes to blogging. But, you know what? I'll give it a shot and I bet that some of them can set up the blogs in a way that will really make sense and be used by all, including me! Hey, look how popular MySpace is."

Twenty-First-Century Outcomes

The teachers list several unit outcomes when they begin the design process, and they refine the list as the unit design progresses. They identify at least one outcome for each of the big twenty-first-century competencies and at least one outcome for each of the multiliteracies. However, they focus most on building in writing tools and explicit teaching of those tools. They decide that students will write during every class period and that they will build comprehension strategies into the journal prompts they give students. Because students have to write supported argument essays in their state reading tests, they build this formal genre into the unit. They ask co-facilitators Ms. Whittier and Mr. Hood to do a day-long workshop in the fall on how to teach argument writing. Ms. Evans insists, "Make us do it! We're English teachers, but we don't teach this" (see Chapter Four for a box presenting the full set of unit outcomes).

(Continued)

Assessments of Student Understanding

Early on in the summer design institute, teachers discuss their students' level of reading proficiency. They plot the scores for both seventh and eighth grades and pinpoint students already receiving additional reading support. The seventh-grade teachers share information and writing samples from some of their students with the receiving eighth-grade teachers. Mr. Hood takes on the role, during the unit design, of anticipating reading problems and building in support ideas.

Teachers make notes for each lesson on how they will look for evidence of understanding of the major essential questions in students' journals and discussion circles. In the fall workshop on supported argument writing, they struggle with their own essays, look at models the facilitators bring, and examine national and state scoring rubrics to adapt one to fit their needs.

While teachers share the goal of learning how to teach supported argument writing, they continue—throughout the design process and over the next months, as they teach and reflect on the lessons—to pursue individual goals for their own teaching. Mr. Stein works to become comfortable with the many roles of writing in the unit; Ms. Alverez works to teach her students how to read a novel. And not everyone makes drastic changes. They all agree that the most striking part of the design experience was their collaboration and mutual support and the ways they could bring different kinds of expertise and professional goals of their own (Hindin et al., 2007).

In your curriculum design processes, you and your colleagues will also think through your vision, essential questions, Meaning-Making Cycles, resources for teaching and learning, twenty-first-century outcomes, and assessments of student understanding. You will decide how and when to teach the multiliteracy skills students need to read for deep understanding, to write to build and express meaning, to engage in accountable talk, and to build digital and media fluency. The units you develop will bring together a research-based framework with your own invention, enabling you to meet your teaching needs and prepare your students for inquiry learning.

To engage in this two-phase process of building a Supported Literacy community, however, you will need a persistent and energetic commitment from your school principal and other school leaders. In the next section, we present a set of guidelines for leadership that builds a Supported Literacy learning community.

PROVIDING LEADERSHIP FOR SUPPORTED LITERACY

The second pillar for the successful implementation of Supported Literacy in your school is shared leadership. Nothing is more important in promoting improvements in teaching and learning than leaders who have actively dedicated themselves to the goals for change because they are infused with a sense of moral purpose to enable every student to learn (Fullan, 2003). Such leaders believe in "having a system where all of your students learn, the gap between high and low performance becomes greatly reduced and what your students learn enables them to be successful citizens and workers in a morally based knowledge society" (p. 29).

You and a few other teachers and a literacy coach within your school can initiate the change process and the development of a learning community. But without a sufficient number of supporters within the school and ardent championship by your principal, changes will be difficult to sustain. Shared leadership is the most powerful, sustainable way to enhance school and classroom practices to improve student learning (DuFour & Eaker, 1998; Lambert, 1990).

To provide this critical shared leadership for Supported Literacy, we recommend that your school, if it does not already have one, create a Literacy Leadership Team that includes the principal and other members of the school's administrative staff, the literacy coach, and teacher leaders like yourself from each of the content areas. The Literacy Leadership Team can assume a number of roles that will support you and other teachers in successfully implementing Supported Literacy across the content areas. These roles include

- Develop and articulate a clear vision of what students should know and be able to do (such as preparing adolescents for life and work in the twenty-first century).

- Engage in planning and providing resources, including supportive organizational arrangements as well as time, people, equipment, space, and assistance.

- Arrange for or provide ongoing professional development.

- Engage in monitoring and evaluation using a wide variety of aggregated and disaggregated data at the school, classroom, and student level.

- Respond effectively to emerging concerns and issues (Hall & Hord, 2001; Louis & Miles, 1990).

Develop and Articulate a Clear Vision

Your school's Literacy Leadership Team needs to understand the Supported Literacy framework so that members can plan with teachers how to incorporate Supported Literacy into the school culture and into content area classrooms. One way for your team to get ready to implement Supported Literacy is by participating in the twelve-session seminar series described earlier in this chapter. Supported Literacy works best as a whole-school change model. Your leadership team is responsible for making sure that all their colleagues, as well as parents and other members of the community, have a clear vision of what it means to prepare adolescents for the twenty-first century and how multiliteracy skills can enhance student learning across the content areas.

One way to get buy-in from your content area colleagues is for them to learn the essentials of the Meaning-Making Cycle. By using the cycle in a few of their lessons and monitoring results, teachers in history, science, and math can begin to see how the skills provide tools for deep understanding of important content and learning that is fueled by essential questions and motivates students to investigate and learn. Another way to motivate and engage teachers is to focus on one of the multiliteracies, such as writing to build and express understanding or accountable talk. Teachers from across the curriculum might participate in a seminar on peer-led discussions, for example, and then apply this strategy in their classrooms and share their experiences. Witnessing their students participate in lively, thoughtful discussions of meaningful content is likely to whet teachers' appetite for implementing Supported Literacy.

Engage in Planning and Providing Resources

Your school's Literacy Leadership Team has overall responsibility for coordinating appropriate and timely professional development for Supported Literacy. This involves arranging for trained Supported Literacy staff to deliver the necessary professional development and ongoing support. It also includes providing the necessary time and space for teachers to engage in professional development activities and collaborate with each other, as well ensuring that teachers have the materials, equipment, and other resources they need to implement the approach. It is not easy to allocate time for professional development institutes, workshops, and collaborative planning in middle and high schools. Yet it is essential for changing teacher practice and improving student learning. As we noted in Chapter Six, some of your students might need intensive support to learn the basic foundation skills required for reading. Your leadership team needs to find and coordinate resources (staff, time, and money) to support these struggling students, who may need individual diagnostic assessments and additional Supported Literacy Intensive tutorials.

Arrange for or Provide Ongoing Professional Development

Your school's Literacy Leadership Team is charged with developing and coordinating Supported Literacy professional development activities. For Supported Literacy to be effective, the team needs to ensure equitable access to professional development opportunities for all teachers including special education teachers, teachers of English language learners, and other specialists. The team must also provide the structures and training for you, other teachers, and reading specialists to work together to respond effectively to students with reading difficulties.

The Literacy Leadership Team must also work to build and sustain a professional learning community and a culture of innovation and change by providing structured, institutionalized time for you and other teachers and coaches to interact within the school schedule on a regular daily or weekly basis. One way to ensure productive use of teachers' time in study groups is to ask teachers to take on various roles, such as the chair, who sets the agenda with input from others; a facilitator, who runs the meeting and ensures that everyone has a voice; a timekeeper, who keeps the group on schedule; and a recorder, who takes notes and shares them after the meeting. Teachers also benefit from having a set of focus questions. ("Which students are struggling with writing in your classroom?" "Who is struggling with reading?" "What particular difficulties are you observing?" "What questions do you have about these students?") Using structured protocols also helps teachers collaborate effectively. For example, a teacher can learn one of a number of procedures for assessing students' understanding by looking at their work (Blythe, Allen, & Powell, 2008).

Skilled literacy coaches and teacher leaders are also a key ingredient in the successful implementation of Supported Literacy. These individuals can help provide professional development activities and facilitate ongoing teacher learning. According to a joint report prepared by four major professional associations representing language arts, mathematics, science, and social studies (IRA et al., 2006), effective literacy coaches at the secondary level have the following characteristics:

- Skilled collaborators who function effectively in middle or high school settings

- Skilled instructional coaches for secondary teachers in the core content areas of English language arts, mathematics, science, and social studies

- Skilled evaluators of literacy needs within various content areas who can collaborate with leadership teams and teachers to interpret and use assessment data to inform instruction

- Accomplished secondary school teachers who are skilled in developing and implementing instructional strategies to improve academic literacy in their specific content area

If you are a coach or other teacher leader who wants to contribute to your school's Supported Literacy effort, you must participate actively in initial professional development activities so that you understand the approach and experience it firsthand. Once you are fully trained, you can help conduct professional development activities so that other teachers can learn the Supported Literacy approach. You can also facilitate teacher meetings during which you and your colleagues plan Supported Literacy lessons and curriculum units, evaluate the results, and discuss changes needed to improve their practice. In addition, you can visit teachers' classrooms to demonstrate ways of teaching and integrating multiliteracy tools to build content understanding.

Engage in Monitoring and Evaluation

Your school's Literacy Leadership Team will support you in gathering informal assessments by examining your students' writing, observing their peer discussions, talking with students individually, and assessing exhibitions or projects. The team can also facilitate the collection and analysis of formal reading and writing assessment data and share that data with staff to enhance instruction and improve student outcomes. This combination of progress monitoring (formative) and summative assessment strategies can help your school make informed decisions about the professional development activities and other supports you and other teachers need for success.

In addition, Literacy Leadership Team members need to take responsibility for learning the Supported Literacy approach to varied content areas by observing in classrooms and talking with you to better understand how you use the Meaning-Making Cycle and other Supported Literacy practices. One of the principals in the Massachusetts schools participating in the development of Supported Literacy found that classroom observations were among the most powerful forms of feedback. The principal came to an after-school teacher meeting to say that he had never heard such extended and deep discussions of literature as he observed in the Supported Literacy classroom. When teachers came to a school board and community meeting to talk about their Supported Literacy work, the principal described what he was seeing in classrooms and why the approach was building literacy skills *and* content understanding. By communicating results to everyone in the school community and the larger community as well, the leadership team can note successes and enlist support in the continuous improvement process.

Respond Effectively to Emerging Concerns and Issues

Effective leadership requires understanding the change process that teachers go through in implementing a new initiative like Supported Literacy and making supportive changes where necessary. Researchers (Hall & Hord, 2001; Louis & Miles, 1990) find that responsive leaders hold these beliefs about change:

- Change is an ongoing process, not a short-term event, and requires persistence.

- As people implement a new initiative like Supported Literacy, their concerns and needs change, so professional development needs to change accordingly. Moreover, people go through change at different rates and in different ways, and learning opportunities must allow for that variation.

- All successful schools experience an "implementation dip." Effective leaders understand that this dip is caused by people experiencing two things: the fear of change and the "lack of technical know-how or skills to make the change work." Teachers need coaching and other professional development opportunities to address these problems.

- Leaders need to proactively identify and address staff concerns to minimize resistance to change (Fullan, 2001; Hall & Hord, 2001).

Successful leaders understand that the change process is complex and nonlinear, so they expect to experience setbacks. They are willing and able to solve problems when they do arise.

MOVING FORWARD: AN EVOLVING FRAMEWORK FOR THE FUTURE

Supported Literacy works to build learning communities at several levels—in your classroom, in your school, in school reform communities, and at a global level.

Your Classroom

Within your classroom, your students collaborate to read about and investigate big questions that matter in the content areas. Those questions also matter outside the classroom—not just in their neighborhoods but in the larger world your students are stepping into. In learning the power of putting their minds together rather than mainly competing as individuals, your students learn that the most difficult and important questions require information, careful thinking, and varied viewpoints. They understand that solutions are based not only on analysis of information but also on creative invention. Supported Literacy enables students to develop a shared language that they can use to talk about their thinking and the tools that help them.

Your School

Supported Literacy connects you with your colleagues by providing you with a common set of principles and practices that you can adapt to your discipline. As with students, Supported Literacy enables you to develop a shared language; you use this language with your colleagues—to talk about your content area teaching goals and how to be more successful with every student. In a profession where practitioners tend to stay within their own classrooms—and certainly within their content areas—Supported Literacy offers a framework where you can talk with colleagues throughout the school about the students you are all teaching. You can communicate about the reading, writing, discussion, and digital media tools that enable your students to be agile learners within and across content areas.

School Reform Communities

Supported Literacy offers a framework and shared vision for creating twenty-first-century schools where adolescents are competent and creative thinkers. In a reform world that often shifts from building skills to exploring ideas, Supported Literacy emphasizes skills that can serve as tools for rigorous investigation. The approach to teaching, learning, and curriculum design that teachers use in this book articulates with policy demands from the business world; the careers of the twenty-first century call for a marriage of conceptual understanding and creative thinking with social responsibility.

In a world where all of our futures hang together, Supported Literacy suggests that addressing important questions can lead to purposeful investigations and problem solving. Supported Literacy calls into question government policies that define outcomes and assessments too narrowly or emphasize reading to the exclusion of the other multiliteracies. The framework's emphasis on building communities of teachers who can design curricula together challenges the paucity of government funds directed to these purposes.

Global Level

Supported Literacy and other approaches that emphasize collaborative inquiry can have an impact beyond our own communities. As presumptuous as it might sound, when your students engage in thinking together about issues as complex and far-reaching as global warming, immigration, the impact of war, and an individual's struggles to fit into her local culture, they catalyze global connections. Adolescents already possess broader, more global identities than their parents because of the diverse cultures they represent and the ways they use technologies to connect beyond school, community, and national borders. Supported Literacy builds on that global mobility to prepare adolescents to take on unlimited roles in the changing kinds of business, scientific, artistic, and social environments that are becoming the workplace of the twenty-first century.

AN EVOLVING FRAMEWORK

Because the world truly is changing—in ways that are both dangerous and potentially liberating and hopeful—adolescents need to acquire ways of thinking and tools for asking questions, understanding, and communicating with others. If Supported Literacy is a useful framework, it means that it can evolve to respond to new questions and new literacy needs. The multiliteracy skills we outline in Chapter One and illustrate throughout the book do not form a fixed set. They will change and expand as new fields of study and new technologies become available. As you tailor the unit design framework for your students, you, too, will emphasize different and additional essential questions and inquiry tools.

We hope that this book creates fertile ground for teacher dialogue within and across your content areas. We want you to consider the implications for English language learners of integrating oral discourse activities with reading and writing in Supported Literacy classrooms. As you seek to meet the needs of the students in your increasingly culturally diverse classrooms, we want you to explore how global essential questions and important curriculum topics enable your newcomer students to bring their unique experiences and perspectives into the meaning-making process. We want your school to see the value of giving students the responsibility and tools they need to tackle issues—such as war and climate change—that they think about daily. We believe that motivation to read, write, talk, think, and use the Internet responsibly will follow.

In Chapters Five and Six, we devote a relatively small amount of space to talking about how Supported Literacy offers a context for providing special support to students with reading and learning difficulties. We were only able to begin to show you how you can use the Meaning-Making Cycle as a scaffolding for differentiating support to students. We have not been able to follow individual learners in depth in this book, and while Ms. Alverez's classroom (Chapter Five) provides a glimpse of how a special education teacher can help students with cognitive disabilities beat the odds and engage in intellectually challenging and personally fascinating learning, there are many more stories yet to be told. You can contribute to these Close-Ups as you explore and communicate with other teachers and coaches in and beyond your school.

Finally, by showing you these classrooms, we hope we are helping you realize there are no limits to what your students can learn if they see themselves as contributors to change. We can't predict their adult futures, but we can captivate their imaginations with dynamic questions. We can create opportunities for them to think and learn with other students, using multiliteracy skills that they can hone the rest of their lives.

KEY TERMS

Blog: A log of one's thoughts, ideas, and questions that is posted on a Web site.

Critical Inquiry: An active, analytic learning process and the way a democratic society examines and renews itself. The linking of the personal development that happens with inquiry with social critique and action.

Decodable Text: Text that is age-appropriate in content but contains decoding patterns and rules that teachers have already taught or words that the students have learned as sight word vocabulary.

Discourses: The norms for how members of groups participate, interact, and use language in different contexts (drawn from the work of Gee; see the term *New Literacy Research* below).

Discourse of Science: Organizing claims and evidence into arguments expressed in a scientific way of talking or writing.

E-book: An electronic book—the digital media equivalent of a conventional printed book.

Essential Questions: A key component of the *Supported Literacy framework,* these are broad questions that are important in a discipline and that propel students into exploring a broad landscape of information and issues. Can include questions that content area experts continue to grapple with without finding final answers, as well as children's naive questions.

Inquiry: An active learning process in which individuals gain knowledge by trying to find answers to important questions.

Meaning-Making Cycle: The Supported Literacy cycle of critical inquiry that moves students through a process of building understanding, using the multiliteracies as their tools. Includes the following steps: engage, respond, elaborate, revisit, and represent.

Metacognition or Metacognitive Awareness: The "ability to monitor one's current level of skill or understanding and decide when it is not adequate" (Bransford et al., p. 47).

Millennials: The name for the generation born between 1982 and 1998.

Multiliteracies: Intellectual tools and techniques that enable learners to access, process, and communicate information and ideas. These include reading for deep understanding, writing to build and express meaning, accountable talk, and digital and media fluency.

Multimedia Messages: Key points communicated through sound and image.

Multiple Literacies: Competence in using new technologies such as digital texts, Internet search engines, film and video, and integrated multimedia presentations.

Nativism: Local people's fears that immigrants will disrupt their jobs and way of life.

New Literacy Research: A branch of research that examines the social contexts in which literacy occurs and the *discourses* that people use within these contexts.

Podcasting: A method of publishing audiovisual or plain audio presentations via the Internet so that users can download and watch or listen to them at will. Individual presentations are called podcasts.

Progress Monitoring: Using students' performance data to continually evaluate the effectiveness of teaching and to permit a teacher to make more informed instructional decisions.

Science Literacy: The knowledge and understanding of scientific concepts and processes required for personal decision making, participation in civic and cultural affairs, and economic productivity.

Supported Literacy Framework: An instructional framework to guide students' classroom learning, as well as a curriculum framework to create rigorous new units in any subject or to modify and enrich existing units to better address the twenty-first-century competencies. The framework contains six components: Vision, Essential Questions, Meaning-Making Cycles, Resources for Teaching and Learning, Outcomes, and Assessment.

Supported Literacy Intensive Tutorial: Small group tutorials in which teachers engage homogenous groups of students in mastering phonemic awareness, phonics skills, and sight word vocabulary—with practice to build fluency—to accelerate their reading skills as quickly as possible and to enable them to benefit from content area instruction.

Twenty-First-Century Competencies: Multiliteracies, conceptual understanding, critical thinking, creative thinking, and collaboration and communication.

Vision of Supported Literacy: Key beliefs that guide you in using the *Supported Literacy framework:* (1) Students are capable of engaging in critical inquiry into important questions in the traditional content areas and newer global content. (2) Students can gather, analyze, and synthesize information in science, history, or literature. (3) Students build conceptual understanding by thinking critically about what they read and using creative thinking to connect concepts. (4) When students work collaboratively with each other, they learn to listen and communicate with others in many different ways.

Visual Texts: Texts that integrate graphs, data tables, still media images and photographs, and moving images to convey information. Students need to know how to read and interpret visual texts; writing strategies can help them do so. To keep pace with the demands of the twenty-first-century workplace, students also need to be able to create visual texts to represent their knowledge and to express their ideas.

Web Quests: Guided information searches on the Internet.

APPENDIX

LESSON UNIT FOR "UNDERSTANDING CLIMATE CHANGE"

Essential Question 1. What climate changes are taking place? What is the evidence?

Lesson 1: What do we know about the "big picture" of climate change?	Students write about what they currently know about climate change in their science notebooks. They view and discuss photographs comparing glaciers in different parts of the world from earlier years to present times. They start building a list of questions they have about climate change. After viewing selected chapters of the DVD *An Inconvenient Truth,* they write about what they saw and discuss their responses in their discussion circles. The class adds new questions to the class list.
Lesson 2: How do we interpret climate change data?	The class clarifies the terms *weather* and *climate* and discusses the weather and climate of their area. The teacher models how to read and interpret climate charts and graphs and then has students work with partners to interpret climate data from New Hampshire and Arizona. Students compare interpretations of the climate data in their discussion circles. Each group researches climate data for a new state and presents this information in a poster session for the class.

Essential Question 2. What causes climate change? How do humans contribute?

Lesson 3: What makes Earth habitable?

Students read and talk about how the greenhouse effect contributes to making life possible on Earth. They draw diagrams to show their understanding of what happens to the Sun's light energy that is transmitted to Earth. Then students read about the greenhouse effect and add this additional information to their drawings. In discussion circles and follow-up class discussion, students clarify how the reflectivity of different surfaces influences heat absorption and climate in different regions.

Lesson 4: How does the greenhouse effect influence climate?

Students perform and analyze an experiment that compares the amount of heat energy absorbed by carbon dioxide to the amount of heat energy absorbed by air. They write up their lab results and relate their findings to the greenhouse effect in Earth's atmosphere.

Lesson 5: Who is to blame? What are the natural versus human contributions?

Students learn about both natural and human contributions to the greenhouse effect. Each discussion circle studies a different natural or human process (carbon flux) that affects the inflow and outflow of Earth's carbon. Then students teach each other the flux processes. The class constructs a drawing that shows how each carbon flux process affects the flow of carbon into and out of the atmosphere. Then students interpret reports of long-term data about carbon emissions and relate them to reported global warming data.

Lesson 6: How can we evaluate what we read about global warming?

Students use criteria (such as credible source, date, evidence included) to compare and evaluate several articles about global warming and climate change. They write an analysis comparing two different articles and they describe, in writing, one piece of evidence for climate change. To summarize their thinking about this essential question, they write about their understanding of the carbon cycle and human contributions to climate change.

Essential Question 3. What are the impacts of climate change?

Lesson 7: How is climate change affecting different regions of the world?	Students respond in writing to *Bogus or Believe It?* statements about the impacts of global warming and then do a class value line for several statements, explaining their position on the value line. Each team does Internet research on the impacts of climate change for a different region of the United States or the world. Students develop a multimedia presentation for the class. As groups present, the class tracks and summarizes the impacts across sectors such as agriculture, water, health, and biodiversity in order to understand global effects.

Essential Question 4. What can be done about climate change?

Lesson 8: How can we limit our contributions to the greenhouse effect?	Students read and discuss an article about the human impact on global warming trends. They calculate their family carbon footprints using an Internet calculator Web site and calculate the auto emissions for their state using online auto data and a worksheet. They identify measures to reduce carbon dioxide emissions and create an ad campaign, multimedia presentation, or podcast to influence others in the school and community.

APPENDIX

LESSON UNIT FOR "HOW FAR WOULD YOU GO TO FIT IN?"

ESSENTIAL QUESTIONS

Why can it be hard for an individual to fit in? What choices do people have when they are being harassed?

What writing craft can an author use to create characters and show character development?

How can writing help us understand fiction?

Lesson	Description
Pre-assessment: Writing a Supported Argument About Fiction	To assess students' skills in supporting an interpretation of a piece of fiction, Mr. Stein assigns them a section of Richard Wright's novel *Black Boy,* in which the mother bars her young son from the house until he stands up to neighborhood bullies who are stealing his grocery money. Students write the essay without having had any instruction in this kind of writing, so Mr. Stein can see how they do. He will use this to guide him in teaching supported argument writing later in the unit.
Pre-lesson: How do we see ourselves?	To prepare for reading *The Skin I'm In,* students write journal entries about how they see themselves and create self-portrait collages. Students bring their journal entries to their discussion circles. They list norms for participating in the circles and try to follow those norms as they discuss their self-portraits. They talk about the characteristics they chose to focus on in their portraits and discuss how people's self-images might affect how they relate to others. Students set up a class blog with the theme of Teens Fitting In so that they can post their writing and receive replies over the course of the unit.
Lesson 1. How does Maleeka see herself? (Chapter 1)	Students examine the front and back covers of *The Skin I'm In* and write predictions about what Maleeka is like. Mr. Stein asks students to share what they think is the purpose of journaling and does a mini-lesson to demonstrate the idea that journaling helps a person think. He comments that predicting is one kind of thinking that good readers do, and he notes that writing their predictions down is a way to help them understand this novel. Students read the first chapter and journal about what they think Maleeka sees in herself and what Maleeka's self-portrait might look like, based on Maleeka's thoughts about herself. They bring their journal entries to their discussion circles and read and talk about them. Groups discuss how people's views of themselves can affect their relationships, and they predict what Maleeka's relationships might be like.
Lesson 2. What are Maleeka's relationships like? How does the author show us? (Chapters 2–4)	Students share their journal responses to a question about what makes a good relationship and sketch a web diagram of Maleeka's relationships. Then students each select one character in Maleeka's life and use their journals to describe what they know about the character and how Maleeka and this

Lesson	Description
	person treat each other. They also note in their journals how the author shows Maleeka's relationship with the character. In their discussion circles, they review a self-assessment tool for guiding their roles in peer discussion circles. Then, with their discussion partners, they discuss their character's relationship with Maleeka. In the follow-up class discussion, they annotate a web of Maleeka's relationships. Finally, the students each rate their own performance in the discussion circle with the self-assessment tool.
Lesson 3. How can dramatizing characters help us understand them? (Chapters 5–8)	Students deepen their understanding of a character's perspective by dramatizing key scenes from the novel. By taking a small scene and asking students to play it in different ways, Mr. Stein introduces the idea that the actors are expressing their interpretations of the characters. They justify their interpretations by pointing to passages where the author provides information about the character's way of relating to Maleeka. Students read their scenes individually and then discuss and practice their scenes in their discussion circles. For homework, Mr. Stein asks students to take on the point of view of one of the characters and write a monologue expressing what their character is thinking and feeling in the scene. To teach them the monologue form, he rereads some passages that show the character's behavior and he thinks aloud about the character. Then he talks about the author, and writes a monologue on the board as he speaks in her voice.
Lesson 4. What dilemmas about fitting in does the author portray? (Chapters 9–10)	Students share their monologues in pairs, and a few volunteers read their monologues aloud to the class. They volunteer to post their monologues on the class blog. Students write in their journals, listing and posing questions about the dilemmas Maleeka faces for the class to discuss, particularly why she lets Char control her and draw her into violence. The class then reviews this list of questions and selects two questions to discuss in a fish bowl format. Students in the inner circle discuss the questions, while students in the outer circle listen and then discuss what they learned or found interesting. Students summarize Maleeka's dilemmas in a group list.

Lesson	Description
Lesson 5. What are Maleeka's possible choices? (Chapters 11–12)	Students construct a web of the kinds of choices they must make in their lives and what distinguishes good and bad choices. They create a time line of Maleeka's choices and consequences, with each discussion circle taking a different set of chapters. Mr. Stein uses a mini-lesson to explain how constructing a time line is a strategy for seeing how the author shows change in a character or situation over time. He also describes how a time line can help a reader connect important scenes. Students integrate their time lines into one big time line for Chapters 1–12 (they will continue to add to this time line throughout the rest of the unit). They review the time line, analyze the progression of Maleeka's choices in those chapters, discuss the results of those choices, and decide whether her choices are positive or negative.
Lesson 6. What choices do we have when someone we know is being bullied? (Reading)	Students read and discuss an informational article that defines bullying and the ways that others can respond when someone is being victimized. The article argues that bystanders provide direct and indirect support for violence when they instigate, encourage, or passively accept bullying behavior. Students discuss who are the aggressors and bystanders in the scenes they have read so far, including John John, Charlese, and Ms. Saunders. They discuss the role they think Ms. Saunders is playing in Maleeka's struggle to respond to bullying and to stand up for herself. They write individual journal entries about bullying situations they know about and what roles people played in responding. Several students post their entries on the class blog.
Lesson 7. How do characters differ in the ways they cope with fitting in? (Chapters 13–16)	Mr. Stein demonstrates how to use the compare-and-contrast comprehension strategy so that students can use it to help them understand why Maleeka lets Char control her. In a writing lesson, he thinks aloud as he uses the strategy on a topic unrelated to the book. Then he demonstrates how to use a Venn diagram to compare and contrast the two characters. Students organize and write a short essay in which they compare the two students around the questions, "How are Maleeka and Char similar and different?" and "Which one is stronger?" As a class, students discuss their responses and their definitions of *strong*.

Lesson	Description
Lesson 8. How can writing help us resolve a dilemma? (Chapters 17–19)	Students review Maleeka's diary entry for Chapter 5 and journal about why the diary is important to Maleeka. In discussion circles, students review the rest of Maleeka's diary entries through Chapter 19 and discuss what Maleeka's diary persona (Akeelma) might have to do with Maleeka's current life. Does Akeelma have any choice in her fate as a slave? Group reporters summarize their discussions and students discuss how keeping a diary might be helping Maleeka change her relationships and her view of herself. Students discuss how their own regular writing in their journals might be helping them think about the essential question of the unit.
Lesson 9. How can adults help students with dilemmas of fitting in? (Chapters 20–23)	Students write in their journals about an important adult who has helped them become a strong individual. A few volunteers share responses from their journals about the important adults in their lives. The class discusses the qualities that make these relationships important. In discussion circles, students talk about the relationships that Maleeka and Char have with adults in their lives, and they debate the qualities that make each relationship helpful or limiting. Discussion groups share ideas with the whole class and consider how adults can help adolescents respond to harassment and with conflicts related to fitting in. Students begin writing a letter to an important adult in their own lives that describes how this person has been helpful to their growth as an individual. Students post some of their letters on the class blog. Students from a school in another city who are also reading fiction on the theme of fitting in post comments with some of their essays.
Lesson 10. Why does Maleeka engage in vandalism? What clues does the author give us? (Chapters 24–26)	Student pairs do a *Doubters and Believers* activity in which they take opposite positions about whether or not Maleeka had a choice about engaging in the vandalism with Char. Students take a closer look at Maleeka's choices in Chapters 24–26, consider the options she had at each point, and consider why Maleeka might have made the choices she did. They look closely at scenes before and during the vandalism and discuss what the author shows us about Maleeka. They also discuss what Maleeka should do, whether Maleeka should be punished, and why people might engage in vandalism when they believe it is wrong.

Lesson	Description
Lesson 11. How can we support an interpretation in writing? (Full Book)	Mr. Stein prepares students to write a supported position essay by giving them a format for the essay and then thinking aloud about a topic of his own. Students reread the final chapters and, as a group, they practice how they would use the supported position format to write about the question, "Should Maleeka be punished for her role in the vandalism?" Mr. Stein assigns students to choose one of the other open-ended questions they have been discussing about Maleeka and plan and write a supported position essay for the class. Possible questions include: "Did Maleeka have a choice in engaging in vandalism?" "Should she tell on Charlese?" "Does Maleeka change in her way of fitting in?" Students work with a writing buddy to give and receive feedback on their persuasive essays.
Lesson 12. How do authors show character change in fiction? (Full Book; Independent Reading)	Students volunteer to read aloud sections of their completed essays. The class discusses the different ways that writers could have supported the same position and the sections of the book they drew on to support their interpretations. Then students exchange papers and use the supported argument format to write comments to each other about whether their essays reflect the format and which of their arguments were best supported and most helpful to readers. In a subsequent class, students meet in "story-like" discussion groups to talk about examples of character change they see in their immigrant teen stories and how those authors showed change. They post a group summary of their ideas on the blog.

APPENDIX

READING ASSESSMENT

Sample Diagnostic Tests

TABLE C.1. Sample Standardized Diagnostic Tests.

Component	Test Name
Phonemic Awareness	Comprehensive Test of Phonological Processing
Phonics	Woodcock Reading Mastery Tests-Revised/Normative Update (WRMT-R/NU); Woodcock-Johnson III Tests of Achievement (WJ III); Kaufman Test of Educational Achievement, Second Edition (KTEA-II)
Word Recognition	WRMT-R/NU; WJ III; KTEA-II
Contextual (oral) Reading	Gray Oral Reading Tests, Fourth Edition (GORT-4)
Word Meanings	Peabody Picture Vocabulary Test IV; Test of Word Knowledge; Expressive Vocabulary Test, Second Edition (EVT-2)
Comprehension	WRMT-R/NU; WJ III; KTEA-II
Fluency	GORT-4; Test of Word Reading Efficiency; Test of Silent Word Reading Fluency (screening)

TABLE C.2. Sample Nonstandardized Diagnostic Tests.

Component	Test Name
Phonemic Awareness	Diagnostic Assessments of Reading, Second Edition (DAR-2); Test of Auditory Analysis Skills
Phonics	Lexia Comprehensive Reading Test (CRT); Decoding Skills Test; El Paso Phonics Survey; Gallistel-Ellis Test of Coding Skills
Word Recognition	DAR-2; Fry Instant Words
Contextual (oral) Reading	DAR-2; Informal Reading Inventory (IRI), such as Burns/Roe and running records
Word Meanings	DAR-2
Comprehension	DAR-2; IRI
Fluency	Lexia CRT; one-minute oral reading fluency tests; observation

APPENDIX

D

A SCHOOLWIDE APPROACH TO READING DIFFICULTIES

In addition to establishing a shared vision and knowledge base, your school needs to take several important steps before launching Supported Literacy Intensive tutorials. To accomplish this, it will need to ensure that there is a leadership team in place to guide the implementation of a schoolwide reading approach. The team will establish policies and procedures related to reading and coordinate them with other school programs and policies. Leadership teams generally include the principal as coordinator, assistant principals, representative content area teachers, a special education teacher or director, a reading specialist, and a teacher who works with English language learners. The team oversees three primary tasks to support a schoolwide reading program such as Supported Literacy Intensive: developing a schoolwide reading assessment system, scheduling tutorials and identifying tutorial teachers, and training the tutorial teachers.

DEVELOPING A SCHOOLWIDE ASSESSMENT SYSTEM

The school leadership team establishes policies for identifying and responding to students' reading difficulties that are consistent with state and district policies. It also decides how to systematically identify poor readers in the school and determine what kinds of interventions they need.

The multilayered evaluation process we describe here begins with a standardized screening test in reading. At the same time, you and other content teachers might gather informal data from the classroom in the ways we discuss in Chapter Six. Your school can use both the standardized test data and the informal observations to identify a subset of students who appear to have significant reading difficulties. Based on the criterion your literacy team selects, the specialist administers individual diagnostic tests to these students and then creates group and individual student profiles of their reading strengths and difficulties. Table D.1 outlines the roles that the reading specialist, the reading teacher, and you as a classroom teacher all play in identifying, assessing, and responding to your students' reading difficulties in a schoolwide approach.

Steps in the Assessment Process

We discuss the roles of the reading specialist, supplementary and tutorial teachers, and you as the classroom teacher from Table D.1 by providing details about each step of the assessment process. We clarify how each step proceeds in an organized way, culminating with appropriate supplementary and intensive instruction for students with reading difficulties. We also explain how the reading specialist works with the school leadership team to make informed decisions about students.

Screen All Students. In the first step of the assessment process, your school's reading specialist oversees the administration of a schoolwide standardized reading test to determine which students can accomplish their reading goals in the Supported Literacy classrooms without additional help. Schools already obtain data from statewide tests about how well groups of students meet reading standards. However, most of these tests do not provide the detail that schools need to diagnose reading difficulties. The kind of standardized screening test we are recommending compares students to other students across the country in their same age group. Each of these tests yields a reading comprehension score and most also yield a score for vocabulary. The results of the screening test and your informal classroom observations constitute a first cut to identify students who need instruction that goes beyond the Supported Literacy classroom approach.

Determine the Cutoff Criterion. Your school leadership team determines the criterion for selecting a subset of students who will be given additional diagnostic tests and, depending on the results, possibly reading interventions. One common criterion is all the students with scores below the twenty-fifth percentile.

Conduct Individual Diagnostic Testing. Following the screening, your school's reading specialist rank-orders the total scores on the group screening test and administers individual diagnostic tests to the subset of students who meet the cutoff criterion. (See Appendix C for examples of individual diagnostic reading tests.) After scoring the tests, the reading specialist meets with the school leadership team to

TABLE D.1. Assessment and Support for Struggling Adolescent Readers.

Reading Specialist	Supplementary and Tutorial Teachers	Classroom Teacher
Screens all students with standardized test		Conducts informal assessments using observations, student think-alouds, oral reading, and student work samples
Determines criterion for inclusion in individual diagnostic testing		
Conducts individual diagnostic testing of low-performing readers who meet criterion		
Groups students homogeneously for supplementary or intensive reading instruction based on the results of formal and informal assessments		
Develops group reading profiles for supplementary and tutorial groups	Uses reading profiles to determine starting points for instruction	
Develops individual profiles for tutorial students	Uses individual student profiles to inform instruction for individuals within a group	Uses individual student profiles to inform decisions about accommodations for access to class content
	Provides supplementary instruction or intensive tutorials	Coordinates instruction with any ELL or inclusion teacher who is providing Tier 2 supplementary instruction in the classroom

decide which students need supplementary interventions or intensive tutorials. The specialist then makes recommendations to the leadership team for appropriate homogeneous instructional groups.

Develop Group and Individual Profiles. Your school's reading specialist creates group and individual student reading profiles to guide supplementary and tutorial reading teachers in providing interventions for low-performing readers. The group profile summarizes the needs of the students as an instructional group—with some indication of individual variability—and serves as an approximate starting point for instruction. It provides an overview of the instruction—to begin the group instruction at Lesson 1 or Lesson 10 of the phonemic awareness strand, for example, or at the fifth-grade level for sight word vocabulary. The profile makes it easier for reading teachers, many of whom are not reading specialists, to plan and implement instruction.

The specialist also creates an individual reading profile for each student who will participate in a Supported Literacy Intensive tutorial. This is less necessary for the supplementary instruction because it is not usually so individualized. The reading teacher uses the individual profiles to decide exactly what kind of help students need. Whereas the group profile offers an overview and starting points, the individual profile tells the reading teacher the specific reading levels for each component, albeit briefly. As a content teacher, you also receive copies of the individual profiles to assist you in providing appropriate accommodations in your classrooms.

Edward's individual profile is available in Chapter Six. It summarizes both the standardized and nonstandardized test results but displays only the nonstandardized test results in numeric form because they are easier for most teachers to understand. In Edward's case, the reading specialist gave a copy of the profile to Ms. Northrup and to Ms. Michaels, Mr. Jacobs, and Ms. Austin. Ms. Northrup used the Recommendations section of the profile to develop Edward's instructional plan, and the content area teachers used this section to design their classroom accommodations for Edward. The other members of Edward's tutorial group had similar but not identical profiles.

Plan Supplementary and Intensive Instruction. Based on the group and individual profiles, the reading teachers will plan supplementary help that your student can receive either in or outside the classroom. They will also design tutorials with instructional segments that closely map to the reading profiles of the small group.

Scheduling Tutorials and Identifying Tutorial Teachers

One of the biggest challenges in providing the tutorials is fitting them into the daily schedule without pulling students out of essential instruction. The Supported Literacy Intensive approach advocates that students receive all their other classroom instruction. Collaboration among staff members is essential because of the demands of scheduling tutorials and providing training for the tutorial teachers. In all likelihood, your school will need to restructure itself to allocate time for the tutorials.

Schools find time for Supported Literacy Intensive tutorials in different ways. In one school, the day is divided into two-hour blocks, such as math and science or language arts and social studies. This eliminates a good deal of the transition time between periods, thereby providing more instructional time, and it allows flexibility during the instructional blocks. This school designates time for the tutorials during an English language arts and social studies block. Another school adds an extra period for literacy. During this period, *all* faculty and administrators teach a group of students, which reduces class size. While some students are engaged in various kinds of literacy work during this period such as writing or independent reading, others participate in the reading tutorials. The group size needs to be smaller for the tutorials, but because class size has already been reduced by recruiting all teachers and administrators, no class is unusually large.

A third school adds an after-school enrichment period. Again, the tutorial students receive intensive reading instruction while the other students participate in reading, writing, or math activities. These are only three possible scenarios for providing time for the intensive instruction; creative leadership teams can arrive at additional solutions.

A second scheduling challenge is providing enough teaching staff for the small group tutorials. Just as with the issue of scheduling, schools manage to find staff in different ways. Reading specialists, special education teachers, English language arts teachers, and others who are interested can be trained to conduct the tutorials. A relatively simple solution is to designate the inclusion teachers for this role if there are enough of them, especially if the entire grade is engaging in the tutorial at the same time. The difficulty of staffing the groups is not easily resolved, but a school that is committed to bringing all of its readers up to grade level and that has a strong leadership team and a faculty experienced in collaborative planning can find ways to make it happen.

TRAINING TUTORIAL TEACHERS

When Hayes Middle School decided to use the Supported Literacy framework, Ms. Northrup participated in EDC training that prepared her to conduct the tutorials. The twenty-hour in-service training gave her the knowledge and tools she needed to succeed in her important role on the Hayes Supported Literacy team:

- An overview of the research on the need for intensive instruction and on scientifically based reading instruction

- Information about assessment methods and how to use assessment to guide instruction

- A summary of the components of reading and how to teach them, especially foundation reading skills

- Opportunities to practice planning and teaching tutorials

- Scripted materials that guide teachers new to this kind of instruction through the tutorial

Your school's tutorial teachers need to complete the training before the day your school begins to implement the framework—yet as close to it as possible. Holding the training close to the first day of teaching will enable your team to make a smooth transition into the instruction. It is also extremely helpful to set aside group planning time for tutorial teachers to create games and activities that reinforce their instruction and that they can share with each other as needed.

In addition to the training and planning time, your tutorial teachers will need support and reinforcement from mentors—educators who are well versed in the tutorial format and materials, behavior management, and classroom management. Mentors regularly observe tutorials, offer feedback to teachers, and model Supported Literacy Intensive best practices. They also occasionally provide additional coaching and e-mail or telephone consultation. We recommend that during the first two months mentors visit each reading group once a week; groups have different dynamics, so it is optimal to observe each group. If this is not possible, mentors can visit each tutorial teacher once a week. After the first two months, monthly observations and feedback generally suffice, although some teachers might require more frequent support.

APPENDIX

DIGITAL AND MULTIMEDIA TOOLS FOR CONTENT INQUIRY

You can use various media to engage students and give them common background knowledge before beginning an in-depth inquiry. These include DVDs, the blogs that we describe throughout this book, electronic text, and wikis.

Electronic text (e-text) is simply text that is in digital form. It might be saved to a flash drive, burned onto a CD-ROM, downloaded from the Internet, or built into a palm-sized "digital reader." E-text allows students to underline words, highlight sections, and cut and paste key ideas.

A *wiki* is a Web page or a collection of Web pages that can be created quickly and easily by any user without requiring knowledge of HTML or other programming languages. Students can create their own wikis or work with other students in creating classroom wikis as part of the learning process. Wikis allow students to demonstrate their understanding of concepts through the use of video, audio, and many other formats. Since students can update, edit, and modify their wikis at any time, wikis become evolving documents that change and grow richer as new events occur or as knowledge is gained. Each successive modification of the wiki is stored in the history, allowing users to revert to previous versions if necessary and to track the evolution of group knowledge.

These tools have an exciting potential for teaching and for learning. Table E.1 illustrates how one teacher uses various multimedia tools to aid her use of the Meaning-Making Cycle in a seventh-grade science class. We encourage you to think about how you might apply these tools in your own classroom to support your students' learning.

TABLE E.1. **Multimedia and the Meaning-Making Cycle.**

Meaning-Making Cycle	Multimedia Tools	Vignette
Engage students in content area.	Videos or DVDs, podcasts, online materials, blogs	Ms. Johnson's seventh-grade science class is starting work on a unit on ecosystems and biomes. To excite students about the topic, she shows them videos from the National Geographic Web site on the biomes and ecosystems of the world. The videos capture students' attention with the diversity of global flora and fauna. They want to know more.
Respond individually to texts and other resources.	Electronic texts, electronic journals	Students read information on biomes in their textbooks and from several online resources selected by Ms. Johnson. She asks them to record any vocabulary words that are unfamiliar or critical to understanding ecosystems. Students begin finding definitions and information about their vocabulary words using their textbooks and online and print versions of resource materials such as the dictionary, encyclopedia, and thesaurus. Students use information from Bartleby, Wikipedia, and a Web site called Blue Planet Biomes to help them build their entries in their electronic journals.
Elaborate and deepen responses.	Chats on wikis, Internet journals	Ms. Johnson divides the class into six teams, each of which is assigned to research one of the six biomes (marine, freshwater, tundra, desert, grassland, and forest). One group works

Meaning-Making Cycle	Multimedia Tools	Vignette
		together to create a wiki about the freshwater biome. They gather data, keep a record of their data on the wiki, and chat with each other about what they have found during their investigation. They keep track of their understanding by writing in their electronic journals.
Revisit understanding through reflecting.	Writing on wikis, guided chat on blogs, video, audio	After completing their research, the group meets to share information. They compare notes to make sure that all information is included. The students then each write up their own section for the group wiki. Students edit each other's sections and add suggestions. For example, Jake has found images of species found in freshwater biomes that are endangered, so he adds them to Grace's page. Grace has found information about how freshwater wetlands can provide flood protection and help filter water. She includes an audio discussion of this feature in her section on threats to freshwater, and she adds it to Jake's write-up of the importance of freshwater biomes.
Represent understanding.	PowerPoint, video, Internet journals, audio podcasts	After a field trip to the aquarium, Maya returns to the marine mammal rehabilitation center and asks to interview one of the veterinarians about her experiences working with marine wildlife. She takes pictures of the vet examining an injured seal brought in by rescue workers and asks about preparation for becoming an aquarium vet. She includes links on her wiki page, so that she can share the pictures and podcast of the interview.

REFERENCES

Alexander, P. A. (2003). The development of expertise: The journal from acclimation to proficiency. *Educational Researcher, 32*(8), 10–14.

Allen, J. (2007). Mastering the art of effective vocabulary instruction. In K. Beers, R. E. Probst, & L. Rief (Eds.), *Adolescent literacy: Turning promise into practice* (pp. 87–104). Portsmouth, NH: Heinemann.

Allington, R. L. (1977). If they don't read much, how they ever gonna get good? *Journal of Reading, 21*(1), 57–61.

Allington, R. L. (1983). The reading instruction provided readers of differing reading abilities. *Elementary School Journal, 83*(5), 549–559.

Allington, R. L. (2000). *What really matters for struggling readers: Designing research-based programs*. Boston: Allyn & Bacon.

Alvermann, D. E. (2007). Multiliterate youth in the time of scientific reading instruction. In K. Beers, R. E. Probst, & L. Rief (Eds.), *Adolescent literacy: Turning promise into practice* (pp. 19–26). Portsmouth, NH: Heinemann.

Anderson, R. C., Wilson, P. T., & Fielding, L. G. (1988). Growth in reading and how children spend their time outside of school. *Reading Research Quarterly, 23*(3), 285–303.

Applebee, A. N. (2000). Alternative models of writing development. In R. Indrisano & J. Squire (Eds.), *Perspectives on writing research, theory, and practice* (pp. 99–110). Newark, DE: International Reading Association.

Applebee, A. N., Langer, J. A., Nystrand, M., & Gamoran, A. (2003). Discussion-based approaches to developing understanding: Classroom instruction and student performance in middle and high school English. *American Educational Research Journal, 40*, 685–730.

August, D., & Shanahan, T. (2006). *Developing literacy in second-language learners: Report of the National Literacy Panel on Language—Minority Children and Youth*. Mahwah, NJ: Erlbaum.

Beach, R., & Bruce, B. (2005). Using digital tools to foster critical inquiry. In D. E. Alvermann (Ed.), *Adolescents and literacies in a digital world* (pp. 147–163). New York: Peter Lang.

Beck, I. L., & McKeown, M. G. (2006). *Improving comprehension with Questioning the Author: A fresh and expanded view of a powerful approach*. New York: Guilford Press.

Biancarosa, G., & Snow, C. E. (2006). *Reading Next—a vision for action and research in middle and high school literacy: A report to Carnegie Corporation of New York* (2nd ed.). Washington, DC: Alliance for Education.

Block, C. C., Gambrell, L., & Pressley, M. (2002). *Improving comprehension instruction: Rethinking research, theory, and classroom practice*. San Francisco: Jossey-Bass.

Bloom, D. E. (2004). Globalization and education: An economic perspective. In M. M. Suarez-Orozco & D. B Qun-Hilliard (Eds.), *Globalization: Culture and education in the new millennium* (pp. 56–77). Berkeley: University of California Press.

Blythe, T. (and the teachers and researchers of the Teaching for Understanding Project). (1998). *The teaching for understanding guide*. San Francisco: Jossey-Bass.

Blythe, T., Allen, D., & Powell, B. S. (2008). *Looking together at student work* (2nd ed.). New York: Teachers College Press.

Bradley Commission on History in Schools. (1988). *Building a history curriculum: Guidelines for teaching history in schools*. Washington, DC: Educational Excellence Network. (ERIC Document Reproduction Service No. ED 310 008)

Bransford, J. D., Brown, A. L., & Cocking, R. R. (Eds.). (2000). *How people learn: Brain, mind, experience, and school.* Committee on Developments in the Science of Learning. With additional materials from the Committee on Learning Research and Educational Practice. Commission on Behavioral and Social Sciences and Education of the National Research Council. Washington, DC: National Academy Press.

Braun, L. W. (2007). *Teens, technology, and literacy: Or why bad grammar isn't always bad.* Westport, CT: Libraries Unlimited.

Brisk, M. E., & Harrington, M. M. (2007). *Literacy and bilingualism: A handbook for all teachers* (2nd ed.). Mahwah, NJ: Erlbaum.

Bruce, B. C. (2005). Diversity and critical social engagement: How changing technologies enable new modes of literacy in changing circumstances. In D. E. Alvermann (Ed.), *Adolescents and literacies in a digital world* (pp. 1–18). New York: Peter Lang.

Buly, M. R., & Valencia, S. W. (2002). Below the bar: Profiles of students who fail state reading assessments. *Educational Evaluation and Policy Analysis, 24*(3), 219–239.

Burke, J. (2007). Teaching English language arts in a "flat" world. In K. Beers, R. E. Probst, & L. Rief (Eds.), *Adolescent literacy: Turning promise into practice* (pp. 149–166). Portsmouth, NH: Heinemann.

Bybee, R. (1997). *Achieving scientific literacy: From purposes to practices.* Portsmouth, NH: Heinemann.

Cazden, C. (2001). *Classroom discourse: The language of teaching and learning* (2nd ed.). Portsmouth, NH: Heinemann.

Clark, A. A. (2005, February). Making meaning: Literacy in secondary schools. *Principal Leadership, 5*(6), 28–32.

Curtis, M. E., & Longo, A. M. (1999). *When adolescents can't read.* Cambridge, MA: Brookline Books.

Cushman, K. (1989). Performance and exhibitions: The demonstration of mastery. *Horace, 6,* 101.

Cutter, J., Palincsar, A. S., & Magnusson, S. J. (2002). Supporting inclusion through case-based vignette conversations. *Learning Disabilities Research & Practice, 17*(3), 186–201.

Delpit, L. (2006). *Other people's children: Cultural conflict in the classroom* (Updated ed.). Herbert Kohl (Afterword). New York: New Press.

Dlott, A. M. (2007, April). A (pod)cast of thousands. *Education Leadership, 64*(7), 80–82.

Douglas, R., Klentschy, M. P., & Worth, K., with Binder, W. (2006). *Linking science and literacy in the K–8 classroom.* Arlington, VA: National Science Teachers Association Press.

Driver, R., Squires, A., Rushworth, P., & Wood-Robinson, V. (2001). *Making sense of secondary science: Research into children's ideas.* London and New York: Routledge/Palmer.

DuFour, R., & Eaker, R. (1998). *Professional learning communities at work: Best practices for enhancing student achievement.* Bloomington, IN: National Educational Service.

Education Development Center. (2003). *Guide for Supported Literacy coaches: School seminar for educators.* Newton, MA: Author.

Education Development Center. (2004a). Supported Literacy: Institute for Literacy Coaches Online Blog.

Education Development Center. (2004b). *Taking action to stop bullying: A literacy-based curriculum module.* A joint project of Pathways to Adolescent Literacy and Teenage Health Teaching Modules. Hartford, CT: MetLife Foundation.

Education Development Center. (2006). *EDC Foundation Science: Earth Science Curriculum Project.* Newton, MA: Author.

Educational Testing Service. (2007). *America's perfect storm: Three forces changing our nation's future.* Princeton, NJ: Policy Information Center, Educational Testing Service.

Englert, C. S., & Palincsar, A. S. (1991). Reconsidering instructional research in literacy from a sociocultural perspective. *Learning Disabilities Research to Practice, 6*(4), 225–229.

Englert, C. S., & Thomas, C. C. (1987). Sensitivity to text structure in reading and writing: A comparison between learning disabled and non-learning disabled students. *Learning Disability Quarterly, 10*(2), 93–105.

Environmental Protection Agency. (2007). *Personal emissions calculator.* Available online: www.epa.gov/climatechange/emissions/ind_calculator.html. Access date: January 13, 2008.

Flake, S. G. (1998). *The skin I'm in.* New York: Hyperion.

Foorman, B. R., & Torgesen, J. (2001). Critical elements of classroom and small-group instruction promote reading success in all children. *Learning Disabilities Research and Practice, 16*(4), 203–212.

Francis, D., Rivera, M., Lesaux, N., Kieffer, M., & Rivera, H. (2006). *Practical guidelines for the education of English language learners: Research-based recommendations for instruction and academic interventions.* (Under cooperative agreement grant S283B050034 for U.S. Department of Education.) Portsmouth, NH: Center on Instruction, RMC Research Corporation. Available online: www.centeroninstruction.org/files/ELL1-Interventions.pdf. Access date: January 13, 2008.

Franek, M. (2007, September 10). Web pulls world into classroom: Blogs, video-sharing websites, and social-networking sites give students the opportunity to tune their thinking and writing to a larger audience. *Christian Science Monitor.* Available online: www.csmonitor.com/2007/0910/p09s03-coop.html. Access date: January 13, 2008.

Friedman, T. (2005). *The world is flat.* New York: Farrar, Straus & Giroux.

Fullan, M. (2001). *Leading in a culture of change.* San Francisco: Jossey-Bass.

Fullan, M. (2003). *The moral imperative of school leadership.* Thousand Oaks, CA: Corwin Press.

Gallo, D. R. (2004). *First crossing: Stories about teen immigrants.* Cambridge, MA: Candlewick Press.

Garbarino, J., Kostelny, K., & Dubrow, N. (1991). *No place to be a child: Growing up in a war zone.* San Francisco: Jossey-Bass.

Garcia, G. G. (Ed.). (2003). *English learners: Reaching the highest level of English literacy.* Newark, DE: International Reading Association.

Gardner, H. (2006). *Five minds for the future.* Cambridge, MA: Harvard Business School Press.

Gee, J. P. (1999a). Reading and the new literacy studies: Reframing the National Academy of Sciences Report on Reading. *Journal of Literacy Research, 31,* 355–374.

Gee, J. P. (1999b). *An introduction to discourse analysis: Theory and method.* London: Routledge.

Gee, J. P. (2003). *What video games have to teach us about learning and literacy.* New York: Palgrave Macmillan.

Gersten, R., Fuchs, L., Williams, J. P., & Baker, S. (2001). Teaching reading comprehension strategies to students with learning disabilities: A review of the research. *Review of Educational Research, 71*(2), 279–320.

Goatley, V. H. (1997). Talk about text among special education students. In S. I. McMahahon & T. E. Raphael (Eds.), *The book club connection: Literacy learning and classroom talk* (pp. 119–137). New York: Teachers College Press.

Graham, S., Harris, K. R., MacArthur, C., & Schwartz, S. (1991). Writing and writing instruction with students with learning disabilities: A review of a program of research. *Learning Disabilities Quarterly, 14,* 89–114.

Graham, S., & Perin, D. (2007). *Writing Next: Effective strategies to improve writing of adolescents in middle and high schools* (Carnegie Corporation Report). Washington, DC: Alliance for Excellent Education. Available online: www.all4ed.org/publications/WritingNext/WritingNext.pdf. Access date: January 13, 2008.

Guggenheim, D. (Director). (2006). *An inconvenient truth: A global warning* [DVD]. Hollywood, CA: Paramount.

Guthrie, J. T., & Humenick, N. M. (2004). Motivating students to read: Evidence for classroom practices that increase reading motivation and achievement. In P. McCardle & V. Chhabra (Eds.), *The voice of evidence in reading research* (pp. 213–234). Baltimore, MD: Brookes.

Guthrie, J., Wigfield, A., & Perencevich, K. D. (2004). Scaffolding for motivation and engagement in reading. In J. Guthrie, A. Wigfield, & K. C. Perencevich (Eds.), *Motivating reading comprehension: Concept-oriented reading instruction* (pp. 55–86). Mahwah, NJ: Erlbaum.

Hall, G., & Hord, S. (2001). *Implementing change: Patterns, principles, and potholes.* Boston: Allyn & Bacon.

Hillenbrand, L. (2001). *Seabiscuit: An American legend.* New York: Random House.

Hillenbrand, L. (2003, July 7). A sudden illness: How my life changed. Personal history. *New Yorker.*

Hindin, A., Morocco, C. C., Mott, E. A., & Aguilar, C. M. (2007). More than just a group: Teacher collaboration and learning in the workplace. *Teachers and Teaching, 13*(4), 349–376. Abstract available online: http://dx.doi.org/10.1080/13540600701391911. Access date: January 14, 2008.

Intergovernmental Panel on Climate Change, Technical Support Working Group I. (2007a). *Climate change 2007: The physical science basis*. New York: Cambridge University Press. Available online: www.ipcc.ch/ipccreports/ar4-wg1.htm. Access date: February 8, 2008.

Intergovernmental Panel on Climate Change, Technical Support Working Group II. (2007b). *Climate change 2007: Impacts, adaptations and vulnerability*. New York: Cambridge University Press. Available online: www.ipcc.ch/ipccreports/ar4-wg2.htm. Access date: February 8, 2008.

Intergovernmental Panel on Climate Change, Technical Support Working Group III. (2007c). *Climate change 2007: Climate change mitigation*. New York: Cambridge University Press. Available online: www.ipcc.ch/ipccreports/ar4-wg3.htm. Access date: February 8, 2008.

International Reading Association. (2006). *Standards for middle and high school literacy coaches*. In collaboration with the National Council of Teachers of English, National Council of Teachers of Mathematics, National Science Teachers Association, and National Council for the Social Studies. Newark, DE: Author. Available online: www.reading.org/resources/issues/reports/coaching.html. Access date: January 14, 2008.

International Reading Association and National Council of Teachers of English. (1996). *Standards for the English language arts*. Newark, DE, and Urbana, IL: Authors.

Jenkins, J. R., Fuchs, L. S., van den Broek, C. E., Espin, C., & Deno, S. L. (2003). Accuracy and fluency in list and context reading of skilled and RD groups: Absolute and relative performance levels. *Learning Disabilities Research & Practice, 18*(4), 237–245.

Kadjer, S. (2007). Unleashing potential with emerging technologies. In K. Beers, R. E. Probst, & L. Rief (Eds.), *Adolescent literacy: Turning promise into practice* (pp. 213–230). Portsmouth, NH: Heinemann.

Kamil, M. L. (2003, November). *Adolescents and literacy—reading for the 21st century*. Washington, DC: Alliance for Excellent Education.

King, J. R., & O'Brien, D. G. (2005). Adolescents' multiliteracies and their teachers' need to know: Toward a digital détente. In D. E. Alvermann (Ed.), *Adolescents and literacies in a digital world* (pp. 40–50). New York: Peter Lang.

Kos, R. (1991). Persistence of reading disabilities: The voices of four middle school students. *American Educational Research Journal, 22,* 757–798.

Kotula, A. W., & Morocco, C. C. (2006). *Reach for reading: Developing a middle school model of instruction for the bottom 25 percent of readers*. Paper presented at the American Educational Research Association, San Francisco, CA, April 8, 2006.

Kutz, E., & Roskelly, H. (1991). *An unquiet pedagogy: Transforming practice in the English classroom*. Portsmouth, NH: Heinemann.

Lambert, M. (1990). When the problem is not the question and the solution is not the answer: Mathematical knowing and teaching. *American Educational Research Journal, 27,* 29–63.

Langer, J. A. (1986). *Children reading and writing: Structures and strategies*. Stamford, CT: Ablex.

Langer, J. A. (2001). Beating the odds: Teaching middle and high school students to read and write well. *American Educational Research Journal, 38*(4), 837–880.

Leach, J. M., Scarborough, H. S., & Rescorla, L. (2003). Late-emerging reading disabilities. *Journal of Educational Psychology, 96*(2), 211–224.

Linares, G. (2006). *Findings from the Mayor's Office of Immigrant Affairs*. Address delivered at the Conference on Race and Immigration: Challenges and Opportunities for the New American Majority, New York City, December 9, 2006.

Louis, K. S., & Kruse, S. D. (1995). *Professionalism and community: Perspectives on reforming urban schools*. Thousand Oaks, CA: Corwin Press.

Louis, K. S., & Miles, M. B. (1990). *Improving the urban high school*. New York: Teachers College Press.

Mayher, J. S., Lester, N., & Pradl, G. M. (1983). *Learning to write, writing to learn*. Portsmouth, NH: Heinemann.

Montague, M., Graves, A., & Leavell, A. (1991). Planning, procedural facilitation, and narrative composition of junior high students with learning disabilities. *Learning Disabilities Research & Practice, 6,* 219–224.

Morocco, C. C., Brigham, N., & Aguilar, C. M. (2006). *Visionary middle schools: Signature practices and the power of local invention*. New York: Teachers College Press.

Morocco, C. C., & Hindin, A. (2002). The role of conversation in a thematic understanding of literature. Special Issue by the REACH Institute. *Learning Disabilities Research and Practice, 17*(3), 144–159.

Morocco, C. C., Hindin, A., Mata-Aguilar, C., & Clark-Chiarelli, N. (2001, Winter). Building a deep understanding of literature with middle-grades students with learning disabilities. *Learning Disability Quarterly, 24*(1), 47–58.

Morocco, C. C., & Solomon, M. Z. (1999). Toward a new vision of staff development: From solo practice to the cultivation of professional communities. In M. Z. Solomon (Ed.), *The diagnostic teacher: Revitalizing professional development* (pp. 247–267). New York: Teachers College Press.

Morocco, C. C., & Zigmond, N. Z. (Eds.). (2006). Good high schools for students with disabilities. Special Series. *Learning Disabilities Research and Practice, 21*(3), 135–190.

Morocco, C. C. & Zorfass, J. (1996). Unpacking scaffolding: Supporting students with disabilities in literacy development. In C. L. Warger & M. C. Pugach (Eds.), *Curriculum trends, special education, and reform: Refocusing the conversation* (pp. 164–178). New York: Teachers College Press.

Mustacchi, J. (2007, March 24). Comment on A. Carvin, "*Discussing Media Literacy with Dan Rather.*" PBS Learning Now, blog entry, March 15, 2007. Available online: http://www.pbs.org/teachers/learning.now/2007/03/discussing_media_literacy_with_1.html. Access date: February 18, 2008.

National Adolescent Literacy Coalition. (2007). *Pitfalls and possibilities in adolescent literacy*. Washington, DC: Author.

National Center for Education Statistics (2003). *The Nation's Report Card: Writing 2002*. Washington, DC: Institute of Educational Sciences. U.S. Department of Education. Available at http://nces.ed.gov/pubsearch/pubsinfo.asp?pubid=2003529. Access date: April 7, 2008.

National Center for Education Statistics. (2005a). *Internet access in public schools and classrooms, 1994–2003*. Issue Brief. Washington, DC: Institute for Educational Sciences, U.S. Department of Education. Available online: http://nces.ed.gov/surveys/frss/publications/2005015/index.asp?sectionID=2. Access date: February 18, 2008.

National Center for Education Statistics. (2005b). *The Nation's Report Card: Reading 2005*. NCES # 2005453. Washington, DC: Institute of Educational Sciences, U.S. Department of Education.

National Center for Education Statistics. (2006). *State nonfiscal survey of public elementary/secondary education, 2004–2005. Enrollment in public elementary and secondary schools, by level, grade, and state or jurisdiction: Fall 2004. Digest of educational statistics, table 34*. Washington, DC: Institute of Educational Sciences, U.S. Department of Education. Available at http://nces.ed.gov/programs/digest/d06/tables/dt06_034.asp. Access date: January 14, 2008.

National Center on Education and the Economy. (2007). *Tough choices, tough times: The report of the New Commission on the Skills of the American Workforce*. San Francisco: Jossey-Bass. Available online for order: www.skillscommission.org. Access date: January 14, 2008.

National Commission on Writing. (2006, May). *Writing and school reform*. Washington, DC: College Board.

National Institute of Child Health and Human Development. (2000). *Teaching children to read: An evidence-based assessment of the scientific research literature on reading and its implications for reading instruction: Reports of the subgroups*. Report of the National Reading Panel. NIH Publication No. 00–4754. Washington, DC: U.S. Government Printing Office.

National Research Council. (1996). *National science education standards*. Washington, DC: National Academy Press.

National Writing Project & Nagin, C. (2006). *Because writing matters: Improving student writing in our schools* (Revised and updated ed.). San Francisco: Jossey-Bass.

New London Group. (1996). A pedagogy of multiliteracies: Designing social futures. *Harvard Educational Review, 66*(1), 60–92.

New Media Consortium. (2005). *A global imperative. The report of the 21st century literacy summit*. Austin, TX: New Media Consortium. Available online: www.nmc.org/publications/global-imperative. Access date: January 14, 2008.

Nystrand, M., & Gamoran, A. (1991). Instructional discourse, student engagement, and literature achievement. *Research in the Teaching of English, 25,* 261–290.

Pahl, K., & Rowsell, J. (2005). *Literacy and education: Understanding the new literacy studies in the classroom.* Thousand Oaks, CA: Paul Chapman.

Palincsar, A. S., & Brown, A. (1984). Reciprocal teaching of comprehension-fostering and comprehension-monitoring activities. *Cognition and Instruction, 1*(2), 117–175.

Palincsar, A. S., Magnusson, S., Marano, N. L., Ford, D., & Brown, N. (1998). Designing a community of practice: Principles and practices of the GIsML community. *Teaching and Teacher Education, 14,* 5–19.

Partnership for 21st Century Skills. (2006, March). *Results that matter: 21st century skills and high school reform.* Available online: www.21stCenturyskills.org; scan "Publications" for title. Access date: January 14, 2008.

Pearson, P. D., & Camperell, K. (1994). Comprehension of text structures. In R. B. Ruddell, M. R. Ruddell, & H. Singer (Eds.), *Theoretical models and processes of reading* (4th ed., pp. 448–468). Newark, DE: International Reading Association.

Pink, D. (2006). *A whole new mind: Why right-brainers will rule the future.* New York: Penguin.

Probst, R. E. (2007). Tom Sawyer, teaching, and talking. In K. Beers, R. E. Probst, & L. Rief (Eds.), *Adolescent literacy: Turning promise into practice* (pp. 43–60). Portsmouth, NH: Heinemann.

RAND Reading Study Group. (2002). *Reading for understanding: Toward a R& D program in reading comprehension.* Prepared for the Office of Educational Research and Improvement (OERI). Santa Monica, CA: RAND.

Raphael, T., Kehus, M., & Damphousse, K. (2001). *Book club for middle school.* Lawrence, MA: Small Planet Communications.

Ravich, D., & Finn, C. E. (1987). *What do our 17-year-olds know?* New York: HarperCollins.

Resnick, L. B. (1999). Making America smarter. *Education Week Century Series, 18*(40), 38–40.

Reznitskaya, A., Anderson, R. C., McNurlen, B., Ngyyen-Jahiel, K., Archodidou, A., & Kim, S. (2001). Influence of oral discussion on written argument. *Discourse Processes, 32,* 155–175.

Robinson, T. (2001). *Out of our minds: Learning to be creative.* Oxford, England: Capstone.

Robinson, T. (2006). *Talk: Do schools kill creativity?* For RED Ideas Work Spreading. Video filmed February 2006, Monterey, CA. Available online: www.ted.com/index.php/talks/view/id/66. Access date: January 14, 2008.

Roschelle, J. M., Pea, R. D., Hoadley, C. M., Gordin, D. N., & Means, B. M. (2000). Changing how and what children learn in school with computer-based technologies. *Future of Children, 10*(2), 76–101.

Schmoker, M. (2006). *Results now: How we can achieve unprecedented improvements in teaching and learning.* Alexandria, VA: Association for Supervision and Curriculum Development.

Snow, C. E., Burns, M. S., & Griffin, P. (1998). *Preventing reading difficulties in young children.* Washington, DC: National Academy Press.

Snow, C., & Biancarosa, G. (2003). *Adolescent literacy and the achievement gap: What do we know and where do we go from here?* Unpublished report, Carnegie Corporation of New York.

Stanovich, K. E. (1986). Matthew effects in reading: Some consequences of individual differences in the acquisition of literacy. *Reading Research Quarterly, 21*(4), 360–407.

Stewart, V. (2007). Becoming citizens of the world. *Educational Leadership, 64*(7), 9–14.

Suarez-Orozco, M. M., & Qin-Hilliard, D. B. (2004). *Globalization: Culture and education in the new millennium.* Berkeley: University of California Press.

Suarez-Orozco, M. M., & Sattin, C. (2007). Wanted: Global citizens. *Educational Leadership, 64*(7), 58–62.

Sutherland, L. M., McNeill, K. L., Krajcik, J. S., & Colson, K. (2006). Supporting middle school students in developing scientific explanations. In R. Douglas, M. P. Klentschy, & K. Worth, with W. Binder (Eds.), *Linking science and literacy in the K–8 classroom* (pp. 163–181). Arlington, VA: National Science Teachers Association Press.

Thier, M., with Davis, B. (2002). *The new science literacy: Using language skills to help students learn science.* Portsmouth, NH: Heinemann.

Torgesen, J. K. (2006). *Adolescent literacy: An overview of skill and knowledge requirements*. Paper presented at K–12 Literacy Seminar for Regional Centers, Boston, MA, February 15, 2006.

Torgesen, J. K., Houston, D. D., Rissman, L. M., Decker, S. M., Roberts, G., Vaughn, S., et al. (2007). *Academic literacy instruction for adolescents: A guidance document from the Center on Instruction*. Portsmouth, NH: Center on Instruction, RMC Research Corporation.

U.K. Department for Environment, Food, and Rural Affairs. (2006). *Attitudes to climate change: Youth sample*. Available online: www.climatechallenge.gov.uk/multimedia/climate_change_toplines_YOUTH.pdf. Access date: February 8, 2008.

Union of Concerned Scientists. (2002, February). *Confronting climate change in the Gulf Coast region: Prospects for sustaining our ecological heritage. Curriculum guide for high school courses in biology, geography, general science, earth science, and other courses focusing on the society/environment interface.* Cambridge, MA: Author.

Union of Concerned Scientists. (2006a). *global warming and California agriculture and global warming and California's water supply. California climate choices: Fact sheets of the Union of Concerned Scientists*. Available online: www.climatechoices.

Union of Concerned Scientists. (2006b). *Global Warming Facts: Human Fingerprints*. Available online: www.ucsusa.org/assets/documents/global_warming/humanfingerprints.pdf. Access date: January 14, 2008.

U.S. Census Bureau. (2004). *Exports from manufacturing establishments. Table 2* (p. 8). Washington, DC: U.S. Department of Commerce.

U.S. Global Change Research Program. (n.d.). *U.S. national assessment of the potential consequences of climate variability and change*. Available online: www.usgcrp.gov/usgcrp/nacc/default.htm. Access date: January 14, 2008.

Van Sledright, B. (2002). *In search of America's past: Learning to read history in elementary school*. New York: Teachers College Press.

Watkins, Y. K. (1994). *My brother, my sister, and I*. New York: Simon & Schuster.

Watson, J. L. (2004). Globalization in Asia: Anthropological perspectives. In M. M. Suarez-Orozco & D. B. Qun-Hilliard (Eds.), *Globalization: Culture and education in the new millennium* (pp. 141–172). Berkeley: University of California Press.

Wilson, W. T. (2005). *The dawn of the India century: Why India is poised to challenge China and the United States for global economic hegemony in the 21st century*. Chicago: Keystone India.

Wineberg, S. (2001). *Historical thinking and other unnatural acts: Charting the future of teaching the past*. Philadelphia: Temple University Press.

Wolf, M. K., Crossen, A. C., & Resnick, L. B. (2006, January). *Accountable talk in reading comprehension instruction*. Unpublished paper. Center for the Study of Evaluation; National Center for Research on Evaluation, Standards, and Student Testing; Graduate School of Education & Information Studies; University of California, Los Angeles.

Wong, B., Wong, R., & Blenkinshop, J. (1989). Cognitive and metacognitive aspects of learning disabled adolescents' composing problems. *Learning Disability Quarterly, 12*(4), 300–322.

Woods Hole Research Center. (2007). *The warming of the Earth: A beginner's guide to understanding the issue of global warming*. Woods Hole, MA: Woods Hole Research Center. Available online: www.whrc.org/resources/online_publications/warming_earth/index.htm. Access date: January 14, 2008.

Wright, R. (1998). *Black boy: A record of childhood and youth*. New York: HarperCollins. (Originally published 1945.)

Zinsser, W. (1988). *Writing to learn*. New York: HarperCollins.

Zorfass, J., & Copel, H. (1998). *Helping middle school students become active researchers*. Alexandria, VA: Association for Supervision and Curriculum Development.

INDEX